Hot Beignets & Warm Boudoirs

The formal dining room at Annadele's Plantation & Restaurant.

HOT BEIGNETS & WARM BOUDOIRS

A Collection of Recipes from Louisiana's Bed and Breakfasts

Chef John D. Folse, CEC, AAC

CHEF JOHN FOLSE
& COMPANY
PUBLISHING

Gonzales, Louisiana

Library of Congress Catalog Card Number: 98-093980

ISBN 0-9625152-6-4

First Printing: February 1999
Second Printing: June 2000
Third Printing: May 2002
Fourth Printing: May 2003
Fifth Printing: August 2009

If this book is not available at your local bookstore, copies may be ordered directly from:

Chef John Folse & Company
2517 South Philippe Avenue • Gonzales, LA 70737
225.644.6000 • www.jfolse.com

Other Chef John Folse cookbooks include:

Hooks, Lies & Alibis
After The Hunt: Louisiana's Authoritative Collection of Wild Game & Game Fish Cookery
The Encyclopedia of Cajun & Creole Cuisine
Something Old & Something New
Louisiana Sampler
Plantation Celebrations
The Evolution of Cajun & Creole Cuisine

Designer: Philip Toups for Bird Graphic Design, Washington, D.C.
Typefaces: Baskerville MT and Shelley Allegro Script
Software: Adobe Indesign

Printed and bound in Canada by Friesens Corporation

Foreword

I remember well that rustic farmhouse on the mountainside in Pennsylvania. As I drove up the winding road in the late evening, the sun was just sinking behind the mountain peak and a springtime frost was in the air. Thus began my first bed and breakfast experience.

I have often asked myself what made this experience so unforgettable. Was it the down-filled comforters, hand-hewn beams or cobblestone fireplace there in the Carriage House? Was it the early morning walk through the rows of lettuces in the vegetable garden with the twin ponds as a backdrop? Was it the two antique corn silos where I enjoyed my early morning coffee while watching a family of mallard ducks shower under a waterfall? Whatever it was, it was enough to make me remember vividly my experience at Glasbern Inn in Fogelsville, and from that day forward I was a B&B aficionado.

As I stood there, I could not help but think of how fortunate we are as travelers today. The variety of options for overnight accommodations and services is endless. I reminisced about the early adventurers who passed this way generations before without the benefit of such luxury and security.

History tells us that the earliest inns were established about 3,000 years before Christ. Most of them were private homes where owners provided rooms for overnight travelers. These quarters were often unclean and only crude meals were served. Frequently, guests not only had to share the same room with strangers, but many times they shared the same bed. In ancient Egypt, beds were used only by the most privileged classes. Commoners slept on the ground with a wooden pillow similar to those still used in many parts of the world today.

The word "hotel" or "hostel" is of ancient origin and refers to a building providing lodging and sometimes meals. These early accommodations were commonplace along the Roman highways and were used by government officials and merchants traveling these routes. During the Middle Ages, brotherhoods from the monasteries often assumed the operation of hostels in order to guarantee safe haven for those traveling in dangerous regions. The quality of inns, especially those in Europe, improved during the 1700s when more people began to travel for pleasure. The rapid growth of travel during the 18th century, especially by stagecoach, stimulated the development of inns here in America.

The first building in the United States specifically designed as a hotel was the City Hotel, which opened its doors in 1794 in New York City. Early hotels such as this had many rooms, but no locks, guest services or lobbies. Later, as a means of marketing beverages and maximizing income, hotels had customers enter through a tavern or bar. In 1829, the Tremont House in Boston became the first hotel to provide private rooms with locks, indoor plumbing and a lobby for registration. With the advent of railroads and the continued expansion of travel for business and pleasure, hotels were most often located near the railroad depots or other transportation centers. Today, hotels are usually larger than inns or bed and breakfasts, provide a variety of guest services and are most often found in urban areas.

The origin of the bed and breakfast in America is a bit elusive. However, we do know that prior to the founding of this country, homeowners provided overnight accommodations with meals to overland travelers. Many of us have visited historical homes that prominently display plaques stating, "George Washington Slept Here." It only stands to reason that early statesmen rested in private homes as they traveled to Williamsburg or to Philadelphia for the signing of the Declaration of Independence. It was probably from these colonial entrepreneurs who opened their homes as a means of livelihood that the idea of the bed and breakfast in America was born.

There are basically two kinds of B&Bs in this country–the B&B homestay and the B&B inn. The homestay is normally a home with a few empty bedrooms to fill, allowing the owner to provide a service guaranteeing extra income and company for the family. These services may include a bedroom with a private bath and a breakfast as simple as continental or as elaborate as a full, gourmet buffet with regional flair. Guests often have the opportunity to share in the main meals with the owners, which adds a bit of warmth and local flavor to the experience. Many owners of out-of-the-way homestays are renovating barns and outbuildings into suites with lavish furnishings, thereby creating the personality and expanded services of an inn.

The B&B inn is operated as a free-standing enterprise, often professionally marketed and subject to local ordinances and licensing. Here, owners provide dedicated common areas for guests' use, but do not share the living quarters as in the homestay. Inns normally serve breakfast, lunch and dinner on a regular basis to the overnight guest and to the public as well. Today, with the expansion of the B&B industry, it is often hard to tell a homestay from an inn.

In the process of researching this book, I had the opportunity to travel the state searching out Louisiana's unique B&B homes. The road took me to more than a hundred establishments stretching from the Red River in North Louisiana to the mouth of the Mississippi at the Gulf. I traveled to Bois des Chênes, a beautiful B&B under the magnificent live oaks of Acadiana, and to the Lanaux Mansion, an 1800s home filled with priceless antiques on the edge of New Orleans' French Quarter. I discovered centuries-old homesteads on Bayou Teche and JuJu's, a quaint cabin on the shore of Toledo Bend. Each home I visited had a unique charm and mystique that transformed an ordinary night into an extraordinary experience.

B&Bs come in many sizes, shapes and colors–from the Victorian-style "painted ladies" to the one-room sharecroppers cabin. In Louisiana, these accommodations range from antebellum plantation estates with formal gardens and statuary to swampland hunting camps. Some rooms are filled with antiques and oversized clawfoot bathtubs, while others are small garrets with a shared bath down the hall.

If this experience taught me one thing, it is that B&Bs differ as much as the Louisiana landscape. In order to guarantee a pleasant experience, you must determine what is attractive to you and find a home that suits your personal tastes. All B&Bs are not created equal! You must express your preferences clearly to the innkeeper when making a reservation and ask pertinent questions. Decide what is important to you, articulate it, and you will not be disappointed upon arrival. If you have not seen the B&B firsthand or been given a recommendation from a friend or relative, you should request brochures, photographs or

OPPOSITE: *Eggs À La Crème…the champagne of egg dishes. Recipe page 158.*

guest testimonials. You should also inquire whether the inn is a member of any professional association of innkeepers. Membership in such organizations often guarantees that these facilities follow rigorous standards governing safety, sanitation, insurance and other issues that protect overnight guests. Ask about the safety of the neighborhood, renovations in progress, wedding receptions or bachelor parties that may be scheduled during your stay. If your reservation is at an antebellum plantation, inquire about the high-traffic months or pilgrimages that could disturb your stay. If you expect to check-in late, say so. Many B&Bs make special arrangements for late arrival. Ask about credit cards, room deposits, personal check cashing policy and in-house security for jewelry and valuables. Inquire about parking, smoking, wheelchair accessibility, air conditioning, room phones and television. If you have special dietary needs, let the innkeeper know prior to your arrival. Request maps and literature about the local historical attractions, restaurants, shopping areas and outdoor sports. These can be mailed in advance, so you can properly plan your itinerary.

I have stayed at B&Bs and inns around the country and around the world. While most innkeepers try desperately to operate reputable facilities, there are those I would never recommend. Generally, the houses that do not make my preferred list, share some of the same anomalies. My most common disappointment is the issue of cleanliness: sinks, bathtubs and showers that need an extra dose of scouring powder. Another pet peeve is cobwebs and dirt-dauber nests attached to porches, windows and eaves. Peeling paint, water-stained walls and ceilings, torn wallpaper, mildewing carpets and musty-smelling halls are a turn-off to me as they would be to you. Roadway noise, neon lights, obnoxious house guests and uncontrolled pets do not enhance the B&B experience. I like collectibles, antiques and family heirlooms, but as we say in jazz, "More ain't better." Bedside lamp tables, bathroom lavatories and in-room coffee tables overcrowded with family pictures and knickknacks too numerous to mention becomes an irritation to this guest rather than an enhancement to the room. These decorative pieces are the highlight of sitting rooms, sun porches and libraries, but in the bedroom these dainty decorations make the guest feel like a bull in a china shop, unable to unpack and feel comfortable during the stay. High at the top of my list of complaints is poorly prepared food taken from a can or freezer and then presented with a lack of creativity and care. Oh sure, I'm a chef, but that does not mean I expect gourmet fare, elegantly prepared every time I sit down to dine. What I want from a meal is a taste of the regional cuisine. I want a food experience, a memory, that I can take home with me. When I'm in New England, I expect lobster and a clambake. In Seattle, I want salmon and Pacific Coast oysters just as those visiting me in South Louisiana can expect steaming bowls of seafood gumbo and bread pudding with whiskey sauce for dessert. For breakfast in New Orleans you should expect to find bran muffins in a basket and a traditional omelette, but wouldn't you love to entice your palate with pecan praline muffins with muscadine butter and a crawfish-andouille omelette? After all, this is the Big Easy where you can expect a little flair and flambé! Guests love to sample indigenous foods presented in a familiar yet delicious fashion.

Of the B&Bs I remember and long to visit again, a few touches were apparent. There was an enthusiastic owner or manager on premise. The best managers stay in each room periodically when vacant to experience the B&B from the guest's perspective. They also employed

OPPOSITE: *Ahhhh Louisiana…where our days last a week and our nights are forever.*

maintenance personnel, gardeners and housekeepers, in many cases the owners themselves, ensuring a fresh, bright, beautiful place. The staff was knowledgeable about the area from the economic as well as the historical standpoint and suggested itineraries with an added emphasis on what to avoid. There was great signage, and the perimeters were well-lit for late-night arrivals with courtesy snacks and drinks available.

Louisiana is home to hundreds of fabulous B&Bs that I would highly recommend to visitors and residents alike. The quality of these bayou state B&Bs is exceptional, in most cases, making the task of choosing the 26 featured here extremely difficult. For this reason I am including a complete list of the homes registered in the Louisiana Bed & Breakfast Directory. I have tried my best to feature B&Bs in this book that will provide a memorable experience for you as they did for me. Inevitably, there may be some disappointments. As owners change, so may the quality of the visit. Unforeseen circumstances may lead to an unpleasant stay. Quite often you may disagree with my definition of a great B&B simply because there was not a good "fit" between the B&B and your personal taste. Just one more reason to check it out in advance. In the introduction to each chapter, I give you a history of the building, personal impressions of the home, unique menu items when appropriate and attractions in the area. I include phone numbers to call ahead for pricing, reservations and for further directions to the home.

But, this book is so much more than a B&B travel guide. It is an anthology on the origin of breakfast as an event in the city of New Orleans. It is a cookbook featuring nearly 200 fabulous recipes from unique breakfast items to desserts–dishes you will only find at a Louisiana B&B. I even include a few "Recipes for Romance" scattered throughout the book to add a little pizzazz to your next romantic rendezvous. And speaking of romance, if there is one thing I have discovered about staying at a B&B, whether alone or with a companion, it is that romance is a permanent guest in every home. From the moment you arrive, she greets you in the Spanish moss draping the trees, in the flames of an antique lantern casting its glow onto the front porch swing and in the scent of camellias and sweet olives on the evening breeze. She places chocolate kisses on the pillows and chills the Cristal Champagne. She is hidden in the battenburg lace covering the canopy bed, and she bathes the room in candlelight in anticipation of your arrival. Romance lives here for those who seek her.

Now, pour the champagne, put on a little soft jazz and turn the page.

Chef John D. Folse, CEC, AAC

Chef John D. Folse, CEC, AAC

Chef John Folse was born in St. James Parish in 1946. From his uncle's hunting camp on Cabanocey Plantation to Mémère Zeringue's country kitchen, John learned early that the secrets of Cajun cooking lay in the unique ingredients of Louisiana's swamp floor pantry. John seasoned these raw ingredients with his passion for Louisiana culture and cuisine, and from his cast iron pots emerged Chef John Folse & Company.

John opened Lafitte's Landing Restaurant in 1978 at the foot of the Sunshine Bridge in Donaldsonville. Located 50 miles from the nearest metropolitan area, John set out to

ABOVE: *Chef John Folse holds an antique painter's palette courtesy of the late Marie Celeste Robertson Spiess.*

market his restaurant by taking "a taste of Louisiana" worldwide. He introduced Louisiana's indigenous cuisine to Japan in 1985, Beijing in 1986 and Hong Kong and Paris in 1987. In 1988 John made international headlines with the opening of "Lafitte's Landing East" in Moscow during the Presidential Summit between Ronald Reagan and Mikhail Gorbachev. In 1989 John created the first Vatican State Dinner in Rome. Promotional restaurant openings also included London in 1991 and 1993, Bogota in 1991, Taipei in 1992 and 1994 and Seoul in 1994. It is little wonder he was named "Louisiana's Marketing Ambassador to the World" in 1988 by the Louisiana Sales and Marketing Executives and "Louisiana's Culinary Ambassador to the World" by the Louisiana Legislature that same year.

The international success of Lafitte's Landing Restaurant spawned the incorporation of several other Chef John Folse & Company properties. White Oak Plantation, established in 1986, houses his catering and events management company. Chef John Folse & Company Publishing has produced eight cookbooks in his Cajun and Creole series since 1989. *"A Taste of Louisiana"* is John's international television series produced by Louisiana Public Broadcasting. Broadcast since 1990, the series is seen throughout the United States, parts of Canada, Asia and via the Armed Forces Network. Chef John Folse & Company Manufacturing, established in 1991, is one of the only chef-owned and -operated food manufacturing companies in America. Named in honor of "Louisiana's Culinary Ambassador to the World," the Chef John Folse Culinary Institute at Nicholls State University in Thibodaux, La., is dedicated to the preservation of Louisiana's rich culinary and cultural heritage. John and Nicholls State dedicated the institute in October 1994. In August 1996 John began broadcasting his radio cooking talk show, *Stirrin' It Up...The Best Tasting Show on Talk Radio.* In 2001, *Stirrin' It Up* expanded to a television cooking segment during the 5 p.m. newscast on WAFB-TV Channel 9 in Baton Rouge, La. Exceptional Endings, the pastry division of his corporation, was launched in 1996 to create specialty desserts, pastries and savories. In the year 2000, Folse incorporated Digi-Tek Productions, a full service digital recording studio. In 2002, Bittersweet Plantation Dairy opened, offering a full line of fresh and aged cheeses, yogurts and other dairy products.

John has received numerous national and international accolades. In 1987 he was named "Louisiana Restaurateur of the Year" by the Louisiana Restaurant Association. In 1989 Lafitte's Landing Restaurant was inducted into *Nation's Restaurant News'* "Fine Dining Hall of Fame." In 1990 John was named the "National Chef of the Year" by the American Culinary Federation, the highest honor bestowed upon an American chef. In 1991 he was inducted into "The Order of the Golden Toque." In 1992 John was recognized with an honorary Doctor of Culinary Arts Degree from Johnson & Wales University in Providence, R.I., and again in 1995 from Baltimore International Culinary College. In 1994 he assumed the role of national president of the American Culinary Federation, the largest organization of professional chefs in America. In 1995 John was one of 50 people recognized in *Nation's Restaurant News'* "Profiles of Power." In 1996 Lafitte's Landing Restaurant received the Award of Excellence from Distinguished Restaurants of North America. In 1998 *Food Arts Magazine* awarded John the "Silver Spoon Award" for his sterling performance and contributions to the food service industry.

Thirty years of culinary excellence later, John is still adding one more ingredient to the corporate gumbo he calls Chef John Folse & Company, which is as diverse as the Louisiana landscape, and he would not want it any other way.

THE WRITER/RESEARCHER:

Michaela D. York was born in 1968 with a writer's soul and a lover's heart. Since she first learned to scrawl lopsided letters on notebook paper, she has written poetry, essays, short stories and children's stories. As a student, her poetry and essays won local writing contests and at least one piece was published in a poetry anthology. Her short story, "Childhood Memories," was published in Baton Rouge's Sunday Advocate in 1994.

Hot Beignets & Warm Boudoirs is her first writing endeavor with Chef John Folse. When Michaela is not busy with writing projects, she is the Director of Communications for Chef John Folse & Company. Before joining the organization in 1997, Michaela worked in the broadcast industry, first as the producer and hostess of a children's show, then as creative writer and commercial producer for a Baton Rouge cable company. Michaela earned a Bachelor of Arts degree in Journalism from Northeast Louisiana University in 1991 and a Master of Mass Communication degree from Louisiana State University in 1996.

Michaela lives in Baton Rouge where she spent most of 1998 poring over dusty volumes in remote corners of libraries, rummaging through historic collections, conducting interviews and finally sitting in front of her computer to slowly weave the text of *Hot Beignets & Warm Boudoirs*. As Michaela reflects on the book she says with a twinkle in her eye, "It was good for me. I hope it's good for you, too."

THE PHOTOGRAPHER:

Ron Manville was the chief photographer for *Hot Beignets & Warm Boudoirs*. Ron specializes in food and travel photography. He is the principal culinary photographer for Johnson and Wales University in Providence, Rhode Island. He has worked on a dozen cookbooks, including location work in Louisiana, Alabama, Chicago, Florida, Rhode Island, Boston, Ireland and France. He lives in Rhode Island with his wife, Christine, and his children, Joel and Sarah.

THE ADMINISTRATIVE ASSISTANT:

Pamela Castel has exemplified the meaning of the word "quality" in her role as Administrative Assistant to Chef John Folse over the past 10 years. Often regarded as Chef Folse's "right hand," Pam has overseen the production of Folse's six cookbooks and his *A Taste of Louisiana* PBS series. She has gained invaluable experience from her vast responsibilities as executive assistant to the "on-the-go" international chef. *Hot Beignets & Warm Boudoirs* is an example of Pam's dedication to a project and her creative spirit.

Employed by Chef John Folse & Company since 1988, Pam is a graduate of Cabrini High School in New Orleans and attended Louisiana State University majoring in Special Education. Born and reared in the Crescent City, she currently calls Baton Rouge home.

It is with much regret that Pam leaves Chef John Folse & Company at the completion of this work. She moves on embarking on a new career with fond memories of the past decade and excited at the opportunities that lay ahead.

THE GRAPHIC DESIGNER:

Philip Toups was born and raised in Houma, LA, and received a degree in advertising from Louisiana State University. An accomplished graphic designer, Philip is currently an art director for a leading trade association in Washington, D.C. His work has earned awards of excellence from the Printing and Graphic Communications Association of Washington, D.C., the International Association of Business Communicators, and *Association Trends.*

Philip enjoys cooking and operates a small catering business in his spare time. He is also a freelance graphic designer for his own design studio, Bird Graphic Design.

Dedication

To Mike Abel, a talented videographer who worked on my *"A Taste of Louisiana"* television show for 10 seasons. Mike died of a heart attack during the taping of our Bed and Breakfast series. During the hectic days of production, he was always the first to bear the load, and his calming personality brought tranquility to our group. Mike will be sadly missed and impossible to replace.

To Pamela Castel, who served as my administrative assistant for 10 years. Her commitment to my projects was unsurpassed. This book is an example of her talent and dedication. Pam organized the selection of the homes in this book, facilitated recipe choices and proofing. In addition, she coordinated photography for the book and the production of the Bed and Breakfast series on Louisiana Public Broadcasting. Thanks Pam for all your hard work on this project and so many others.

The heart of the home is always the kitchen, especially at T'Frere's House & Garçonnière.

Contents

Couples have frequented the coffee stalls for
generations. However, it was not until the 1920s
that New Orleans society adopted the custom of
dropping in for coffee as the smart thing to do.
Courtesy of The Historic New Orleans Collection

BREAKFAST IN THE BIG EASY:
The Quintessential Love Affair

The first ray of daylight saunters through the French Quarter, casting aside shadows of darkness as though they were last night's lover. She slips in softly through shuttered windows and glides gracefully over tables laid with sultry Southern pleasures. Daylight gently cups the tall, steaming mugs of thick, black chicory already in place on the table, drinking deeply of the rich elixir. Beads of moisture swell on crystal goblets of freshly squeezed juice, plunging drowsily onto dainty drapings and frilly frocks of lace. Slowly, morning awakens. Her passions rise, and certain satisfaction lies just ahead, piled high atop platters of crabmeat omelettes, Eggs Sardou, grillades and hot beignets. Morning arrives in the Crescent City, and nothing seduces her sensuous soul more than breakfast.

Wake with her. Let morning take you. Let her lead you through the streets of Old New Orleans. Slip into the stalls of the French Market for a little foreplay disguised in cups of café au lait and platters of beignets. Sip Mimosas in restaurant courtyards while the tinkling of silver and crystal and the mellow drone of the trombone whisper promises of bedroom bliss. Dream of scandalous escapades aboard the steamboats wavering in port, laden with myriad Southern comforts. Let morning take you to the tables of royal repasts during Carnival season or down River Road for a Réveillon feast. Drink deeply of life, liquor and lust at the planter's table, while morning tosses her coquettish glances from every corner of the room. Whether you eat "Breakfast at Brennan's" or breakfast in a remote cafe, the banquet never ends until your thirst is quenched, your hunger satisfied. Let morning take you.

In New Orleans, breakfast is not just a meal. It is the quintessential love affair everyone dreams of, but few have the pleasure of partaking.

DRINKING THE NIGHT AWAY:
Hot Cups of Café au Lait

Café Du Monde is one of the city's oldest coffee stands. Many people believe that the sidewalk cafe began in the 1830s.
Courtesy of Louisiana State Museum

OPPOSITE: *Café au lait is a mixture of dark roasted café noir with chicory diluted with equal parts of steaming hot milk, then sweetened.*
Courtesy of Robert Hennessey

You never forget your first time…the first time your lips press against the pillow-shaped dough covered with powdered sugar…the first time your lips sip deeply of the intoxicating elixir known as café au lait…the first time you visit any one of New Orleans' oldest coffee stands.

For well over a century a coffee house has been comfortably nestled alongside the Mississippi River in the heart of the Vieux Carré at the corner of St. Ann and Decatur, standing sentinel over the entrance to the New Orleans French Market. In 1782, Spanish colonists established the first make shift stalls of the market. In 1813, a permanent meat and fish market was built, which included the building containing present-day Café Du Monde. The Market was originally known as "Les Halles des Boucheries" or "The Meat Shops." It was here, at the entrance to the French Market, that the butchers peddled their pork, beef and fresh-cut mutton. "Les Halles des Boucheries" was the first market building and it led to the fruits and vegetables and fish markets. Even before New Orleans was founded in 1718, this same area along the Mississippi River was used by Choctaw, Creek and Natchez Indians as a trading post.

From its inception the French Market appears to have housed coffee stands. The coffee stand at the entrance was once known as "Café Rapide," where patrons drank cups of coffee or chocolate. Throughout the market, vendors and visitors could find marble-top tables with four-legged stools beside them. The tables were dressed with white cups and saucers, pewter-lidded bowls of white or brown sugar, and large, steaming urns of coffee. In 1885 coffee sold for a nickel a cup. The coffee stands offered a variety of menu items, notably beefsteaks, bread, bacon and greens, pies, cakes and crullers of puff paste.

The coffee vendors, dressed neatly in white shirts, were considered the elite of market merchants. They communicated well with the ethnic gumbo of the market, replicating the favorite slang phrases of the patrons who drank coffee throughout the business day.

The coffee stands seem to have always been a community collection plate of personalities and professions that daily observed the activities of the populace. It is said that often times as Pere Antoine, also known as Antonio de Sedilla, a Spanish priest, passed the marketplace, people would hold out their cups of coffee for him to touch with his lips to bring them luck. It is also believed that the infamous Madame La Laurie, whose mansion on Rue Royal is still haunted by the slaves she tortured, frequented the coffee stands daily to drink café noir. Young ladies and gentlemen visited the coffee stalls after an evening opera performance, chaperoned of course, to partake of café au lait or café noir. However, it was not until the early 1920s that New Orleans society adopted the custom of dropping in for coffee and doughnuts as the smart thing to do.

"Morning Call…New Orleans' Most Famous Coffee Drinking Place" thrives on tradition. It was established in the French Quarter in 1870 by the Jurisich family

CC's Gourmet Coffee House on Magazine Street in New Orleans.

who still own and operate it today. Though Morning Call was originally located on Decatur Street, renovations to the French Market and a widening of the street in the 1970s eliminated Morning Call's curb service and forced the coffee stand to relocate to Metairie in 1974. Even in a different location the locals, business owners and natives enjoy the traditional cups of café au lait and heaping platters of beignets Morning Call has served for more than a century.

Though historical records do not establish exactly when the French Market's corner coffee stand became Café Du Monde, it is thought that the sidewalk cafe began in the 1830s. In 1932 Hubert N. Fernandez bought the French Market coffee stand along with the recipe for beignets that Café Du Monde has become famous for serving.

Beignets, the forerunner of the doughnut, were brought to New Orleans by the Ursuline Nuns who came to Louisiana in 1727. Many believe the Creole-style beignet is derived from Beignets Viennois, a French classical version filled with cream or fruit, then sprinkled with sugar after frying. Others maintain beignets were adapted from the Spanish sopapilla. Regardless, every culture has had some form of fried dough.

Beignets are made with flour, milk, water and, often, yeast. Some versions are pan-fried, although most are deep-fried; regardless, they are always smothered in powdered sugar and served hot, or they are simply not worth eating. Café au lait is a mixture of dark roasted café noir with chicory diluted with equal parts of steaming hot milk, then sweetened. Chicory was first used more than a century ago by New Orleans Creoles as a filler in their coffee when coffee supplies were scarce.

The tradition of the local coffee stand transgresses time and establishes coffee as the common denominator of humanity. New Orleans hosts approximately 10 million guests every year from all over the world, and nearly every visitor takes a break at one of New Orleans' coffee stands. Though Morning Call and Café Du Monde have dominated the cafe scene over the last century, today many Parisian-style coffee houses are appearing on just about every street corner. Coffee shops such as CC's Gourmet Coffee House, P.J.'s and Starbucks are reminiscent of those early "Penny Universities" where the famous and infamous sat to exchange conversations and controversies while tipping a cup. The poignant, aromatic fragrance of coffee incessantly captivates passersby to partake of the pleasures these charming cafes offer.

Through the decades both Café Du Monde and Morning Call have welcomed the masses to their tables—from poets to playwrights, paupers to prostitutes. Amid the chatter of the city, where the seasons of change are measured in hot cups of café au lait and heaping platters of beignets, almost all strata of society have enjoyed a first time at one of the famous coffee houses…where it's a New Orleans tradition to eat breakfast all night long.

Café au Lait

No coffee can compare to the coffee of South Louisiana and none is more famous than Café au Lait! In early Louisiana, dark, swarthy Creole chicory coffee was enjoyed throughout the day by hard-working Cajuns and Creoles. In order to make the coffee more palatable for the children, hot milk was *(Continues on page 5)*

(*Continued from page 4*) blended with the coffee to create a beverage enjoyed by all and unparalleled outside of Cajun Country. Today, Café au Lait has become world-famous as the beverage of choice when enjoying powdered sugar-coated beignets in the New Orleans French Quarter.

INGREDIENTS:

- 4 cups dark roast coffee
- 2 cups hot milk or cream
- 6 tbsps sugar

METHOD:

In a small sauce pot, combine all of the above ingredients and bring to a low boil, stirring constantly. Pour the steaming Café au Lait into 6 warm mugs and serve alone as a breakfast drink or alongside beignets.

PREP TIME: 15 Minutes   SERVES: 6

A study break at CC's.

New Orleans Beignets

This classical fried doughnut of the Crescent City was made famous in restaurants such as Morning Call and Café Du Monde. Thought to have been brought to New Orleans by the Ursuline nuns, fried dough was found in every culture from Native American to Chinese. However, when dusted in powdered sugar and dipped in hot café au lait, this simple breakfast confection is debatably the best-known of all breakfast foods in Cajun Country.

INGREDIENTS:

- 1 package dry yeast
- 4 tbsps warm water
- 3 1/2 cups plus 2 tbsps flour
- 1 tsp salt
- 1/4 cup sugar
- 1 1/4 cups milk
- 3 eggs, beaten
- 1/4 cup melted butter
- Vegetable oil for deep frying
- Powdered sugar

METHOD:

In a measuring cup combine the yeast and warm water. Using a teaspoon, stir to blend well then set aside. In a large mixing bowl, combine flour, salt and sugar. Using a wire whisk, stir until all ingredients are well blended. Add blossomed yeast, milk, eggs and butter. Mix with a wooden spoon until dough is formed. Cover dough with a dish towel and set in a warm place. Allow dough to rise for 1 hour. Place vegetable oil into a home-style deep fryer, such as a Fry Daddy, and heat to 350°F according to manufacturer's directions. Dust a work surface with additional flour and turn the dough onto the floured surface. Knead dough once or twice and roll out to approximately 1/2-inch thickness. Cut the dough into 3-inch squares and return to a lightly floured pan. Allow the dough to rest, covered, for approximately 10 minutes. Deep fry the beignets, 2-3 at a time, for approximately 2 minutes on each side or until golden brown and puffed. Remove beignets from oil, drain and dust generously with powdered sugar. Beignets should be served 3 to an order with a cup of steaming hot café au lait.

PREP TIME: 1 1/2 Hours   SERVES: 10-12

The Penny University

Legend has it that in the early days of Oxford and Cambridge universities many would-be students found admission standards difficult, because they could not afford tuition or they did not have the "blue blood" required. These individuals, who yearned for knowledge, made it a habit to frequent the local coffee houses conveniently situated near the universities. These casual meeting places became known as "Penny Universities." For a pence these knowledge seekers would purchase a cup of coffee and sit around discussion tables with scientists, philosophers, writers and students of the university. So, for the price of a cup of coffee and the time engaged in scholarly conversation one could quickly become a learned man.

AND ALL THAT JAZZ:
"Second Breakfast," the Origin of Brunch

A traveling street merchant in Congo Square.
Courtesy of The Historic New Orleans Collection

OPPOSITE: *Madame Elizabeth Kettenring Dutrey Bégué with her husband, Hypolite Bégué. Madame Bégué was famous for her three-hour "second breakfasts."*
Courtesy of Louisiana State Museum

It is a drowsy, slumberous, lovers kind of morning. The gentle breeze in the courtyard is dipped in wisteria scent, its coolness draping the lovers like satin sheets. The rhythmic pulse of the jazz orchestra keeps perfect time with her reflections, and she calls his name instinctively with the crescendo. With each gentle glide of the slide trombone he nibbles her alabaster neck and caresses the silky sleekness of her long legs. It is the morning after the night before when the mind is completely lost in forbidden fantasies and the soul satisfied only with the ecstasies of brunch.

The British upperclass, it is believed, developed the tradition of brunch, a combined breakfast and lunch, around 1895, though the tradition most likely existed long before, when sportsmen returned home from the hunt. Though the word "brunch" was not used in the United States until twenty or thirty years later, brunch certainly existed and thrived in the heart of New Orleans.

After the War Between the States, steamboat captains prided themselves on the elaborate champagne brunches provided for passengers. But brunch was popular in New Orleans long before the extravagant riverboat breakfasts were served.

Brunch is a New Orleans tradition born from the heart of Catholic faith. Until the mid-twentieth century, Catholics were prohibited by church law from eating or drinking anything after midnight on Saturday, if they intended to go to Communion on Sunday morning. After Mass, those who had been fasting were hungry and ready for a meal, though in many cases it was too late for breakfast and too early for lunch. Hence, brunch became a favorite Sunday meal for Catholics in New Orleans.

This Catholic hunger created a niche for the many savvy street vendors. These traveling merchants conveniently strolled through the Place d'Armes in front of St. Louis Cathedral each Sunday morning as Mass ended, with sundry foods to sell. It was not unusual to see black women parading through the square with large baskets of goodies balanced on their heads. Among the savory street foods were ginger cake, calas cakes, almond sticks, sweet potato cakes, pralines, coffee cake, peanuts and boiled shrimp. Later years saw snowballs, taffy candy and gumbo being peddled on the streets. There were small stands where fresh fruit, candied fruit and Ginger Beer were sold, and Greek Sherbet was a favorite Sunday treat. Along the levee oyster men opened fresh oysters for hungry customers. Street vendors capitalized upon New Orleans' need for brunch, but they were not the only ones to manipulate the hungry masses.

Each day when business slowed at the French Market, the butchers crossed old Levee Street and climbed the stairs to Madame Bégué's "Coffee House" where platters of delectables awaited their devourment.

In the stalls of the French Market, workers gathered early to arrange their produce, prepare their seafood counters and slaughter the beef and mutton to be sold in the market that day. To service the vendors and early morning patrons of the market, two types of eatinghouses emerged, adding another dimension to New Orleans brunch. Scattered throughout the buildings were small cafes serving café noir, café au lait, chocolate, cake and biscuits. The second type of establishment was nearly a restaurant but served a limited, cheap bill of fare, including soup, roast ham, pork sausage, beef stew, tripe stew, fried catfish, baked beans, potato salad and eggs. Although many vendors patronized these smaller market eatinghouses, by mid-morning the merchants were famished and needed a hearty meal to sustain them through the rest of the day.

The butchers in particular yearned for the hearty sustenance a "second breakfast" provided. They had drunk only a cup of coffee or glass of wine and eaten a mere chunk of French bread before reporting to the market at dawn. Each morning when business slowed at about 11 o'clock, they left the French Market, crossed old Levee Street and climbed the stairs to Madame Bégué's "Coffee House" where platters of delectables awaited their devourment. This "second breakfast" was hearty and lasted three or four hours.

The "Coffee House," as it was customarily called, was established in 1863 by a Creole named Louis Dutrey. While he tended the bar and greeted the guests, his wife, Elizabeth Kettenring Dutrey, a German immigrant from Bavaria, prepared the delicious meals in the kitchen. She so thoroughly combined her German culinary skills with the cooking art of Old New Orleans that the world considered her a Creole cook. In 1875 Louis Dutrey died, but his widow kept the place and her fame as a cook grew as did the butchers' desire for her "second breakfasts."

In 1877 Hypolite Bégué, a Frenchman, gave up the butcher business to tend bar for the Widow Dutrey. In 1880 Hypolite married Elizabeth and the coffee house became "Bégué's." It was as "Madame Bégué's" that the place received culinary recognition.

Legend has it that the smells permeating the air about Madame Bégué's were like no other, "with aromas that, some swear, no other woman ever coaxed out of food." Her meals usually began with a heavy soup followed by bouilli (boiled meat from the soup) with spiced sauce. If crawfish were in season, steaming platters were set on the table followed by sweetbread omelettes. There was usually a platter of redfish in Creole sauce served with potatoes in butter. Then, chicken in red-brown sauce with mushrooms was served, with a salad and shrimp. And no meal was complete without Madame Bégué's famed liver. The succulent strip of meat was larded with bacon, pre-broiled in butter, then merged with bay leaf, cloves, herbs and red wine. Besides the liver dish, Madame Bégué was also known for her Snails á la Créole, Artichokes á la Bégué, tripe in a yellow peppered sauce, fried chicken, fried boiled potatoes, half a tomato topped with parsley and other specialties no one could get anywhere else west of Paris. After such a sumptuous fare, most patrons sat around and smoked or nibbled cheese and fruit while waiting for the café noir laced with brandy to be set aflame.

Madame Bégué's breakfasts did not gain prominence beyond the French Market until the Cotton Centennial Exposition in 1884. Tourists to the Vieux Carré "discovered" Madame Bégué's "second breakfasts," and within a few years her fame had spread across the continent.

In time the restaurant closed, but the sturdy brick building still stands on the original site. Today, the downstairs of the building is the home of Tujague's Restaurant.

Breakfast at Bégué's did not gain prominence beyond the French Market until the Cotton Centennial Exposition in 1884. The restaurant closed after the deaths of Madame Bégué and Hypolite. Today, the downstairs of the building is the home of Tujague's Restaurant.
Courtesy of Louisiana State Museum

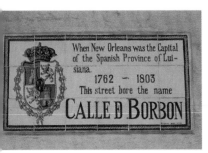

The original Spanish name for Bourbon Street.

Whether is was Catholicism, the street vendors or the "second breakfast" at Madame Bégué's that inspired brunch in New Orleans, the tradition continues at many restaurants of the Crescent City.

ARNAUD'S RESTAURANT was established in 1918 by a Frenchman named Leon Bertrand Arnaud Cazenave. Count Arnaud, as he was called by friends and patrons, came to America with intentions to study medicine. His plans changed and he opened a successful cafe on Bourbon Street instead, which eventually led to his fabulous restaurant on Bienville.

Count Arnaud was a vivacious presence in the French Quarter, a man of distinction with a charming personality. He never forgot a name or a face, and he welcomed guests to his dining room with his wisdom and wit.

With his chefs, Count Arnaud created some of New Orleans' signature dishes such as Shrimp Arnaud and Oysters Bienville. Upon his death in 1948, his daughter, Germaine Cazenave Wells, helped her mother operate the restaurant, eventually controlling it herself. Her first love was theater, but Germaine transferred this affection to the restaurant. Many referred to lunch as her first act of the day, followed by intermission, with dinner as act two. Germaine's spirit kept the French flavor alive, and the restaurant flourished as it always had.

Germaine created many of Arnaud's classic dishes such as Cornish Game Hen Twelfth Night, Canapé á la Irma (after her mother) and Watercress Salad á la Germaine. In 1979 Germaine granted Archie Casbarian a long-term lease to operate Arnaud's.

Brunch is served every Sunday at Arnaud's from 10:00 to 2:30 and should always begin with an apéritif such as a Bloody Mary or Fuzzy Navel. Appetizers of Crawfish Mousse Bourgeois, Shrimp Arnaud or Oysters Arnaud should always follow. Choose from a large selection of entrées including poached egg dishes, omelettes, pain perdu, Creole crab cakes, Fettuccine Barataria or Creole stuffed pork loin. Complete the meal with Bread Pudding Fitzmorris or Strawberries Arnaud and a hot cup of café brûlot–a perfect finish to a perfect feast.

Charm Gates guard the entrance to the COURT OF TWO SISTERS at 613 Royal Street. Legend has it that Queen Isabella had the gates blessed so that "their charm would pass on to anyone who touched them." Charming indeed is the Court of Two Sisters, where an elaborate jazz brunch buffet is a daily occurrence.

But the Court of Two Sisters was not always a restaurant. In fact, in the late 1800s it was the home of two cultured, aristocratic Creole sisters, Emma and Bertha Camors. The restaurant derives its name from these two inseparable sisters who owned a notions shop, the "Shop of the Two Sisters," on the ground floor of their home. They outfitted many women with formal gowns, carnival costumes, lace, novelties and perfumes imported from Paris. Their special customers were treated to tea and cakes in the courtyard, the largest in the French Quarter.

The 600 block of Rue Royale was once known as "Governor's Row" and was the home of five governors, two State Supreme Court Justices and one future Justice of the U.S. Supreme Court. The original resident of 613 Rue Royale was Sieur Etienne

The front entrance to the Court of Two Sisters.

de Perier, the royal governor of colonial Louisiana between 1726 and 1733. It is also believed that the outrageous Marquis de Vaudreil, the colonial royal governor who transformed New Orleans into a "petit Paris," was once a resident as well.

After the Camors sisters died in 1924 the property was inherited by the Delvalle family, and purchased by New Orleans writer Natalie Scott in 1925. The property passed through five ownerships in which time it developed into a restaurant. Joe Fein, Jr., acquired the property in 1963 and nurtured the Court of Two Sisters to its exemplary reputation in the restaurant community. His sons, Joe and Jerry, continue the tradition today.

Brunch begins at 9 each morning and lingers through 3 in the afternoon. Guests are entertained by a live jazz trio while they sample a profusion of foods displayed in pirogue buffets. More than 80 of New Orleans' favorite dishes can be savored, such as chicken and andouille gumbo, seafood omelettes, artichoke salad, shrimp mousse, jambalaya, boiled crawfish, boiled shrimp, Oysters Bienville, grillades and grits, oyster pasta, shrimp pasta, pecan pie, bread pudding with whiskey sauce and crêpes Suzette. A host of other delectables includes duck, roast beef, Eggs Benedict, sausages, salads, vegetables, fresh fruits, pâtés, imported cheeses, biscuits and breads.

Newcomers are often as bashful as newlyweds, but it's not long before they become clandestine lovers rendezvousing in mid-afternoon.

The commanding presence of COMMANDER'S PALACE entreats visitors to the heart of the historic New Orleans Garden District. It was here in the shadows of the ancient oaks and Louisiana magnolias that the institution of "jazz brunch" was born.

In 1880 Emile Commander opened the restaurant in the beautiful Victorian mansion. The restaurant passed to the Giarrantano family in the early 1920s. During these days of Prohibition, Commander's had a spicy reputation. While the dining room downstairs remained respectable for families and meals after church, the upstairs area, entered by a secret side door, hosted riverboat captains and sporting gentlemen who were likely entertaining their "lady of the hour." Ella and Dick Brennan, present owners of Commander's Palace, remember their mother telling them, "Now don't you go in that restaurant." How ironic that is now.

In 1944 Commander's was purchased by Elinor and Frank Moran. The Morans transformed the second floor into dining rooms and created a large patio from the adjacent lot. After Frank Moran's death, Commander's Palace was sold to Ella, Adelaide, John and Dick Brennan who originated "jazz brunch."

Commander's Palace, recipient of the 1996 James Beard Outstanding Restaurant Award, offers numerous appetizers, entrées, desserts and drinks for Sunday brunch. However, you have not eaten until you experience Commander's traditional jazz brunch consisting of a Bloody Mary, Eggs Sardou, Roasted Mississippi Quail and Creole Bread Pudding Soufflé.

New Orleans Brunch...where the sweet sounds of jazz combine with the subtle flavors of champagne to consummate the purest of impure thoughts.

Gas lamps light the way to the patio at the Old Coffee Pot on St. Peter.

Madame Bégué's Liver & Onions

Madame Bégué's Coffee Shop was located in the French Quarter on the present day site of Tujague's Restaurant. She became famous for her "second breakfast" or brunch, which was served to the workers during mid-morning break. One of her best known dishes was smothered liver and onions. The liver was carefully selected and cut by her husband—the French Market butcher, Hypolite Bégué.

INGREDIENTS:

- 3 pounds calves liver, sliced
- 2 large onions, thinly sliced
- 1/2 pound bacon
- 1 cup seasoned flour
- 2 cups chicken stock (see recipe)
- Salt and black pepper to taste

METHOD:

In a heavy bottom skillet, cook bacon over medium-high heat until crispy. Remove, drain and allow to cool. Chop bacon and reserve drippings for sauteing. Season liver using salt and pepper. Dust liver in flour, shaking off all excess. Reheat bacon drippings over medium-high heat. Pan-fry liver until golden brown on each side, approximately 10 minutes. Remove from pan to a drain board and keep warm. Into the same skillet, add onions and saute over medium-high heat. Stir-fry onions until caramelized, approximately 20 minutes. Return chopped bacon and liver to the skillet. Pour in chicken stock, bring mixture to a rolling boil and cook for 10 additional minutes. Season to taste using salt and pepper. When ready to serve, place liver in the center of a 10-inch dinner plate and top with caramelized onions and bacon.

PREP TIME: 1 Hour   SERVES: 6

Street musicians entertain French Quarter visitors daily.

Free Lunches

There really was such a thing as a "free lunch," and it existed in the first-class saloons of the Crescent City. A man named Alvarez, who ran the barroom at the old St. Louis Hotel, instituted the free lunches in 1837. Gentlemen conducting business in the city found they did not have time to travel to their homes for lunch, and they did not want to pay restaurant prices for a simple bowl of soup and a sandwich. To accommodate these gentlemen, and to acquire their business, many first-class barrooms of the city, such as those at the St. Louis Hotel, Hewlitt's (afterward City Hotel), Arcade, Veranda and St. Charles Hotel, served free lunches daily.

The meal was served on narrow tables and consisted of soup, a piece of beef or ham, potatoes, meat pie or oyster patties. The free lunches gained popularity and the menu choices increased. Many restaurateurs complained that these free lunches hurt their business, but that did not destroy the concept. The free lunch was generally served from noon to 1 p.m., though some places served from 10 a.m. to 2 p.m.

The concept of free lunch is prevalent today, though now it is referred to as "happy hour." Local bars and restaurants often offer free food with drink specials to the business crowd after work, instead of during the traditional lunch hour. The more things change, the more they really stay the same.

French Market Pork & Sweet Potato Breakfast Sausage

Many types of sausages were created by the different nationalities settling the Crescent City. The marriage of two cultures can be seen in this creative blend of the ground pork and flavoring of the Germans and sweet potatoes from the Africans.

INGREDIENTS:

- 5 pounds ground pork
- 1 (16-ounce) can yams, drained
- 1 tbsp black pepper
- 1 1/2 tbsps rubbed sage
- 1 tsp ginger
- 1 1/2 tsps nutmeg
- 2 tsps dried thyme
- 2 tbsps salt
- 1 tbsp cayenne pepper
- 1 1/2 tbsps granulated garlic
- 1/4 cup chopped parsley
- 1 cup iced water

METHOD:

When making sausage of any type, it is always best to keep the meat chilled to 35-40°F. The iced water in the recipe maintains the cold temperature in the meat and sets the fat in the sausage. Slice the drained yams and dice into 1/4-inch cubes. Place the cubes on a cookie sheet and freeze for later use. In a large mixing bowl, combine all of the above ingredients except yams. Using your hands, mix well turning and pushing the meat 10-15 minutes to ensure proper blending. Gently fold in the frozen yams into the meat mixture. NOTE: Freezing the yams will guarantee a solid 1/4-inch cube which will be visible in the finished sausage. Roll the sausage into 3-inch patties or stuff into hog casings and tie off at 6-inch links. Cook patties in the same manner as any other breakfast sausage or grill the links over charcoal.

PREP TIME: 1 Hour

MAKES: 25-30 (3-ounce) Patties

A skillet of yam sausage awaits the guests.

"I'LL NEVER BE HUNGRY AGAIN:"
Pleasures of the Plantation Table

A misty fog lingered about the towering oaks, embracing the shadowy outline of the plantation home like a sheer negligee. It was daybreak on the plantation and the field hands were already working the soil. After a few toddies of Tafia, a rum drink, or Mint Juleps, the gentlemen planters made early rounds to survey the plantation grounds, then returned home for a bountiful breakfast.

And so it was in the days before these Confederate brothers declared war on their Northern antagonists. Breakfast was the sustenance that helped them endure their labors in the delta heat and through the languid hours of afternoon.

When the planter returned home from his sunrise surveillance, the mahogany, oak or cypress tables were covered with foods for the morning meal. Breakfast was served between 8 and 9 and the typical menu might include a salad of mixed greens with an oil and vinegar dressing, eggs scrambled with calf brains or crawfish, tripe fried in fritter batter, boudin blanc, beef grillades and grits, oysters in pastry shells, beef pies, kidneys in wine, wild game, rice fried in egg batter, bacon strips, yam sausage, soft cheeses, cheese toast, stewed apples with cream, battercakes drowned in butter and honey, French bread, cathead biscuits and corn pone, strawberry preserves, crab-apple jelly, muscadine jelly, molasses and coffee. Breakfasts were hearty, and each meal ended with the service of "eau de sucre," or sugared water, to aid digestion.

It was the responsibility of the plantation mistress to obtain all the foods necessary for the lavish planter's meals. Menus for the family and guests had to be planned well in advance, because there were no local grocery stores to quickly fetch forgotten food items. The mistress had to be sure the pantry, storehouse and smokehouse were adequately stocked. Each morning the mistress discussed menus with the cooks, then doled out the food supplies needed for that day's meals. If a dish was not cooked properly or garnished well, it reflected poorly on the mistress.

William Howard Russell, a guest at Houmas House in 1861, wrote in his diary about the elaborate breakfasts he enjoyed during his visit. "Breakfast is served: there is on the table a profusion of dishes—grilled fowl, prawns, eggs and ham, fish from New Orleans, potted salmon from England, preserved meats from France, claret, iced water, coffee and tea, varieties of hominy, mush and African vegetable preparations." At plantation homes throughout South Louisiana, each day was christened with an elaborate morning breakfast.

The gentleman planter was perhaps best regarded for the elaborate soirées or dances he hosted at his country plantation, which always featured a lavish assortment of food. Often, guests stayed at the plantation several days. No matter what time guests arrived, food was waiting—coffee, cakes or steaming bowls of gumbo. The plantation parties were followed by midnight suppers in the dining room. The huge oak tables, sideboards and side tables were covered with whole turkeys, roasts, cold meats, salads, salmis or game pies, galantines, cheeses, gelatins, fruits, cakes in richly iced pyramids, custards, pies, jellies, nougat or caramel, sorbets, sherbets and ice creams in baskets

Boudin, hot or cold…it's perfect for breakfast.

OPPOSITE: *A bounty awaits the planters.*

carved from orange peel and decorated with candied rose petals or violets. At dawn it was customary for gumbo and black coffee to be served before everyone retired.

If the weekday breakfasts were elaborate, the Sunday morning menus were sublime. Following the Saturday evening soirées many young gentlemen stayed as guests at neighboring homes, so they could escort the young plantation belles to church Sunday morning. The young lady's family was sure to host a magnificent breakfast to begin the day. A Sunday morning menu might include eggs poached in cream, fried chicken with gravy, hot biscuits, hot buttered muffins, sausage and gravy, steak and gravy, fried sweet potatoes, assorted preserves and jellies, fried apples with cream, apple pie, pound cake and coffee…a religious experience to be sure, long before the priest made the sign of the cross at Mass.

So that was the way of life on the plantation homes of the Old South. And as day waned into night the planter returned home to end his day just as he had begun it… with his whiskey, his wife and his warm boudoir.

Smothered Breakfast Chops with Oyster Mushrooms

Many debate that the original grillades—that magnificent breakfast meat dish—began as smothered pork chops in a cast iron skillet. Fact is, the dish does find its roots with the early butchers of Bayou Country who took strips of pork meat, not chops, and slowly braised them in a rich tomato-based brown sauce.

INGREDIENTS:

- 12 center-cut pork chops, sliced thin
- 1/2 pound oyster mushrooms
- 1 cup flour
- 1/2 cup shortening or bacon drippings
- 2 cups chopped onions
- 2 cups chopped celery
- 1 cup chopped bell pepper
- 1/4 cup diced garlic
- 1 cup diced tomatoes
- 4 cups beef or chicken stock (see recipe)
- 1 bay leaf
- 1/2 tsp dried thyme
- 1/2 tsp dried basil
- 1/2 cup sliced green onions
- 1/2 cup chopped parsley
- Salt and black pepper to taste

METHOD:

Season pork chops well using salt and pepper. Dust chops in flour, shaking off all excess. Set aside. In a dutch oven, heat oil or bacon drippings over medium-high heat. Saute pork chops until golden brown on each side. Once browned, remove from dutch oven and keep warm. Into the same oil, add onions, celery, bell pepper, garlic, tomatoes and mushrooms. Saute 3-5 minutes or until vegetables are wilted. Add beef or chicken stock, bay leaf, thyme and basil. Bring mixture to a rolling boil, reduce to simmer and cook 3-5 additional minutes. Return pork chops to the dutch oven and top with green onions. Cover dutch oven and allow pork chops to cook 45 minutes to 1 hour until tender, but not falling apart. Season to taste using salt and pepper. Add parsley and serve over rice or Cheese Garlic Grits (see recipe).

PREP TIME: 1 Hour   SERVES: 6

A centerpiece of fruit enhances the breakfast table.

Cheese Garlic Grits Soufflé

While basic boiled grits is perfect in its simplicity for breakfast, at bigger meals cheese grits are more likely to appear. Adding cheese is the first "company" thing done to grits when it's time to show off a little. Grits and garlic have an ancient affinity in the South. Cooks who wouldn't use garlic in any other form have been slipping a bit into cheese grits for years. Many cooks add a lot more garlic by roasting it first and often refer to it as their "secret ingredient." Cheese Garlic Grits Soufflé is usually served as a brunch or luncheon dish and is very much like a sharply-flavored spoon bread.

INGREDIENTS:

- 1 1/2 cups shredded sharp Cheddar cheese
- 1/2 cup freshly grated Parmesan cheese
- 1 cup stone-ground grits
- 2 cups water
- 2 cups milk
- 1/2 tsp salt

- 2 tbsps unsalted butter
- 1/2 tsp ground white pepper
- Dash of Worcestershire sauce
- 1 garlic clove, crushed
- Hot sauce to taste
- 4 eggs, separated

METHOD:

In a large sauce pot, heat water and milk over medium-high heat. Bring mixture to a rolling boil then add salt. Slowly stir in grits and reduce heat to simmer. Continue to cook grits approximately 20 minutes, stirring often, until done. The grits should be quite thick and creamy. Preheat oven to 350°F. Remove grits from heat and stir in butter, pepper, Worcestershire sauce, garlic, hot sauce and cheeses. Allow cheese grits to cool slightly. Butter a deep 2-quart baking dish. In a small mixing bowl, beat egg yolks lightly with a fork. Pour beaten yolks into grits and stir until well incorporated. In a separate mixing bowl, whip egg whites until soft peaks form and fold into grits. Pour the batter into the buttered dish and bake until lightly browned and well-puffed, approximately 30 minutes.

PREP TIME: 1 Hour   SERVES: 6

A crock bowl filled with piping hot cheese garlic grits.

RIVERBOAT REPAST:
Breakfast Aboard a Mississippi Paddle Wheeler

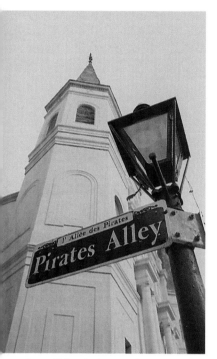

One of the city's most famous streets.

OPPOSITE: *Passengers dined or were entertained in the long main cabin of the J.M. White, which was lined by staterooms.*
Courtesy of Thomas H. and Joan Gandy

She's been more than one man's mistress, enticing suitors with her soft, gentle curves and rhythmic caresses. What is the allure of this love affair between man and the Mississippi? Perhaps it's her unpredictable, foreboding waters. Perhaps it's her delicate scent after a hard rain. Perhaps it's her subdued strength that plays her prey like a calliope. Whatever her mystique, she seems to have been most intriguing during the golden age of steamboat travel when thousands of vessels steadily plied her, exploring every inch of her beguiling waters.

The first steamboat arrived in New Orleans in January 1812 and was appropriately named for the city. Though early steamships were concerned more with freight than passenger accommodations, post-Civil War steamers were renowned as "floating palaces." The elegant staterooms, ballrooms, dining rooms, salons, casinos and bars were ornately furnished with chandeliers, oil paintings and massive furniture. Food, drink, entertainment and the luxurious accommodations were comparable to the best hotels of the day, and the Southern hospitality extended aboard the steamers welcomed visitors to the Crescent City long before the ships arrived.

Planters often chartered steamboats for gala events or reserved staterooms for their families to live aboard the riverboat for weeks at a time. These plantation owners were sometimes the special guests of the steamboat proprietors whose lavish generosity was an attempt to obtain the business of these affluent gentlemen. Owners instructed the captain and staff to give these guests whatever they desired, sparing no expense and the "Bill of Fare" was certainly no exception. Guests feasted on the finest food available in whatever quantity they desired.

On many ships, such as the steamer *America*, the main cabin was converted into a dining room for meal service. The black cabin boys, dressed in white jackets, removed the square oak tables from their stored positions against the walls and dressed the tables with red and white checked tablecloths and matching napkins. Each table was set for twelve with china plates, water goblets and silver engraved with the ship's name. Down the center of the table were bread trays, cake stands containing pastries, dishes of butter, silver canisters for the vinegar and oil cruets, a mustard jar, and containers of pickles, chow chow, catsup and hot sauces. Once the tables were in place, passengers of the *America* trickled into the dining hall for breakfast service. The meal consisted of bacon, sausage, eggs to order, grits, lye hominy, jambalaya, rolls, milk and coffee. But breakfast was not over until the pancakes were served, complete with butter and Louisiana cane syrup. With the conclusion of breakfast, the waiters dismantled the tables and returned the cabin to a social hall for dancing and card playing.

Though first-class passengers on steamships were treated with dignity and delightful accommodations, less affluent passengers often had to furnish their own food and bedding, sleeping among the bales and boxes on the cargo deck. In some cases, leftovers from the wealthier class were pitched into bins, one for meat and potatoes, one for bread and one for dessert—and served buffet style to those less fortunate.

In the antebellum days of steamboat travel, many passengers packed their own provisions and traveled with a man-servant who prepared private meals for the family he tended. When the boat stopped "to wood," these servants bought eggs, chickens, milk and other goods at the woodman's cabin.

The sumptuous meals served on the paddle wheelers complimented the ship's luxurious accommodations. During the golden age of steamboat travel (1870 - 1900) the finest food and drinks were served to travelers, and breakfast was no exception. In first-class passage, breakfast was usually served between 7 and 10. Mixed drinks were served early, followed by a variety of courses. A menu from the *Thompson Dean* recounted the bountiful breakfast available to passengers. In the category of broiled foods for breakfast the menu listed ham, breakfast bacon, calf's liver with onions and mackerel. Beefsteak was served plain, with onions, tomatoes and mushrooms or with a variety of sauces including bordelaise and Creole. Also served were pork and mutton chops, plain or breaded. Fried foods for breakfast were calf's brains, potatoes, onions, fish, tripe, mush, codfish balls, plantains, hominy fritters and sausage balls. Passengers could also select grits, potatoes stewed, potatoes fricasséed, hash, jambalaya, hominy, stewed kidney, fricasséed tripe and stewed chicken. There were offerings of waffles, muffins, buckwheat cakes, dipped toast, corn bread, hot rolls, buttered toast, dry toast, graham rolls and white rolls. Beverages included green tea, black tea, oolong tea, Java, Mocha, hot chocolate, milk and claret. Of course, breakfast was the least extravagant meal of the day.

A modern-day paddle wheeler docks at the Port of New Orleans.

Great pride was taken aboard the steamboats in the presentation of the food and in the service to passengers. On the little Saint Joseph, waiters copied the style of the larger steamboats by balancing the silverware in front of each place setting.
Courtesy of Thomas H. and Joan Gandy

Today, few steamboats travel the Mississippi River. Even fewer, the *American Queen, Delta Queen* and *Mississippi Queen,* provide overnight passenger accommodations. When aboard these majestic vessels, prepare for morning on the river and a scrumptious breakfast bill of fare. Choose the Plantation Breakfast consisting of two eggs prepared any style, sugar-cured ham, sausage or bacon, grits, hash browns or biscuits with saw mill gravy. The Carpetbagger Special, smoked salmon and onions cooked into scrambled eggs, might be more your style. The steamships also offer fresh fruits, omelettes, Eggs Benedict, hot cakes, lox, bagels and cream cheese and Steamboatin' Tall Stacks, which are hot cakes topped with two eggs and two strips of bacon.

Though the luxurious era of "floating palaces" has ceased, the intrigue of the River rolls on. So, what is this love affair between man and the Mississippi? It is a legacy...of motion, of memories, of a Mistress and days gone by.

Fillet of Catfish St. Charles

Often on the floating palaces of the Mississippi River, a fishing line or two dangling over the decks would produce enough Blue Channel catfish to serve this elegant breakfast dish. The unlikely combination of pan-sauteed fish, spicy Creole sauce and poached eggs creates a delicacy that has outlasted the steamboats by more than 100 years.

A streetcar carries passengers on St. Charles Avenue.

INGREDIENTS FOR SAUCE:

- 12 Roma tomatoes, peeled and seeded
- 1/4 cup extra virgin olive oil
- 2 tbsps vegetable oil
- 10 garlic cloves, sliced
- 1 cup fish or chicken stock (see recipe)
- 6 large basil leaves, julienned
- 1 tbsp fresh thyme leaves
- 1/2 tsp cayenne pepper
- Creole seasoning to taste
- Hot sauce to taste

METHOD FOR SAUCE:

In a saute pan, heat oils over medium-high heat. Using a wooden spoon, stir-fry garlic slices until lightly browned around the edges, approximately 2 minutes. Add tomatoes, bring to a low simmer and cook 5-7 minutes, adding stock to retain moisture. Add basil and thyme and season to taste using pepper, Creole seasoning and hot sauce. Additional stock may be used to thin sauce to preferred consistency. This recipe yields 3 cups of sauce.

INGREDIENTS FOR FISH:

- 6 (7-ounce) catfish fillets
- 1 egg, beaten
- 1/2 cup milk
- 1/2 cup water
- 2 cups seasoned flour
- 1/4 cup vegetable oil
- Salt to taste
- Pepper to taste
- 12 poached eggs (see recipe)
- 1 cup Hollandaise Sauce (see recipe)
- 1/4 cup chopped chives

METHOD FOR FISH:

Prepare Hollandaise according to recipe and keep warm. Poach eggs according to recipe and reheat in hot water. In a large mixing bowl, combine beaten egg, milk and water. Season lightly using salt and pepper. Place each fillet in the eggwash and set aside. Sprinkle seasoned flour on a large baking pan. In a 10-inch saute pan, heat oil over medium-high heat. Remove fillets from eggwash and coat in seasoned flour, shaking off all excess. Saute 2-3 fillets at a time, until golden brown on each side, approximately 5 minutes. NOTE: Do not overcrowd the skillet. Continue until all fish have been sauteed. To assemble dish, place 2 ounces of Creole Sauce in the center of a 10-inch plate. Top with sauteed fillet and 2 poached eggs. Pour Hollandaise on top of eggs and garnish with fresh chives.

PREP TIME: 1 Hour   SERVES: 6

Captain John's Cathead Biscuits

It must have been someone with a great sense of humor who first called these biscuits cathead. I think I first heard the term mentioned by Miss Emily Bruno of the Emily House on Lake Bruin in St. Joseph, Louisiana. Boy, could she make a cathead biscuit! What I like most about this recipe is the number of variations that can come about by adding other ingredients such as cracklin, cheese, herbs or whatever else comes to mind.

INGREDIENTS:

- 2 cups all purpose flour
- 1 tbsp baking powder
- 1/2 tsp baking soda
- 1/2 tsp salt
- 1/3 cup shortening
- 1 tbsp plus 1 tsp butter
- 2/3 cup buttermilk
- 2 tbsps melted butter

METHOD:

Preheat oven to 450°F. In a mixing bowl, sift flour, baking powder, baking soda and salt. Blend well, then cut in the shortening and the butter using a pastry cutter. The particles should remain pea-sized or that of coarse corn meal. Add buttermilk and, using a large cooking spoon, stir just enough to blend the buttermilk into the flour mixture. Sprinkle the work surface with flour and turn the dough out onto the work surface. Knead just until the dough comes together. Do not overwork the dough as the less you handle it, the flakier your biscuits will be. Break the dough into 8 equal portions and pat approximately 1/2-inch thick onto a baking sheet. The biscuits should be irregular in shape, but no more than 1/2-inch high and 1-inch apart. Bake biscuits until golden brown, approximately 10-15 minutes. Remove from oven and brush with melted butter.

PREP TIME: 30 Minutes   **SERVES:** 8

River Rations

The crew and passengers of keelboats and vessels that preceded the steamships in river navigation were not offered a sumptuous bill of fare. They drank whiskey and ate simple skillet dishes such as chowders, stews, game, corn, wheat breads and vegetables picked up en route. Many dishes were branded with "river" names by the crew. Gingerbread became "stage planks," doughnuts were "elephant ears," stew became "witch-water," bread pudding was "heavy devil" and meat was known as "bullneck."

Cathead biscuits soon to be smothered with fig and blackberry preserves.

THROW ME SOMETHING, MISTER:
Carnival, King Cake and Queen's Breakfast

Mardi Gras parade at the corner of Canal and St. Charles Avenue about 1866.
Courtesy of Louisiana State Museum

Piety always follows pleasure, and every Ash Wednesday morning finds the Crescent City on her knees–begging for mercy, begging for more. Mardi Gras is like no other time of year. It is as gaudy as it is elegant, as decadent as it is refined. For centuries the natives of the "City That Care Forgot" have held in highest regard their licentious, sensuous Carnival.

Mardi Gras was brought to Louisiana from Paris where it had been celebrated since the Middle Ages. In 1699 when Iberville and his explorers were traveling the Mississippi River, they remembered that Mardi Gras was being celebrated back home, and named the spot where they made camp that night "Point du Mardi Gras."

We believe that Mardi Gras balls began during New Orleans' colonial days, shortly after the city's founding in 1718. The celebrations, known as "Soirée du Roi," or "King's Party," were held in private homes on Twelfth-Night, January 6. The guests would cut a cake called King's Cake, or twelfth-cake, and the person finding the bean would host the next party, thus beginning a series of balls. The early carnival balls were masquerade dances that lasted until Shrove Tuesday or Mardi Gras.

By 1769 balls and costume soirées were an established part of the Creole social life of the city, and it was not uncommon for the dancing to last until morning. The Creoles loved their parties and the masked balls flourished under French rule. The Spanish and early American governors of Louisiana prohibited these masquerades until Creole sentiment prevailed and the balls returned in 1823.

The first recorded New Orleans Carnival occurred in 1827. A group of Creole planters' sons, who had recently returned from their studies in Paris, duplicated France's Mardi Gras festivities with a grand street procession of masqueraders. At this time Mardi Gras was nothing more than a group of maskers on foot, in carriages or on horseback traveling through the streets. It was not until 1837 that a costumed group of revelers walked in the first "parade." However, the violence among maskers during the next two decades incited the press to request a ban on Mardi Gras. Fortunately, in 1857, the Mistick Krewe of Comus was established, saving Mardi Gras from total discard and setting the standards of Carnival today. The six New Orleans men who founded the Comus organization presented a themed parade through the streets of New Orleans with floats and costumed maskers. Comus staged a tableau ball following the parade and then a banquet that lasted until morning.

OPPOSITE: *Breakfast fit for a King!*

A leather-bound volume identifying the early Mardi Gras krewes.

Rex, the King of Carnival and Monarch of Merriment, made his debut at Mardi Gras in 1872. The Rex organization began as part of the festivities surrounding the Russian Grand Duke Alexis Romanoff's visit to the city. Rex became the international symbol of Mardi Gras. Unique to the Rex parade is the "Boeuf Gras," or fatted bull or ox, which is the ancient symbol of the last meat eaten before the Lenten season begins. A live bull was used in the parade until 1909. A papier-mâché version appeared in 1959 and remains one of Carnival's most recognizable symbols.

Each year the Carnival organizations choose themes for their parade floats. Not surprisingly, food has been the principal symbol on more than one occasion. In 1859 the Mistick Krewe of Comus chose as its theme "The English Holidays." The tableaux embraced Christmas, which was represented by various drinks and dishes of Christmas dinner, notably plum pudding, mince-pie, the wassail-bowl, ale, port and champagne. In 1867 Comus featured "The Feast of Epicurus." The parade was a personification of various dishes and wines that make up a grand dinner: the Heralds of Appetite, the Knights of the Shell and the Rulers of the Roast. Rex chose a food theme for Mardi Gras on several occasions. In 1882 the theme was "The Pursuit of Pleasure;" in 1898 "The Harvest Queen" was showcased; and in 1903 "Fetes and Feasts" were celebrated.

Germaine Cazenave Wells, daughter of Count Arnaud of Arnaud's Restaurant, reigned as queen more than twenty times for more than seven krewes. During her reign of Sparta in 1954 Wells dressed as "Vintage Champagne." For the "Royal Repast" ball the entire court dressed as delicious dishes and wines. The maids dressed as shrimp cocktail, Creole gumbo, de luxe artichokes, sizzling broiled steak, cherry flambeaux, cheese and crème de menthe. In 1963, when she reigned again as Queen of Sparta, the court celebrated a "Royal Repast Relived." The mantle of Wells' dress featured a cornucopia of fruits, vegetables and seafood.

The visiting of Rex is an important Mardi Gras custom that began in 1874. Each year around midnight, Rex, his queen and their court leave their ball to join the Court of Comus. A blast of trumpets announces the arrival of Rex. Comus, the God of Joy and Mirth, toasts the health of Rex and his Queen. The two courts and their majesties perform a grand march before the guests to Carnival's theme song, "If Ever I Cease to Love." It would seem that this parade of royalty would be the grand finale to the Carnival season, but there's still the matter of breakfast.

In most krewes it is the responsibility of the Queen and her family to provide a breakfast for her King and Court following the ball. It seems that this breakfast has always been a New Orleans tradition. Laura Locoul, the namesake of Laura Plantation in Vacherie, Louisiana, was a maid at the Rex ball of 1884. She wrote that after the Rex ball, the Court rushed to the French Opera House for the ball of Comus where the courts met, exchanged queens and moved in a procession before the guests. Afterward, she and members of the Rex court went to Queen Annie Howard's home for a "sumptuous supper."

Antique Mardi Gras ball dance cards from the turn of the century.

Perhaps the most renowned Queen's Breakfast each year is that of the Rex and Comus krewes. Until 1949 these were separate breakfasts held at the private home of each queen. In 1949 a queen's father was dying, so a breakfast at her home was impossible. The queens of Comus and Rex held a joint breakfast at a local hotel, establishing a tradition that continues through today.

The Queen's Breakfast is private. Not even all members of the krewes are invited because the groups are so large. The queen and her parents determine the guest list, choose the flowers and band and select a breakfast menu. The menu of a Queen's Breakfast varies from year to year. The breakfast is sometimes served by waiters, or it can be arranged buffet-style. Menu items may extend to fresh fruits and berries, scrambled eggs, Eggs Sardou, Eggs Benedict, crawfish omelettes, crabmeat omelettes, tomato nests, crêpes Barbara, Harlequin Soufflé, grillades and grits, bacon, sausage, lamb chops, steaks, blueberry muffins, sweet rolls, prussians and an assortment of breads. Platters of food fill the hall and libations flow freely through the morning. It is then, after the last member of the court eats breakfast, that the rapture of food and flesh, liquor and lust slowly surrenders to the lean Lenten season. It seems that after centuries of bidding "farewell to flesh" a pious New Orleans would have emerged, but instead, repenting the deed merely revives the desire, and the flagrancy of Carnival parades on.

Mardi Gras King Cake

The king cake has a long tradition associated with the Carnival season. Originally served as a dessert on the Feast of the Epiphany, this cake was baked with unique ingredients. A bean was pressed into the dough prior to cooking and whoever got the slice containing the bean had to host a party for all guests in attendance. Today, the bean has been replaced with a plastic baby signifying the New Year.

INGREDIENTS:

- 1/2 ounce instant yeast
- 1/2 cup warm water
- 1/2 cup granulated sugar
- 5 cups all purpose flour
- 1/2 cup dry milk (powdered)
- 2 tsps salt
- 2 eggs, beaten
- 1 cup melted butter
- 1 cup warm water

METHOD:

In a measuring cup, combine yeast and 1/2 cup of water. Set aside. In a large mixing bowl, combine all dry ingredients and sift together. Using a dough hook on an electric mixer, blend ingredients on low speed for 2-3 minutes. In another mixing bowl, combine eggs, butter and remaining warm water. Slowly pour liquids and blossomed yeast into the dry ingredients, gradually increasing the mixing speed. Mix until dough separates from the bowl, approximately 8-10 minutes. An additional 1/2 cup of flour may be sprinkled into the bowl if dough is too wet. Brush a large stainless bowl with melted butter then place dough inside. Brush dough with more butter and cover tightly with plastic wrap. Allow dough to proof in a warm place until double in size, approximately 1 hour.

INGREDIENTS FOR GLAZE:

- 2 pounds powdered sugar
- 1 pinch salt
- 1 tbsp almond extract
- 3/4 cup water
- 3 tbsps cinnamon

METHOD FOR GLAZE:

In a large mixing bowl, combine sugar and salt. Place mixture in the bowl of an electric mixer and slowly pour in almond extract and water while mixing on low speed. Add cinnamon and continue to blend until glaze is smooth. Set aside.

TO ASSEMBLE:

- 1/4 cup melted butter
- 1/2 cup sugar
- 1 tbsp cinnamon
- Eggwash (1/2 cup milk, 2 eggs, beaten)
- Purple, green and gold sugars

Preheat oven to 350°F. After dough has proofed, roll out onto a well-floured surface into a rectangle shape 18" x 12". Brush the top of the dough with melted butter then sprinkle with mixture of sugar and cinnamon. *(Continues on page 29)*

Miss Varina Anne (Winnie) Davis, 1892 Queen of Comus, with Maids. Miss Davis dressed in Oriental robes for the theme, "Nippon, the Land of the Rising Sun."
Courtesy of Louisiana State Museum

(Continued from page 28) Cut cake into three even sections vertically. Fold edges tightly together in the middle. Form into a basic three-strand braid then into a circle. Brush the entire cake with eggwash and proof in a warm place until the cake doubles in size. Bake 20-25 minutes or until golden brown. Drizzle glaze over the entire cake and sprinkle with purple, green and gold sugars. These sugars are available at pastry and cake decorating outlets.

PREP TIME: 2 1/2 Hours   SERVES: 10

Gold jewelry and glittering sugar garnish this carnival confection.

Beaten Biscuits with Ham

Beaten biscuits are actually more of a scone or shortbread. Once the dough is made, the biscuits are beaten with a broomstick or small rolling pin until blisters appear on the dough. This process gives the biscuit its unique texture and prevents it from rising too high during baking. Many old timers say that the biscuits need to be beaten 20 minutes for family and 30 minutes for company.

INGREDIENTS:

- 1 cup all purpose flour
- 1 cup cake flour
- 1 tbsp sugar
- 1/2 tsp salt
- 1/4 tsp baking powder
- 6 tbsps lard or shortening
- 1/4 cup finely minced ham
- 1/2 cup skim milk

METHOD:

Preheat oven to 325°F. In the bowl of a food processor, combine flours, sugar, salt and baking powder. Pulse for 5 seconds then add shortening and ham. Process mixture until it resembles coarse crumbs, approximately 10-15 seconds. Add milk and process until dough forms into a ball. Wrap dough in plastic wrap and let rest for 10 minutes. Place dough on an unfloured surface and beat with the smooth side of a meat mallet for 15-20 minutes, until blistered. Fold the dough over occasionally while beating. You will notice that the dough becomes less sticky and stronger. To make each biscuit, pinch off small pieces of dough about the size of a walnut, between your thumb and forefinger. Place pieces on a baking sheet, close but not touching. Flatten slightly to even the cooking surface. Prick each biscuit with the tines of a fork twice. Bake for 30-40 minutes or until tops begin to color.

PREP TIME: 1 1/2 Hours   SERVES: 12

A festive invitation to a royal repast.

Crab Cakes Rex

Normally, in Bayou Country crab cakes are dense in texture because of the amount of bread crumbs in the recipe. Because they are served over poached eggs, I've cut back the bread crumbs for a looser texture.

INGREDIENTS:

- 1 pound lump crabmeat
- 3 tbsps butter
- 1/2 cup diced onions
- 1/2 cup diced celery
- 1/2 cup diced red bell pepper
- 1/4 cup diced garlic
- 1 cup seasoned Italian bread crumbs
- 1/4 cup scallions, minced
- 1/4 cup mayonnaise
- 1 egg

- 2 tbsps minced parsley
- 2 tsps Worcestershire sauce
- 2 tsps lemon juice
- 2 tbsps Old Bay seasoning
- 1 tsp dry mustard
- 1/2 tsp salt
- 1/2 tsp salt
- 1/2 tsp cracked black pepper
- Hot sauce to taste
- 10 poached eggs (see recipe)

METHOD:

Preheat oven to 500°F. Using your fingers, pick through crabmeat to remove any bone or cartilage. In a saute pan, melt butter over medium-high heat. Add onions, celery, bell pepper and garlic. Saute 3-5 minutes or until vegetables are wilted. Remove and allow to cool slightly. In a large mixing bowl, combine sauteed vegetables along with all remaining ingredients except crabmeat and eggs. Gently fold in crabmeat with your fingers continually checking for bone or cartilage. Blend carefully into the bread crumb mixture until all ingredients are well incorporated. Adjust seasonings if necessary. Gently form crab mixture into a 1" x 2 1/2" patty and place on a cookie sheet. Place in the refrigerator and chill for at least 1 hour. Remove cakes from the refrigerator and broil each 3-4 minutes or until browned. Turn each cake over gently so they don't fall apart, and broil the other side of the cake for 3-4 additional minutes. Place crab cake in the center of a dinner plate and top with one poached egg and Hollandaise Sauce (see recipe).

PREP TIME: 30 Minutes   SERVES: 8

Miss Rosa Florence Febiger. Queen of Rex, 1900.
Courtesy of Louisiana State Museum

LE RÉVEILLON:
Christmas Eve Around the Fire

Santa mugs overfilled with eggnog.

Against the cold nakedness of a winter's eve, timber pyramids rise into the virgin night. In an instant these pyramids are set ablaze to light the path for passersby traveling to Midnight Mass. The desire of lovers walking near the bonfires is reflected in the burning passion of the flames that lick the levee and cast shadows down the riverbank. The lovers dream of their return journey home and their early morning feast yet to come.

Le Réveillon, or the awakening, the morning feast following Midnight Mass on Christmas or New Year's Eve, was an age-old custom inherited by the Louisiana Creoles from their European ancestors and adopted by the Germans who settled in the River parishes. Réveillon was a time of family reunion and thanksgiving, which began early in the evening with family members converging on households for hours of conversation. In the French Quarter of New Orleans when the church bells began to ring at about 11 o'clock, the Creoles and their families strolled to St. Louis Cathedral for Christmas Mass. A man might miss any service during the year, but he would be certain to join his family for Midnight Mass at Christmas.

Christmas Eve was recognized as a day of fasting and abstinence by most Catholics. By the end of Midnight Mass the Creoles were hungry and ready to celebrate with a Réveillon feast. Family members returning from church were greeted with an elaborate meal of daube glacé, chicken and oyster gumbo, salmis or game pies, egg dishes, sweetbreads, soups and soufflés, grillades, grits, hominy, homemade breads, crystallized fruits, fruitcake and lavish desserts, wine, brandy, eggnog and New Orleans coffee. The Creole table emulated what might have been found on the tables of France during that same hour. The ladies and children usually celebrated until about 3 o'clock in the morning, but the gentlemen smoked cigars, sipped cordials and conversed until the dawn of Christmas Day.

The children received small token gifts and candies stuffed in their stockings on Christmas; the more elaborate gifts were to be given on New Year's Day. A small tree with a tiny crèche beneath it decorated the home. On Christmas the children were taken to the Cathedral and other small churches in the French Quarter to view the crèches and to say prayers for the Christ Child.

In rural South Louisiana, Le Réveillon was celebrated by many families into the 1950s and 1960s. People gathered at the house of the family matriarch or patriarch to visit, then to walk to Midnight Mass. Often, the trip was lighted by bonfires along the levee, and a hearty breakfast always followed.

A second more elaborate, more festive Réveillon with singing and dancing was celebrated on New Year's Eve. Tables were adorned with platters of oysters, steaming bowls of gumbo and bouillabaisse, fish, fowl, wild game, daube glacé,

OPPOSITE: *The fireplace in the boardroom at Zatarain's is the perfect place to enjoy Réveillon delicacies on Christmas Eve.*

The French Quarter sports Christmas-colored neon year-round.

cream puff pyramids called croquembouche and wine and rum cakes filled with jellies.

The Réveillon celebration disappeared from New Orleans and rural South Louisiana perhaps during the Reconstruction days following the Civil War or during the social change following the world wars when many of the old ways were lost. The relaxation of Church law concerning fasting and abstinence may have also contributed to the demise of Réveillon. In 1986, this old-world tradition was revived in New Orleans as a way to attract visitors to the French Quarter during the holidays. Many restaurants and hotels adopted Réveillon menus during this festive season.

While the Réveillon repast is being revisited in Louisiana, it never lost its vitality in European countries. The traditional Réveillon feasts are still celebrated at homes, in restaurants and even in country chateaus.

While Christmas morning may be for children, Christmas Eve is definitely for lovers. Candlelit caresses. Intimate kisses under Spanish moss and mistletoe. Whispered conversations over warm winter drinks and late-night desserts under goose down quilts…

Daube

Although a less tender, inexpensive cut of beef, daube is commonly found on the tables in South Louisiana. The slow cooking process combined with the many vegetable seasonings tends to make this dish a very full-flavored entree.

INGREDIENTS:

- 1 (5-pound) beef shoulder roast
- 1/4 pound salt pork fat
- 1/4 cup salt
- 1/4 cup black pepper
- 1/4 cup finely diced garlic
- 1/2 cup bacon drippings or vegetable oil
- 2 cups chopped onions
- 2 cups chopped celery
- 1 cup chopped bell pepper
- 1/4 cup diced garlic
- 1/4 cup tomato sauce
- 2 cups diced carrots
- 1 cup dry red wine
- 1 quart beef stock (see recipe)
- Salt and black pepper to taste

METHOD:

Cut the salt pork fat into 1/4-inch strips about 2-inches long. Combine 1/4 cup salt and 1/4 cup black pepper. Using a sharp paring knife, cut six to eight 1-inch deep slits into the shoulder roast. Open these slits with two fingers and stuff with generous amounts of garlic, salt, pepper and pork fat. Continue until all slits have been stuffed. Season roast well on all sides using salt and pepper. In a cast iron dutch oven, heat bacon drippings over medium-high heat. Brown roast well on all sides. When golden brown, add onions, celery, bell pepper and garlic. Saute 3-5 minutes or until vegetables are wilted. Add tomato sauce, carrots and red wine, blending well into the vegetable mixture. Add beef stock, bring to a rolling boil and reduce heat to simmer. Cover dutch oven and allow roast to simmer 2 1/2 hours. Season to taste using salt and pepper and continue to cook until roast is tender. Slice and serve with natural sauce.

PREP TIME: 3 Hours   SERVES: 6-8

Daube shaped into a Christmas wreath with garlic croutons.

Daube Glacé

Daube Glacé is the most classical of the Creole hors d'oeuvres. Usually made with leftover daube (see previous page), further cooked with additional seasonings, this dish is also found in most retail markets around the City of New Orleans.

INGREDIENTS:

- 1 (3-pound) cooked daube (see recipe)
- 2 quarts beef stock (see recipe)
- Reserved sauce for pre-cooked daube
- 1/2 cup finely diced onions
- 1/2 cup finely diced celery
- 1/2 cup finely diced red bell pepper
- 1/4 cup diced garlic
- 1/2 cup finely diced carrots
- 1/2 cup finely minced parsley
- Salt and cayenne pepper to taste
- 3 envelopes gelatin, dissolved

METHOD:

Cut cooked daube into 1-inch cubes. In a cast iron dutch oven, bring beef stock and sauce from cooked daube to a light boil. Add cooked meat, onions, celery, bell pepper and garlic. Reduce heat to simmer and allow to cook until meat begins to string apart. Strain all ingredients from liquid through a fine sieve and set aside. Return liquid to heat and reduce to 1 1/2 quarts. Add carrots and parsley. Season to taste using salt and cayenne pepper. Using a wire whisk, blend dissolved gelatin into sauce. Remove from heat and allow to cool slightly. Break the meat into small pieces and place equal amounts in two terrine molds. Divide cooked vegetables from the original sauce in previous Daube recipe between the two molds. Ladle stock over the meat, cover with clear wrap and allow to gel in the refrigerator. Daube glacé is best when allowed to sit for 24 hours for flavors to develop. The Daube glacé should be sliced and served with garlic croutons.

PREP TIME: 2 1/2 Hours   MAKES: 2 (4" x 8") Terrine Pans

A bonfire waiting to light the night sky at Laura Plantation in Vacherie.

Bonfires on the Levee

Building bonfires on the levee has long been a family tradition in St. James and St. John the Baptist parishes. The construction of these timber pyramids usually began around Thanksgiving in anticipation of the Christmas Eve night spectacular. Every Cajun boy knew to surround the willow branch structure with cane reeds or bamboo, because once ablaze, these reeds popped louder than firecrackers and shot sparks into the sky brighter than the stars.

Bonfires on River Road date back to the settlement of the French and Germans in the 1700s. Local legends contend that the bonfires were lit Christmas Eve to guide Papa Noel and his alligator-drawn pirogue into the darkness of Cajun country.

The origin of bonfires dates centuries before Christ, when the Celts inhabited France and the British Isles. In Germany, the bonfires are accompanied by wheels, wrapped in straw, ignited and rolled down a hill. In Louisiana's German settlements near Lutcher, a similar custom exists of soaking cotton bales with kerosene, lighting them and rolling them down the levee.

In Louisiana, Christmas is never complete until the bonfires are set ablaze on the levee, and every guest has been served a bowl of chicken, oyster and andouille gumbo.

Salmi of Rabbit

Although this stew was always made from leftover game, especially game birds, we often made creative entrees in the same fashion. In this version, wild or tamed boned rabbits are used to create a wonderful game pie. Try this recipe with a combination of game meats as the perfect way to clean out the freezer and make unique gifts for friends.

Game pies have been a Christmas Eve tradition for centuries.

INGREDIENTS:

- 2 large wild rabbits
- 2 large onions, quartered
- 2 carrots, sliced
- 1 celery stick, quartered
- 1 head garlic, split
- 1 tbsp peppercorns
- 1 bay leaf
- Salt to taste
- 1/4 pound butter
- 1/4 cup flour
- 1 cup diced onions
- 1 cup diced celery
- 1/2 cup diced red bell pepper
- 1/4 cup chopped garlic
- 1 quart reserved rabbit stock
- 1 ounce Burgundy wine
- 1 tbsp chopped thyme
- 1 tsp chopped basil
- 1/2 tsp rubbed sage
- Salt and cracked pepper to taste
- 3/4 cup sliced green onions
- 1/2 cup chopped parsley
- 2 (9-inch) prepared pie crusts

METHOD:

Cut each rabbit into 8 pieces and place in a stock pot along with quartered onions, carrots, celery, garlic, peppercorns, bay leaf and salt. Cover ingredients by 2-3 inches with cold water. Bring to a rolling boil, reduce to simmer and cook until rabbit is tender and falling from bones. It is important to skim the impurities that rise to the surface during the cooking process. Once rabbit is tender, remove from stock and allow to cool. Strain approximately 1 quart of the rabbit stock and set aside for later. When rabbit is cooled, debone and discard bones. Preheat oven to 375°F. In a large cast iron skillet, melt butter over medium-high heat. Add flour and, using a wire whisk, stir until golden brown roux is achieved. Add onions, celery, bell pepper and garlic. Saute 3-5 minutes or until vegetables are wilted. Slowly add stock, a little at a time, until stew-like consistency is achieved. Add wine, thyme, basil and sage. Season to taste using salt and pepper. Break the boned rabbit into small pieces and place into simmering sauce. Allow rabbit to cook approximately 1 hour, adding additional stock as necessary. The majority of the sauce should be absorbed by the rabbit toward the end of the cooking time. Add green onions and parsley and adjust seasonings if necessary. Pour the contents onto a large baking pan and allow to cool to room temperature. Press one of the pie shells into the bottom of a pie pan. Spoon in rabbit then cover with second pie crust. Crimp the edges of the crust together and cut away the excess. Using a paring knife, pierce the crust in 3 or 4 places to allow steam to escape. Bake 30 minutes or until golden brown. Allow to cool slightly, prior to serving.

PREP TIME: 2 1/2 Hours   SERVES: 6

WHEN THE ROOSTER CROWS,
It's "Breakfast at Brennan's"

The front entrance to Brennan's on Royal Street.

She tips her glass, sipping the last of her Mr. Funk. Catching her lover's attention with a mischievous twinkle in her eye, she leans over the linen tablecloth and whispers in a lustful voice, "Was it good for you, too?"

Breakfast at Brennan's is like breakfast in bed following a naughty night of indiscreet passion...long, intoxicating and never disappointing.

Owen Edward Brennan, "The Happy Irishman of the French Quarter," founded Brennan's Restaurant in 1946 at the challenge of Count Arnaud, a good friend and owner of Arnaud's Restaurant. At the time, Brennan owned the Old Absinthe House on Bourbon Street. The pub, built in 1798, had been a secret hangout of pirate Jean Lafitte, who was instrumental in protecting the city during the Battle of New Orleans. Owen would relay complaints overheard at the Absinthe House to offending restaurant owners. Finally, Count Arnaud told Brennan that he should open a restaurant if he thought he could do better, and he taunted Brennan that no Irishman could run anything more than a hamburger joint. Brennan accepted the challenge, vowing to prove to the local aristocrats that an Irishman could create the finest French restaurant in the city.

In July 1946, Brennan leased the Vieux Carré Restaurant across the street from his tavern. He named it Owen Brennan's French & Creole Restaurant. It became known as Owen Brennan's Vieux Carré, and eventually Brennan's Restaurant. He hired his dad to greet lunch customers, his sister Adelaide to do the bookkeeping and his sister Ella to supervise the kitchen. Chef Paul Blangé created many of Brennan's original signature dishes.

In a few years Brennan had established himself as one of New Orleans' best known hosts and his restaurant as one of the finest French food eateries in the city. He welcomed to his restaurant tourists, political figures, writers and celebrities such as Walt Disney, Vivien Leigh, John Wayne and Tennessee Williams.

Breakfast at Brennan's was one of Owen's ingenious marketing strategies, born after the 1948 publication of Frances Parkinson Keyes' novel, *Dinner at Antoine's.* Owen was envious of his rival's celebrity but intrigued. He was confident that if dinner could entice the culinary crowd, so could breakfast. He revived the nineteenth-century custom of a three-hour breakfast, and became the first one of his time to promote breakfast as an event. The meal was advertised as "an old New Orleans tradition dating from the great days of the Creoles," and the rooster, or chanteclair, became symbolic of "Breakfast at Brennan's." Surely, Owen must have had the elaborate breakfasts of Madame Bégué's in mind when breakfast at Brennan's was conceived and the menu determined. Madame Bégué was a distinguished Creole cook of German descent who attained national prominence in the late nineteenth century for her fabulous "second breakfasts."

OPPOSITE: *Eggs Hussarde, a Brennan's tradition.*

The rain-swept patio at Brennan's.

Owen's friends watched in wonder as he set about popularizing a restaurant breakfast at a time when people wanted quick morning meals. Many were astonished when they discovered that his menu consisted of broiled pompano, lamb chops with béarnaise sauce, shirred eggs, café diable, gin fizz, claret, champagne, fruit in brandy and a dessert flamed in Kirsch and strawberry liqueur.

But Brennan resolved that if nobody else intended to enjoy his breakfasts, he certainly would. He even had his portrait painted opening a bottle of the best champagne for breakfast, which still hangs in Brennan's today.

Brennan's Restaurant became so successful that when the lease was to be renewed on the building, the landlord demanded fifty percent of the business. In 1954, Owen E. Brennan decided to move the restaurant to its present location at 417 Royal Street and renovations on the property began.

The site on Royal Street was part of the original city of New Orleans designed by Adrien de Pauger in 1721. The structure was rebuilt by Don Vincente Rillieux after a 1794 fire destroyed more than two hundred buildings in the French Quarter. The building served as a residence, a place of business, the Banque de la Louisiane and the Louisiana State Bank. It was once the home of Martin Gordon, a prominent Virginian and clerk of the United States District Court, who entertained General Andrew Jackson regularly at fashionable Creole parties. In 1920, the property was donated to Tulane University. The Brennan family rented the building from Tulane before purchasing it in 1984.

Owen E. Brennan never saw the opening of his restaurant at the Royal Street location. He died in his sleep of a massive coronary the November before the May 1956 opening. He was gone, but his family maintained the tradition of excellence that had made Brennan's world-famous. Despite his absence, his friends still patronized the restaurant. The business prospered on Royal Street as it had on Bourbon. Breakfast at Brennan's and the famous dishes created in the kitchen, such as Bananas Foster and Eggs Hussarde, are Owen's legacy to the world.

Breakfast at Brennan's is served any time of day or night in one of the twelve dining rooms or in the courtyard. Executive Chef Lazone Randolph continues Brennan's culinary standard of excellence with traditional favorites while creating imaginative masterpieces that would make Owen proud. Brennan's maintains a classic wine cellar in what was once the slave quarters of the pre-Civil War mansion. For its outstanding wine cellar Brennan's has received the "Wine Spectator Grand Award."

Breakfast at Brennan's is relaxed, unhurried and certainly unforgettable. A traditional Brennan's Breakfast is reminiscent of a Planter's Breakfast beginning with an Absinthe Suissesse, followed by Oyster Soup Brennan, Eggs Benedict, a hearty sirloin with fresh mushrooms and hot French bread, accompanied by Perrier-Jouet, Grand Brut. Of course, Breakfast at Brennan's is never complete without Bananas Foster.

Among the array of egg dishes on the menu are Eggs Hussarde, Eggs Sardou, Eggs Bayou Lafourche, Eggs St. Charles, Eggs Ellen, Eggs Owen, Eggs Shannon, Eggs Portuguese and Eggs Nouvelle Orléans. There are numerous omelettes such as Omelette Florentine, Crabmeat Omelette, Cajun Tasso Omelette with cheddar cheese and Cajun Grilled Andouille Omelette with cheddar cheese. Breakfast items range from grillades and grits and grilled ham steak to Brennan's Blackened Redfish or Trout Nancy.

Whatever you choose to eat, begin the meal with an "eye opener" such as Brandy Milk Punch, a Mimosa or Mr. Funk of New Orleans. Then, indulge in a long, leisurely Breakfast at Brennan's, where there are as many exotic egg dishes on the menu as there are provocative pleasures in the boudoir.

Eggs Hussarde

SERVES: 6

INGREDIENTS:

- 2 cups veal stock (see recipe)
- 1/2 cup Burgundy Wine
- 1 tbsp softened butter
- 2 tbsps butter
- 12 slices Canadian bacon
  (ham can be substituted)
- 12 Holland rusks or English Muffins
- 12 poached eggs (see recipe)
- 1 cup Hollandaise Sauce (see recipe)
- 6 grilled or broiled tomato halves for garnish

METHOD:

Combine veal stock and Burgundy Wine in a saucepan and bring to a rolling boil. Reduce to simmer and cook until sauce is thickened and approximately 1 cup in volume. Add the 1 tablespoon of softened butter and whisk into the sauce. Remove from heat and keep this Marchand de Vin Sauce warm.

Melt the 2 tablespoons of butter in a large saute pan and warm the Canadian bacon over low heat. Place 2 Holland rusks on each plate and cover with slices of warm Canadian bacon. Spoon Marchand de Vin Sauce over the meat, then set a poached egg on each slice. Ladle Hollandaise Sauce over the eggs; garnish the plates with grilled tomatoes and serve.

RECIPE MODIFIED FROM *BREAKFAST AT BRENNAN'S AND DINNER, TOO.* COOKBOOK
COPYRIGHT 1994, BRENNAN'S INC.

Legendary chef Michael Roussel, now deceased, prepares his world-famous breakfasts.

Oyster Soup Brennan

SERVES: 10-12

INGREDIENTS:

- 2 cups (about 48) shucked oysters
- 3 quarts cold water
- 3/4 cup (1 1/2 sticks) butter
- 1 cup celery, finely chopped
- 1 1/2 tbsps garlic, finely chopped
- 1 cup scallions, finely chopped
- 4 bay leaves
- 1 tbsp thyme leaves
- 1 cup all purpose flour
- 1 1/2 tbsps Worcestershire sauce
- 1 tsp salt
- 1 tsp white pepper
- 1/2 cup fresh parsley, finely chopped

METHOD:

In a large saucepan, combine the oysters and 3 quarts cold water. Bring the water to a boil, then reduce the heat and simmer about 5 minutes; skim any residue from the surface. Strain the oysters, reserving the stock. Dice the oysters and set aside. Melt the butter in a large pot and saute the celery and garlic over medium heat about 5 minutes until tender. Add the scallions, bay leaves, and thyme, then stir in the flour. Cook the mixture for 5 minutes over low heat, stirring constantly. Using a whisk, blend in the oyster stock, then add the Worcestershire, salt, and pepper. Cook the soup over medium heat about 20 minutes until thickened, then add the parsley and oysters. Simmer until the oysters are warmed through, about 5 minutes. Remove the bay leaves prior to serving.

RECIPE TAKEN FROM *BREAKFAST AT BRENNAN'S AND DINNER, TOO.* COOKBOOK COPYRIGHT 1994, BRENNAN'S INC.

The personality of the Crescent City.

Mr. Funk of New Orleans

Mr. Funk of New Orleans was created in memory of Brennan's Restaurant's late Cellar Master, Herman Funk.

SERVES: 1

INGREDIENTS:

- 3 ounces champagne
- 2 1/2 ounces cranberry juice
- 1/2 ounce peach schnapps
- 1 whole ripe strawberry

METHOD:

Pour the champagne into a stemmed glass, then add the cranberry juice and schnapps. Garnish with strawberry and serve.

RECIPE TAKEN FROM *BREAKFAST AT BRENNAN'S AND DINNER, TOO.* COOKBOOK

COPYRIGHT 1994, BRENNAN'S INC.

The author enjoys a somber moment with a glass of Mr. Funk at Brennan's.

EAT YOUR HEART OUT:
Casual Breakfasts in the Crescent City

Links of spicy boudin. *Oh, yes.*
   Dirty rice. *Don't stop.*
      French toast with powdered sugar. *Oh, that's it!*

Keep it coming…overfilled platters of omelettes with fried potatoes, bowls of grits with homemade biscuits, waffles smothered in thick cane syrup. A casual breakfast in New Orleans is like naughty casual sex—it always seems to satisfy just the right spot and gets better the later it's served.

The Crescent City is rife with casual breakfast places, and one of the most famous "dirty girls" is the HUMMINGBIRD HOTEL AND GRILL on St. Charles Avenue. This little greasy spoon is located on the salty side of the tracks where a little "nasty" constitutes a normal night of business. The Hummingbird, open 24 hours a day, 365 days a year, attracts an eclectic crowd…from cabbies to cops, deadbeats to debutantes.

The Hummingbird has been a late-night crowd pleaser since Harry Hillensbeck opened the place in the late 1940s. As a kid Hillensbeck had been a waiter on the Louisiana and Nashville Railroad. He worked the loop between Baton Rouge and New Orleans known as the "Hummingbird." He quit the line to open a diner by the same name, which he hoped would attract the railroad crew.

The original Hummingbird was located across the street from its present location. It was surrounded by beer joints and sleazy motels and catered to the rougher set. The flashing sign in front of the "Bird" is still a beacon in the night to wanderers and wanton women who need a cheap meal and a cheap night's rest.

Despite its rough and tumble temperament, the "Bird" has served hearty breakfasts to the working class and the late-night ramblers for more than 50 years. The menu is scrawled on the trademark chalkboard on a side wall of the cafe. You can read it from your stool at the old brick counter or from any one of the small tables scattered throughout the room.

Belly-up to the bar for the "Early Bird," a late-night breakfast favorite of three eggs, hash browns or grits, biscuits or toast, ham, bacon or sausage. If you prefer buttermilk hotcakes, choose the "Steam Schooner." Other favorites include "Steak & Eggs" or the "Pork Chop Breakfast." The food is cheap but it's guaranteed to please, and in a world drenched with false fronts and counterfeit comforts, it's nice to know there are some things you never have to fake.

MOTHER'S RESTAURANT, established in 1938 by Simon Landry, is another favorite New Orleans breakfast spot, specializing in authentic home cooking. Located in the Central Business District at the corner of Poydras and Tchoupitoulas, Mother's is a working-class restaurant recognized for generous portions of food served at reasonable prices.

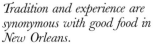

Tradition and experience are synonymous with good food in New Orleans.

OPPOSITE: *Nothing's better than a Ferdi at Mother's!*

Midnight at the Camellia Grill.

New Orleans is a 24-hour city, so breakfast at the Old Coffee Pot is often served to those just waking up or to those who have not yet gone to bed.

But perhaps the most charming lady of all the breakfast nooks is the CAMELLIA GRILL. Demurely perched on South Carrollton and St. Charles this lady of the night has gently gazed upon the crowds sashaying past for more than 50 years. Don't be deceived by her innocent air. Beneath her graceful, perfumed scent and white-columned gown lurks a passionate seductress awaiting her next conquest.

Stepping into the Camellia Grill is like stepping back in time. It has been owned by the Schwartz family for three generations and looks today much as it did when it opened in December 1946. It has never lost its 1950s charm right down to the old-style drug store counter with stools and white linen napkins. The waiters, dressed in white coats and black bow ties, double as entertainers and perform for guests to the sizzle of sausage on the grill and the drizzle of coffee in the pot.

In the early days the Camellia Grill fed customers around the clock. The grill was popular because of its linen napkins and air conditioning, which was rare back then.

Today, the Camellia Grill is especially popular for breakfast on weekends when lines wrap around her skirts and stretch down the city block. House favorites include pecan waffles and Spanish omelettes topped with chili followed by a slice of legendary chocolate pecan pie. And the lady would be alarmed if you departed without having an order of grits on the side.

The lines may be long, but the theatrical waiters turn the crowds over quickly. With a wink of pink neon and the promise of homemade pies, you know in an instant that the Camellia Grill is more than worth the wait.

Kenny & Mary Daze enjoy café au lait and beignets at Robert's Coffee House in Sorrento.

Raised Calas (Rice Cakes)

Calas or rice cakes were introduced to America by the Africans who also brought rice growing techniques from the region of Senegal. These rice cakes although quite different from most breakfast foods do have one similarity, they are much better with the addition of powdered sugar and cane syrup.

INGREDIENTS:

- 1 cup long grain white rice
- 1 1/2 cups cold water
- 1 tsp salt
- 1/2 tsp butter
- 1 package dry yeast
- 1/2 cup warm water
- 3 large eggs, well beaten
- 1/4 cup sugar
- 1/4 tsp freshly grated nutmeg
- 1/2 tsp salt
- 1 1/4 cups flour
- 2 cups vegetable oil
- Confectioners sugar

METHOD:

In a 2-quart cast iron sauce pan, combine water, salt and butter. Bring mixture to a rolling boil and add rice. Reduce heat to simmer, cover and cook 30 minutes. Do not remove cover or stir rice during the cooking process. When done, stir rice and place in a large mixing bowl. Using the back of a wooden spoon, mash rice and allow to cool. Dissolve yeast in water. Add to rice and beat thoroughly with a spoon for approximately 2 minutes. Cover the bowl with a towel and set in a warm place to rise overnight. Add eggs, sugar, nutmeg, salt and flour to rice mixture. Stir mixture well and cover bowl again. Set in a warm place to rise for 30 minutes. In a 14-inch cast iron skillet, heat oil over medium-high heat. Drop the rice batter by heaping tablespoons into the hot oil. Deep fry cakes, 4 to 5 at a time, until golden brown on all sides. Remove and place on drain board. Top each cake with confectioners sugar. Serve hot.

PREP TIME: 30 Minutes   SERVES: 4

The menu board outside the Old Coffee Pot.

EROTIC, EXOTIC
New Orleans

It's home of the quintessential love affair, where passions burn deep into the night and multiple pleasures rise and fall like the crests of the River. Nothing is more arousing than breakfast in the Big Easy, except breakfast in the boudoirs of Bayou Country, where the only thing between you and the sheet is your lover.

Steamboat Gothic architecture graces many buildings in the French Quarter.

WELCOME TO
Louisiana's
BED AND BREAKFASTS...

Lanaux Mansion

THE FRENCH QUARTER

The original gas chandelier graces the entrance hallway at Lanaux Mansion.

ove at first sight. Through the years it has happened to many—a breathless encounter, a serendipitous discovery. It happened to Ruth Bodenheimer on her seventeenth birthday. She fell in love near the French Quarter in New Orleans, right where Esplanade meets Chartres. You may guess that a debonair gentleman won her heart as she strolled along the boulevard, but that would not be entirely true. It was on this day that she visited Lanaux Mansion, an extraordinary historic home that she loved instantaneously and was compelled to someday own.

This turn-of-the-century family home was designed by William Fitzner and constructed in 1879 for a bachelor lawyer, Charles Andrew Johnson, of Connecticut. Though built for Johnson, the home is named for Marie Andry Lanaux, his business partner's daughter, to whom he left all his worldly possessions.

The two-and-one-half-story Victorian townhouse is built in Italianate style with a recessed entrance and a second-level cast-iron gallery. The beautiful home Ruth promptly adored is a favorite among filmmakers who often use it as a background for movies.

Once Ruth purchased Lanaux Mansion she planned to restore the home to its former splendor. Amid long discarded articles in the attic were discovered antiques and hand-painted wall coverings original to the house, which became the cornerstone of her renovation. To these precious heirlooms she has added antiques from her personal collection to complete the home in historic detail.

Today, Lanaux Mansion welcomes visitors with private suites in the main home comfortably arranged with a bath and kitchenette, or guests can request a romantic garden cottage for their stay. To arrive at Lanaux Mansion travel I-10 East to Esplanade Avenue, Exit 236A. The home is located at 547 Esplanade, one block from the Old U.S. Mint, and within walking distance to the old Ursuline Convent and the historic Vieux Carré. Call (504) 330-2826 for advanced reservations, which are required.

While visiting this Mediterranean-flavored city by the Mississippi, stroll through Jackson Square, ride the riverfront streetcar, tour the Superdome, enjoy a historic walking tour of the French Quarter or get a true taste of Bayou Country with a swamp boat ride, but whatever you do, hold on to your heart. The Big Easy is a renowned philanderer—making love, making memories and making departure devastatingly difficult.

OPPOSITE: *The Esplanade Avenue entrance to Lanaux Mansion.*

A century of family photographs adorn the piano at Lanaux Mansion.

FRICASSÉE OF CHICKEN & SMOKED SAUSAGE

Next to Southern Fried Chicken, the fricassée or "stewed chicken" is the most popular dish in the kitchens of New Orleans. The traditional fricassée was always prepared on Sunday, and when the dish needed to be dressed up for special guests, a melange of vegetables and seasoning meats were added.

INGREDIENTS:

- 1 (3-pound) fryer
- 1 pound smoked sausage, sliced
- 3/4 cup vegetable oil
- 1 cup flour
- 1 cup diced onions
- 1/2 cup diced celery
- 1/2 cup diced red bell pepper
- 1/4 cup minced garlic
- 6 cups chicken stock (see recipe)
- 1 cup sliced carrots, (cut 1/2-inch thick)
- 1/2 cup sliced celery, (cut 1/4-inch thick)
- 1 cup diced potatoes, (cut 3/4-inch cubed)
- 1/2 cup sliced green onions
- 1/4 cup chopped parsley
- Salt and black pepper to taste
- Hot sauce to taste

METHOD:

Cut fryer into 8 serving pieces and season well using salt and pepper. In a large cast iron dutch oven, heat oil over medium-high heat. Add flour and, using a wire whisk, whip constantly until dark brown roux is achieved (see roux techniques). Add onions, diced celery, bell pepper and garlic. Saute 3-5 minutes or until vegetables are wilted. Add chicken stock and stir constantly to dissolve roux. Add chicken pieces and sausage and blend well into the roux mixture. Bring to a rolling boil, reduce to simmer and cook 30 minutes. Add carrots, sliced celery and potatoes. Season to taste using salt, pepper and hot sauce. Continue to cook until chicken is tender, adding additional stock if needed. Add green onions and parsley and cook an additional 5 minutes. Serve over steamed white rice.

PREP TIME: 1 1/2 Hours

SERVES: 6

MODIFICATIONS:

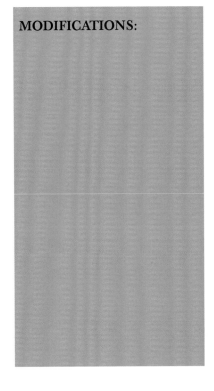

SWEETBREADS IN LEMON CAPER CREAM

Sweetbreads are the thymus glands found in young suckling animals and are considered a delicacy when prepared from veal or young calves. The gland is slightly larger than a man's fist. Once the calf is weaned from the mother and turned out to pasture, the glands shrink and disappear in less than a week. Sweetbreads have always been a sought after delicacy in Creole homes and have been prepared by the hands of Creole chefs in New Orleans for generations.

INGREDIENTS:

- 1 pound veal sweetbreads
- 1 tsp lemon juice
- 2 tbsps capers in juice
- 1 carrot, diced
- 1 small onion, diced
- 1 celery stalk, sliced
- 2 garlic cloves, mashed
- 12 peppercorns
- 1 bay leaf
- 1 cup dry white wine
- 1 quart water
- 1 cup seasoned flour
- 1/2 stick butter
- 1/4 cup minced purple shallots
- 1/4 cup minced garlic
- 1 ounce dry white wine
- 2 cups heavy whipping cream
- 1 cup reserved poaching liquid
- Salt and black pepper to taste
- 1/4 cup chopped chives
- 1 tsp lemon zest

METHOD:

Have your butcher select 3 whole pieces, approximately one pound, of fresh sweetbreads. In a 1-gallon stock pot, create a poaching liquid by combining carrots, onion, celery, garlic cloves, peppercorns, bay leaf, wine and water. Bring liquid to a rolling boil and reduce to simmer. Cover and cook 30 minutes to flavor the liquid. Add whole sweetbreads, turning once or twice until firm to the touch, approximately 3-5 minutes. Do not overcook. Remove sweetbreads and cool. This may be done the day prior to use. Strain and reserve 1 cup of poaching liquid for later use. Once sweetbreads are cool, use your fingers to remove the veil-type membrane covering the sweetbreads. Using a sharp boning knife, slice sweetbreads 1/2-inch thick. The smaller pieces that break away are also usable in this recipe. Season sweetbreads using salt and pepper and then dust in seasoned flour. In a cast iron skillet, melt butter over medium-high heat. Be careful not to brown butter. Add sweetbreads and saute, a few at a time, until lightly browned and crispy. Remove and keep hot. Into the same skillet, add shallots and garlic. Saute 3-5 minutes or until vegetables are wilted. Add lemon juice, capers and deglaze with white wine. Pour in heavy whipping cream and 1/4 cup of poaching liquid. Reduce sauce over medium-high heat until liquid coats the back of a spoon, approximately 7-10 minutes. Be careful as cream may tend to boil over in the early stages. Season to taste using salt and pepper. Add chopped chives and lemon zest. Place sweetbreads in the center of a 10-inch serving plate and surround with a generous portion of the lemon caper cream. If you hold the sauce prior to service, you may need to thin sauce with additional poaching liquid.

PREP TIME: 1 Hour

SERVES: 6

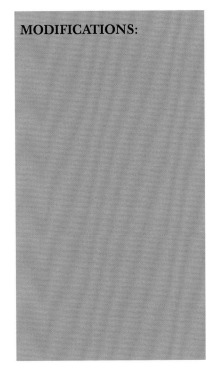

MODIFICATIONS:

BISQUE OF SPINACH & LUMP CRABMEAT

Often in Louisiana we find the union of unlikely ingredients in the pot of innovative Creoles. The reason for this is simple. With the abundance of domesticated meats and seafoods available to the cook and the semi-tropical climate guaranteeing a great amount of fresh vegetables, the need to combine ingredients became necessary. This is one such dish.

INGREDIENTS:

- 3 cups fresh spinach, chopped
- 1 pound claw crabmeat
- 1/2 pound jumbo lump crabmeat
- 1/4 pound butter
- 1/2 cup diced onions
- 1/2 cup diced celery
- 1/2 cup diced yellow bell pepper
- 1/4 cup minced garlic
- 1 tsp fresh tarragon, chopped
- 3/4 cup flour
- 2 quarts shellfish stock (see recipe)
- 1 pint heavy whipping cream
- 1/2 cup sliced green onions
- 1/4 cup chopped parsley
- 1/2 cup minced red bell pepper
- Salt and pepper to taste
- Hot sauce to taste

OPPOSITE: *A stag terrine filled with Bisque of Spinach & Lump Crabmeat.*

METHOD:

Pick through the crabmeat to ensure that all bone and cartilage are removed. In a cast iron dutch oven, melt butter over medium-high heat. Add onions, celery, yellow bell pepper and garlic. Saute 3-5 minutes or until vegetables are wilted. Add 2 cups chopped spinach, tarragon and saute an additional 3 minutes. Remove spinach mixture to the bowl of a food processor. Puree and then return to the dutch oven. Sprinkle in flour and, using a wire whisk, blend well into the mixture. Add shellfish stock, 1 ladle at a time, until soup-like consistency is achieved. Fold in claw crabmeat, bring to a rolling boil and reduce to simmer. Cook for 30 minutes, adding additional stock as needed. Add heavy whipping cream, green onions, parsley and red bell pepper. Season to taste using salt, pepper and hot sauce. Immediately prior to serving, bring mixture to a low boil and add remaining spinach. Cook 2 minutes, remove from heat and gently fold in the lump crabmeat. Adjust seasonings if necessary.

PREP TIME: 1 Hour

SERVES: 6

An antique Richard with plates of veal sweetbreads.

MODIFICATIONS:

GRILLADES & GRAVY SPANISH-STYLE

Grillades, from the French word "to grill," were first created by the butchers in early Louisiana as they carved a freshly killed pig into hams, sausages and other fresh cuts of meat. Tiny slivers of meat "grillade" were cooked in a black iron skillet over the coals of a wood fire. This made a perfect mid-morning meal for the hungry workers, especially when served over steaming grits.

A 1950s-era Chambers Range in the kitchen at Lanaux Mansion.

INGREDIENTS:

- 1 (2-pound) round steak
- 1/4 cup olive oil
- 1 cup diced onions
- 1/2 cup diced celery
- 1/2 cup diced bell pepper
- 1/4 cup minced garlic
- 2 tbsps flour
- 1 (8-ounce) can tomato sauce
- 1 (14.5-ounce) can diced tomatoes in juice
- 1/2 cup sliced black olives
- 3 cups beef stock (see recipe)
- 2 tbsps fresh basil, chopped
- 1 tsp fresh thyme, chopped
- 1/2 cup sliced green onions
- 1/4 cup chopped parsley
- Salt and black pepper to taste
- Hot sauce to taste

METHOD:

Cut round steak into 3-inch cubes and pound lightly. Season to taste using salt and pepper. In a cast iron skillet, heat olive oil over medium-high heat. Brown round steak on all sides. Remove and keep warm. An additional tablespoon of olive oil may be added to the skillet if necessary. Into the same oil, add onions, celery, bell pepper and garlic. Saute 3-5 minutes or until vegetables are wilted. Sprinkle in flour and blend well into the mixture, removing any lumps that may form in the blending process. Add tomato sauce, diced tomatoes and black olives, blending well into the vegetable mixture. Add stock and continue to blend until all is incorporated. Add basil and thyme and season lightly using salt, pepper and hot sauce. Return round steak to the skillet and bring mixture to a rolling boil. Reduce to simmer, cover and cook 1-1 1/2 hours or until meat is fork-tender. Additional stock or water may be needed during the cooking process. Once tender, add green onions and parsley and adjust seasonings if necessary. Serve over hot, buttered grits (see recipe).

PREP TIME: 2 Hours

SERVES: 6

MODIFICATIONS:

A portrait of Charles Andrew Johnson, the original owner of the home.

RIZ AU LAIT

Rice custard, like flan and bread pudding, is considered a premier Creole dessert. Eggs and milk were plentiful in early New Orleans due to the large German settlements surrounding the city, therefore it was just natural that custard-based desserts evolved out of the Cajun and Creole kitchens. Since rice is a staple of bayou country and grown in abundance in our wetland environment, Riz Au Lait became the perfect finish for an elegant Creole dinner.

INGREDIENTS:

- 1 cup long grain rice
- 1 1/2 cups water
- 1 tsp sugar
- 1 tbsp butter
- 4 eggs
- 3/4 cup sugar
- 2 cups milk
- 1 tbsp grated orange peel
- 1/8 tsp ground nutmeg
- 1 tbsp vanilla

METHOD:

In a 1-quart sauce pot with lid, place rice, water, 1 teaspoon of sugar and butter. Bring to a rolling boil, reduce to lowest setting and cover. Cook 30 minutes, being careful not to remove the lid. Remove from heat, making sure the rice is fully cooked. Allow to cool slightly. In a small mixing bowl, blend eggs and sugar. Using a wire whisk, whip until creamy and pale yellow. Combine the rice mixture with milk and bring to a low boil. Add the grated orange peel, nutmeg and vanilla, stirring constantly. Slowly add egg mixture to the boiling milk and cook for 1 minute. Remove from heat and pour into a large fluted custard bowl. You may wish to garnish with additional nutmeg and orange peel. Cover and refrigerate until chilled. If you wish to serve as a baked custard, follow the above instructions then spoon into 8 custard cups. Place custard cups into a pan of water and bake at 350°F for approximately 20 minutes. Custard may be served hot or cold.

PREP TIME: 1 Hour

SERVES: 8

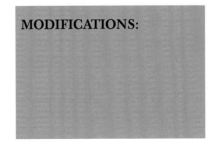

MODIFICATIONS:

Recipe for Romance: Cajun Caviar and Ice-Cold Vodka

McKendrick-Breaux House

NEW ORLEANS

*T*here is nothing more rousing than a knowing stare. The look that tells you intuitively he is undressing you with his eyes in his meticulous weave of seduction. The trance is interrupted only when he takes you in his arms to carry you up the stairs to paradise.

The McKendrick-Breaux House in New Orleans' Lower Garden District features its own winding staircase to heaven in this beautifully restored home on Magazine Street. The three-story masonry home was built in 1865 by Daniel McKendrick, a well-to-do plumber and wealthy Scottish immigrant. Both this home and an 1850s two-story frame townhouse were restored by Eddie Breaux in the early 1990s. The McKendrick-Breaux House, established as a bed and breakfast in 1994, is located in one of the most comprehensive 19th-century Greek Revival neighborhoods remaining in the country.

The house features original plaster arches and medallions, as well as some original fixtures, woodwork and flooring. There are five spacious guest rooms, several which open onto the tropical courtyard and patio that connect the main home with the townhouse. The rooms are furnished with antiques, local artwork, family collectibles and are decorated upon arrival with fresh flowers. Most of the guest rooms have 12-foot ceilings and claw-foot bathtubs and each room has a private bath.

The gracious hosts accommodate guests' every need. Breakfast is provided each morning in the downstairs parlor and adjoining dining room.

The McKendrick-Breaux House is located at 1474 Magazine Street where Magazine and Race streets intersect. It is just four blocks from St. Charles Avenue and six blocks from the interstate. Magazine Street is renowned for its world-class antique, art and collectible shopping. The McKendrick-Breaux House is minutes from Coliseum Square, the Convention Center, the historic French Quarter and the growing Warehouse District, which features excellent restaurants, contemporary art galleries and the Louisiana Children's Museum. For reservations call (504) 522-7138 or (888) 570-1700.

At the McKendrick-Breaux House you will want for nothing—from viewing the Mississippi River from the ornate belvedere to fulfilling your expectations up the winding staircase.

An ornate mantel clock.

OPPOSITE: *McKendrick-Breaux House at Christmas.*
Courtesy of Andy Breaux

OVERNIGHT BREAKFAST COFFEE CAKE

*B*aking certainly is not everyone's forte. However, recipes are often created allowing the novice to deliver a wonderful homemade pastry to the table with little effort. This coffee cake recipe uses the ingredients and flavorings of Louisiana pralines to produce a masterpiece that anyone can make.

INGREDIENTS:

- 2 cups all purpose flour
- 1 cup sugar
- 1 cup firmly packed brown sugar
- 1 tsp baking soda
- 1 tsp baking powder
- 1/2 tsp salt
- 2 tsps ground cinnamon
- 1 cup buttermilk
- 2/3 cup melted butter
- 2 large eggs
- 1/2 cup chopped pecans

METHOD:

Grease and flour a 10" x 10" x 2 1/2" Pyrex baking dish. A 13" x 9" x 2" baking dish may be substituted. In a large mixing bowl, combine flour, sugar, 1/2 cup brown sugar, baking soda, baking powder, salt and 1 teaspoon cinnamon. Using a wire whisk, blend to incorporate ingredients. Add buttermilk, melted butter and eggs. Using an electric mixer, blend on low speed for 1 minute then beat at medium speed for 3 minutes. Spoon batter into baking pan until leveled. In a small mixing bowl, combine 1/2 cup brown sugar, pecans and remaining teaspoon of cinnamon. Blend well and sprinkle evenly over the top of the batter. Cover with clear wrap and refrigerate for 8-12 hours. When ready to bake, preheat oven to 350°F. Uncover pan and bake 45-50 minutes, or until wooden toothpick inserted in the center comes out clean. Serve coffee cake warm with cafe au lait. This cake has the wonderful aroma of an old-fashioned Creole spice cake.

PREP TIME: 1 Hour

SERVES: 9-12

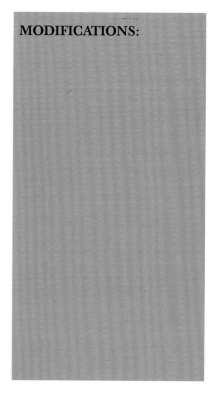

MODIFICATIONS:

Dr. Bob, a local New Orleans artist, says it all in this sign.

CRABMEAT & SHRIMP-STUFFED MIRLITON

The "chayote" squash, as many know it, is commonly referred to in Louisiana as mirliton. This unique vegetable was brought to Bayou Country by the Canary Islanders, who relocated to Louisiana when Spain took ownership of New Orleans from France. Whether called chayote, mirliton or vegetable pear, this Southern Louisiana delicacy is indeed wonderful when stuffed with shrimp and crabmeat.

INGREDIENTS:

- 6 mirlitons, sliced lengthwise
- 1 pound jumbo lump crabmeat
- 1 pound (70-90 count) shrimp, peeled and deveined
- 1/4 pound butter
- 1 cup diced onions
- 1 cup diced celery
- 1/2 cup diced red bell pepper
- 1/4 cup minced garlic
- Salt and black pepper to taste
- Hot sauce to taste
- 1/4 cup chopped parsley
- 2 cups seasoned Italian bread crumbs
- 12 pats butter

METHOD:

Preheat oven to 375°F. Boil sliced mirlitons in lightly salted water until meat is tender enough to scoop from the shells but shell stays intact, approximately 30-40 minutes. Once tender, remove from water and cool. Using a teaspoon, remove the seed pod from the center of the mirliton and gently scoop all meat out of the shell. Since so much water accumulates when scooping the meat, discard excess liquid. Take extra care not to break or tear the outer shell. Reserve meat and save shells for stuffing. In a 12-inch cast iron skillet, melt butter over medium-high heat. Add onions, celery, bell pepper and garlic. Saute 3-5 minutes or until vegetables are wilted. Add shrimp and blend well into the vegetable mixture. Cook 2-3 minutes or until shrimp are pink and curled. Add the reserve meat from the mirliton to the skillet, blending well into the vegetable mixture. Chop the large pieces and cook 15-20 minutes, stirring until flavors develop. After most of the liquid has evaporated, remove from heat and season to taste using salt, pepper, hot sauce and parsley. Fold in crabmeat, being careful to not break the lumps. Sprinkle in approximately 1 1/2 cups of bread crumbs to absorb any excess liquid and to hold the stuffing intact. Divide crabmeat mixture

Mirlitons fresh from the Farmers' Market.

into 12 equal portions and stuff into the hollowed-out shells. Place stuffed mirlitons on baking pan and sprinkle with remaining bread crumbs. Top each mirliton with 1 pat of butter. Bake until golden brown, approximately 30 minutes. Serve 1 mirliton half as a vegetable or 2 as an entree.

PREP TIME: 1 1/2 Hours

SERVES: 6

MODIFICATIONS:

OYSTERS DUNBAR

This dish was named after the great restaurateur, Coreen Dunbar. Coreen had one of the few potluck restaurants. This simply meant that you walked in, pulled up a seat and whatever was in the pot was served that evening—no options, no choices. This dish became a mainstay at her restaurant and went on to become a sought after dish on other New Orleans restaurant menus.

INGREDIENTS:

- 3 dozen oysters
- 1 cup reserved oyster liquid
- 12 oyster shells
- 2 cups artichoke hearts
- 1/4 pound butter
- 1/2 cup diced onions
- 1/4 cup diced celery
- 1/4 cup diced red bell pepper
- 1/4 cup diced yellow bell pepper
- 1/4 cup minced garlic
- 1/4 cup flour
- 2 cups heavy whipping cream
- 1 tsp Worcestershire sauce
- 1 tsp Creole seasoning
- 1/4 cup sliced green onions
- 1 tbsp chopped basil
- 1 tsp chopped thyme
- 1/4 tsp nutmeg

OPPOSITE: This oyster dish was developed by Coreen Dunbar and is captured in the courtyard at McKendrick-Breaux.

- Salt and black pepper to taste
- Hot sauce to taste
- 3 cups seasoned Italian bread crumbs

METHOD:

Preheat oven to 375°F. Wash oyster shells once or twice with hot soapy water then rinse under cold running tap water until all soap is removed. Hold shells in cold water for later use. Chop 2 dozen oysters and artichoke hearts into bite-size pieces and set aside. In a cast iron dutch oven, melt butter over medium-high heat. Add onions, celery, bell peppers and garlic. Saute 3-5 minutes or until vegetables are wilted. Add chopped oysters and artichoke hearts, blending well into the vegetable mixture. Saute 5-7 additional minutes for flavors to incorporate. Sprinkle in flour and blend well to create a white roux (see roux techniques). Add heavy whipping cream and reserved oyster liquid, stirring constantly to blend into the roux mixture. The consistency should be that of a slightly-thickened white sauce. Add Worcestershire sauce, Creole seasoning, green onions, basil, thyme and nutmeg. Season lightly using salt, pepper and hot sauce. Continue to cook 7-10 minutes then remove from heat. Stir in 2 cups of bread crumbs until mixture is thickened and resembles a stuffing. Place 1 whole oyster in the center of each oyster shell and top with equal portions of Dunbar stuffing. Place stuffed oyster shells on a cookie sheet and sprinkle with remaining bread crumbs. Bake oysters until stuffing is heated thoroughly and bubbly, approximately 30 minutes. It is imperative that the oysters in the shells are hot and fully cooked. Serves 4 as an entree.

PREP TIME: 1 Hour

SERVES: 6

MODIFICATIONS:

SUN-DRIED TOMATO & BASIL-STUFFED CHICKEN

I am constantly amazed at the new and interesting methods of preparing chicken. This recipe originated in the Italian communities around New Orleans, but has since found its way onto many low-fat menus because of its method of preparation. I cannot think of any two flavors more intense and accessible when preparing chicken as sun-dried tomatoes and fresh basil. Try this combination with pork loin, lamb or let your imagination run wild.

INGREDIENTS:

- 6 boneless chicken breasts
- 2 1/2 ounces (12 pieces) sun-dried tomatoes
- 12 large basil leaves
- 1 cup chicken stock (see recipe)
- 2 tbsps balsamic vinegar
- 2 tbsps Worcestershire sauce
- 2 tbsps extra virgin olive oil
- 1 tsp chopped thyme
- 2 cloves minced garlic
- 1/8 tsp granulated garlic
- 1/8 tsp crushed red pepper flakes
- Salt and black pepper to taste
- Hot sauce to taste

METHOD:

Preheat homestyle grill according to manufacturer's

An 1880s Victorian Walnut Bed purchased in the antique city of Hessmer, Louisiana.

directions. If using smoked wood to flavor, I recommend apple. Soak the wood in water 1 hour prior to use. In a small sauce pan, place sun-dried tomatoes and 1/2 cup chicken stock. Bring to a low boil, remove from heat and let stand 15 minutes to allow tomatoes to soften. Using a sharp paring knife, cut a large pocket into the side of each chicken breast, being careful not to cut all the way through. Season chicken breasts, including the inner pocket, lightly using salt and pepper. Remove tomatoes from broth, reserve liquid and cut each tomato in half. Place 2 basil leaves and 4 of the tomato halves into each chicken breast pocket. Secure the opening with one or two toothpicks to keep the stuffing intact. In a shallow dish large enough to hold the breasts, combine the remaining chicken stock with vinegar, Worcestershire sauce, olive oil, thyme, minced garlic, granulated garlic and red pepper flakes. Season to taste using salt, pepper and

hot sauce. Place the chicken in the marinating liquid, turning once or twice. Allow chicken to sit in liquid at room temperature for 1 hour. Since the marinating liquid contains items that are high in sugar content, the chicken will brown quickly and burn if cooked directly over hot coals. It is best to cook on a lower heat or off to the side of the fire. When ready to cook, grill chicken 15-20 minutes turning occasionally or until chicken is done to your liking.

PREP TIME: 2 Hours

SERVES: 6

MODIFICATIONS:

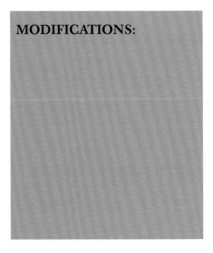

66

ANISE COOKIES

My God, this is a great cookie, but a little challenging. I discovered this cookie by accident. The cookies were sitting in a green Depression glass cookie jar pushed back in the corner of the kitchen counter at McKendrick-Breaux House. It was the lightest textured cookie I had ever eaten, similar to meringue but yet had the unique essence of freshly crushed anise seeds. I knew I had to have this recipe!

INGREDIENTS:

- 1 tsp pure anise extract
- 6 eggs
- 3 cups sugar
- 4 1/2 cups flour

METHOD:

Preheat oven to 350°F. Butter two 9" x 13" baking sheets and set aside. In the bowl of an electric mixer, combine the eggs and sugar. Beat mixture on high speed for 30 minutes. It is essential that the sugar egg mixture whip for a full 30 minutes. Reduce speed to low and add flour, 1 tablespoon at a time, until all is incorporated. Add anise extract and whip 1 additional minute. Using a rubber spatula, scrape down the sides of the bowl to ensure that flour is well mixed. Drop cookie batter onto the buttered baking sheet in teaspoon-size portions. Bake 15-20 minutes or until cookies are lightly browned on the outer edges and cream-colored in the center. Do not overbake as the cookies will become hard if overcooked. Store in an air tight container.

PREP TIME: 1 Hour

MAKES: 3 1/2 Dozen

MODIFICATIONS:

The original plaster archways and medallions of the home painstakingly restored.

Recipe for Romance: Licorice, Lace and a Late-Night Chase

The House on Bayou Road

NEW ORLEANS

Moonlight dances in a secluded hideaway just beyond the city lights, titillating young lovers and arousing comfortable couples on the porches and patios of the French Indigo Plantation. There is nothing like a clandestine tryst in the secluded elegance of the country with the glamour of a beckoning city only a few blocks from the boudoir.

Some primitive folk-art roosters displayed in the kitchen.

The House on Bayou Road, a West Indies-style Indigo Plantation, was built in 1798 for the director-general of the Royal Hospital while New Orleans was under Spanish rule. Guests are pampered with terry cloth robes, fresh cut flowers and decanters of sherry. With the morning sunshine comes a plantation-style breakfast: delicacies such as Eggs Benedict, mixed fruit pancakes, smothered andouille or pain perdu.

Situated on two acres of land just off Esplanade Avenue, The House on Bayou Road features gardens, ponds, patios, decks, brick courtyards and sun porches. Each of the eight guest rooms is named for a Louisiana bayou and is elegantly furnished with antiques and collectibles. There are three rooms in the main house with four-poster feather beds, some with sitting rooms and fireplaces. The Kumquat House, adjacent to the pool and gazebo,

OPPOSITE: The front entrance to The House on Bayou Road.

has four rooms each with private entrances that feature Jacuzzi tubs, fireplaces and sitting rooms. A Creole cottage offers privacy for honeymoon couples or romantic getaways and features fanlight windows, a luxurious whirlpool bath, sitting area and private porch overlooking the grounds.

The House on Bayou Road is listed on the National Register of Historic Places. New Orleans maps and restaurant reviews are always available, and the innkeeper and staff are happy to make restaurant or tour reservations for guests. While visiting the area, tour the historic New Orleans French Quarter, Longue Vue House & Gardens, the Cabildo Museum, the Presbytere Museum and Hermann-Grima/Gallier Houses. Magazine and Royal streets are lined with unique antique shops or enjoy browsing at Canal Place or the Riverwalk. Dine at local establishments including Gabrielle Restaurant, Peristyle or Brigtsen's Restaurant.

The House on Bayou Road is conveniently located at 2275 Bayou Road in New Orleans, just outside the French Quarter and near the New Orleans Museum of Art. For reservations call (504) 945-0992.

Runaway to the city and bask in the serene ambience of the country, where the elegance of The House on Bayou Road enraptures and captures moonstruck hearts.

Eggplants, peppers and radishes fresh from the Crescent City Farmers' Market.

POTAGE FOR EGGPLANT LOVERS

Although eggplant originated in the Middle East, it somehow made its way to the Orient, the New World and eventually was combined with shrimp, crab, crawfish and oysters in Louisiana. The delicate flavor of eggplant marries superbly with the flavor of oysters to create a soup of extremely delectable taste.

INGREDIENTS:

- 1 large eggplant
- 2 pints of oysters, reserve liquid
- 1/4 cup melted butter
- 1 cup diced onions
- 1 cup diced celery
- 1/2 cup diced red bell pepper
- 2 tbsps minced garlic
- 1/2 cup flour
- 1 quart shellfish stock (see recipe)
- 1/4 cup tomato sauce
- 2 bay leaves
- 1 tbsp fresh thyme leaves
- 1 tbsp fresh tarragon
- 1 cup heavy whipping cream
- Salt and pepper to taste
- Hot sauce to taste
- 1/4 cup chopped chives

METHOD:

Peel and dice eggplant into 1/4-inch cubes. One large eggplant should yield 6 cups diced. Place the cubed eggplant in a colander and salt lightly. Allow to drain completely for 15 minutes. In a cast iron dutch oven, heat butter over medium-high heat. Add onions, celery, bell pepper and garlic. Saute 3-5 minutes or until vegetables are wilted. Sprinkle in flour and, using a wire whisk, blend well into the vegetable mixture. Do not brown. Add reserved oyster liquid (approximately 1 1/2 cups) and stock, 1 cup at a time, until soup-like consistency is achieved. Add eggplant, tomato sauce, bay leaves, thyme, tarragon, and 1 pint of oysters. Bring mixture to a rolling boil, reduce to simmer and cook 20 minutes, stirring occasionally. Remove bay leaves from dutch oven and pour soup into the bowl of a blender or food processor. Puree mixture on high until smooth. Return soup to dutch oven, add whipping cream and season to taste using salt, pepper and hot sauce. Place soup over medium-high heat and bring to a low boil. Add remaining oysters and cook 2-3 additional minutes or until oysters are puffy and curled. Adjust seasonings if necessary. Add fresh chives and serve in pre-warmed soup bowls.

PREP TIME: 45 Minutes

SERVES: 6

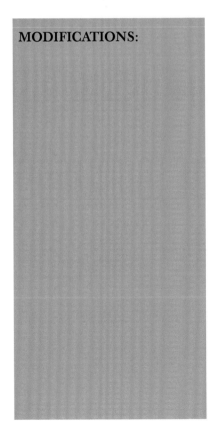

MODIFICATIONS:

SPINACH & STRAWBERRY SALAD PONCHATOULA

Ponchatoula is the strawberry capital of the world. It is surprising to the residents of this sleepy South Louisiana town that the rest of the world considers strawberries a dessert ingredient only. Here, they may be found in soups, sauces, as a flavor ingredient over pork roast or lamb or as the perfect finish to a crisp crunchy spring salad.

INGREDIENTS:

- 10 ounces fresh spinach leaves, cleaned and dried
- 1 pint ripe Louisiana strawberries, sliced
- 1 egg yolk
- 1 tbsp Balsamic vinegar
- 4 tbsps Boone's strawberry wine
- 6 ounces vegetable oil
- 1 tbsp fresh thyme, chopped
- 1 tbsp fresh tarragon, chopped
- Salt and pepper to taste
- 1 tbsp extra virgin olive oil
- 1 cup freshly grated Parmesan cheese

METHOD:

Remember to rinse spinach leaves 2-3 times under cold running water to ensure that all sand and grit are removed from leaves. Dry well and set aside. When selecting strawberries for this salad, Ponchatoula berries are always best and should be slightly over-ripe but not mushy. I prefer to buy a 5-ounce block of Parmesan cheese and hand grate it using the large holes of a grater. Create the sauce by combining egg yolk, Balsamic vinegar and strawberry wine in a stainless steel bowl. Using a wire whisk, combine ingredients until well incorporated. Slowly drizzle the vegetable oil into the egg yolk mixture in a steady stream, whisking constantly. A smooth emulsified dressing will emerge. Add thyme and tarragon and season to taste using salt and pepper. Continue whisking until ingredients are well-blended. The dressing may be stored in a glass jar in the refrigerator until ready to use. When ready to serve, toss spinach with extra virgin olive oil and drizzle with the desired amount of strawberry vinaigrette. Once the leaves are shining from the sauce, but not wilted, add strawberries and cheese and toss once or twice to incorporate. Serve in a large, crystal salad bowl to showcase the vivid colors of this salad.

PREP TIME: 30 Minutes

SERVES: 6

The ingredients for a unique South Louisiana salad.

MODIFICATIONS:

CARIBBEAN SALMON ON OYSTERS ROCKEFELLER SAUCE

Although any quality fish may be sauteed in this recipe, the bright orange color of salmon gives tremendous eye appeal to this dish. The Caribbean influence may be seen in not only the architecture of New Orleans, but certainly the flavor of our food is apparent in this dish. Quickly sauteed or grilled fresh fish placed on a natural sauce of greens and shellfish could not be more Caribbean or at the same time Creole.

INGREDIENTS:

- 6 (5-7 ounce) salmon fillets
- 1 (10-ounce) package frozen spinach, thawed
- 1 pint oysters, reserve liquid
- 1/4 cup melted butter
- 1/2 cup diced onions
- 1/2 cup diced celery
- 2 tbsps minced garlic
- 1/4 cup diced tasso or heavily-smoked ham
- 2 tbsps fresh tarragon, chopped
- 2 tbsps flour
- 3 cups shellfish stock (see recipe)
- 1/4 cup diced red bell pepper
- 1/4 cup diced yellow bell pepper
- 2 tbsps or 1 ounce Herbsaint or Pernod
- Salt and pepper to taste
- Hot sauce to taste

OPPOSITE: *View of the breakfast room at The House on Bayou Road with farmers tables and chairs.*

METHOD:

Since salmon cooks so quickly and requires a medium-rare center for ultimate flavor, I recommend making the sauce prior to cooking the salmon. In a heavy bottom saute pan, melt butter over medium-high heat. Add onions, celery, garlic and tasso. Saute 3-5 minutes or until vegetables are wilted. Add spinach and chop well into the vegetable mixture. Cook 2-3 minutes or until vegetables and spinach are well incorporated. Add oysters along with oyster liquid and tarragon. Bring mixture to a low boil, stirring occasionally, until liquid has evaporated totally from the skillet, approximately 10 minutes. Sprinkle in flour, blending well into the spinach mixture. Add shellfish stock, a little at a time, until all has been incorporated. NOTE: Canned clam juice may be substituted in this recipe. Bring mixture to a low boil, remove from heat and place sauce in a blender or food processor. Add bell peppers and Herbsaint and puree until sauce-like consistency is achieved. Return mixture to the skillet, bring sauce to a low simmer and adjust seasonings if necessary. Should the mixture become too thick prior to serving, add additional stock. When sauce has been prepared, season salmon to taste using salt, pepper and a mixture of your favorite herbs such as thyme, basil and tarragon. In a cast iron skillet, saute salmon quickly in 1 tablespoon of oil or butter or grill on a homestyle barbecue pit according to manufacturer's directions. When ready to serve, place a generous portion of the Rockefeller Sauce in the center of a 10-inch dinner plate and top with sauteed salmon fillet. Garnish the edge of the sauce with quickly sauteed red and yellow pear tomatoes and finely diced carrots or sweet potatoes.

PREP TIME: 45 Minutes

SERVES: 6

MODIFICATIONS:

CREOLE QUESADILLAS

Although quesadillas are Spanish and Southwest in origin, they were a natural addition to Creole country. The Spanish had control of the city of New Orleans in the late 1700s, and many of their cooking techniques are a major part of Creole cuisine today.

INGREDIENTS:

- 1 pound fresh crawfish tails
- 1/2 pound wild oyster mushrooms
- 1/2 pound sliced button mushrooms
- 1/2 pound Chanterelle mushrooms
- 1/2 cup butter
- 1 cup sliced green onions
- 2 tbsps minced garlic
- 1 tbsp fresh thyme leaves
- 2 tbsps chopped cilantro
- 1 cup diced Creole tomatoes
- 1/2 cup diced yellow bell pepper
- 1/2 cup diced red bell pepper
- 1 tbsp Creole seasoning
- Salt and black pepper to taste
- Hot sauce to taste
- 8 large tortilla shells
- 1 pound grated Monterey Jack cheese

METHOD:

Preheat oven to 375°F. You may wish to substitute a local seafood such as shrimp or crab or even chicken if crawfish is unavailable in your area. In a large cast iron skillet, melt butter over medium-high heat. Add green onions, garlic and mushrooms. Saute 3-5 minutes or until mushrooms are wilted. Add crawfish, thyme, cilantro, tomatoes and bell peppers. Continue to saute until juices are rendered and liquids have almost completely evaporated, approximately 10 minutes. Season to taste using Creole seasoning, salt, pepper and hot sauce. Place the tortilla shells on a large cookie sheet and sprinkle with a small amount of Monterey Jack cheese. Top with a portion of the crawfish stuffing and more of the Monterey Jack cheese. Fold each tortilla in half and bake 7-10 minutes or until cheese is melted and tortillas are slightly crisp but not over-browned. NOTE: The quesadillas may be pan sauteed in a hot skillet that has been sprayed with a small amount of vegetable spray. Be careful not to over-brown.

PREP TIME: 30 Minutes

SERVES: 8

MODIFICATIONS:

Hand-painted cooking spoons from Honduras.

The salon where guests savor a cordial or sip cognac before retiring for the evening.

CHOCOLATE JAVA MOUSSE

We love coffee in South Louisiana! Not only do we drink it with our desserts, we add the flavor to many of our sweets. This simple mousse recipe is quite elegant and incorporates the finest from the sweet cart, while borrowing a pinch of instant coffee from the cupboard. What a marriage!

INGREDIENTS:

- 8 ounces Baker's semi-sweet chocolate
- 1 tbsp instant coffee granules
- 2 egg yolks
- 1 tsp Cointreau or brandy
- 8 ounces heavy whipping cream
- 2 tbsps orange zest
- 6 coffee beans, optional
- 1/4 cup finely grated white or dark chocolate
- 6 mint leaves, optional

METHOD:

Chop chocolate into 1/4-inch pieces. In a stainless steel bowl, combine chocolate pieces and coffee granules. Place 1 inch of water into a sauce pot and bring to a low simmer. Do not boil. Place stainless steel bowl containing chocolate over the simmering pot. Do not allow the bottom of the bowl to touch the hot water. Stir chocolate gently using a wooden spoon until completely melted and smooth. Remove chocolate from heat and stir in the egg yolks and Cointreau. The mixture will quickly thicken to a heavy mousse-consistency. Set aside. Place the whipping cream in a large ceramic bowl and whip with a hand mixer until stiff peaks form. Blend 3 tablespoons of the whipped cream into the chocolate mixture to help "loosen" the heavy mousse. Using a rubber spatula, gently fold the chocolate into the bowl of whipped cream. Continue blending chocolate to create a marbling effect. It is important not to overwhip. Cover the bowl with clear wrap and chill for a minimum of 1 hour or preferably overnight. When ready to serve, place an equal amount of the Chocolate Java Mousse into 6 chilled wine glasses or decorative coffee cups. Top with orange zest, a coffee bean and grated chocolate. Garnish with fresh mint leaves.

PREP TIME: 1 Hour

SERVES: 6

MODIFICATIONS:

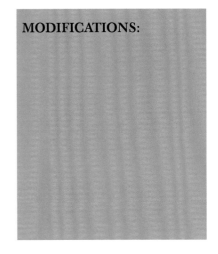

Recipe for Romance: Pecan Pralines on Fluffy Pillows

Degas House

NEW ORLEANS

*F*eeling the gentle slope of her body lying next to you in bed…drinking a cup of coffee and reading the morning newspaper when she is only an arm's length away… picnicking in clover fields and drawing cloud pictures in the sky. Doing nothing at all is invigorating, as long as you are doing nothing with her. This is the romance of everyday life.

A ladies' antique lavatory.

The renowned French Impressionist, Edgar Degas, was an aficionado of everyday life and an artist devoted to the common interests of man and the world around him. For several months in 1872 and 1873 Degas lived with his brothers and maternal relations, the Musson family, in their New Orleans residence known today as the Degas House. This was the only American home of the painter, and the only home/studio of Degas anywhere in the world now open to the public. Degas worked prolifically, creating 17 paintings during his stay including *Portraits in an Office: The New Orleans Cotton Exchange*. This scene depicted his uncle's place of business and was the first Impressionist painting purchased by a museum, marking for the first time the significance of Impressionism as an art movement.

While in New Orleans Degas complained a great deal about his eye disorder, which prevented his drawing or painting outdoors. Consequently, he was unable to paint the Mississippi River, the American railroads or the people of New Orleans. Degas used his bedroom as his studio while living in the house. He made several portraits of his cousin and sister-in-law, Estelle, of whom he was particularly fond, as well as other family members.

The Degas House was built in 1853 by architect and developer Benjamin Rodriguez as part of the Esplanade Ridge neighborhood. (Rodriguez amassed a fortune through real estate and as part owner of New Orleans' first omnibus line, which became New Orleans' famous streetcar. The first of the omnibuses ran on Esplanade Avenue in front of the Degas House.) During the years preceding the Civil War, there was a boom in wealth and population in the South. New Orleans thrived and was the fourth largest city in the United States. The borders of the city were expanded by buying plantations surrounding the city to build neighborhoods with large houses and spacious grounds. As the French Quarter filled with growing families, wealthy Creoles moved to the new areas.

The Degas House, with its square white columns and decorative wrought iron, was one of the most impressive residences in the area. Its grounds occupied almost the entire block. However, it was bitter circumstances that forced the family to move to Esplanade Ridge. Following the Civil War the Musson family, like many others, lost money and property and had to sell their mansion in the Garden District and move to the less

(Continues on page 78)

OPPOSITE: *At the Degas House on Esplanade in 1872-73, Edgar Degas painted many of his favorite subjects.*

(Continued from page 76)

fashionable neighborhood on Esplanade Avenue where they lived for more than a decade.

Reproductions of Degas' work are found throughout the house, which is a Louisiana landmark and listed on the National Register of Historic Places. The wide-planked floors of the home have been preserved as well as much of the original plaster. The walls of the spacious rooms have been painted in colors found in Degas' original paintings. The original mansion was cut in two in the 1920s, and one wing was moved several feet to the side. This smaller wing today is the reservations desk of Degas House and a part of the future expansion.

Just three miles from I-10, Degas House is conveniently located at 2306 Esplanade Avenue in New Orleans. While touring the area, visit the New Orleans Museum of Art (where the portrait of Estelle may be viewed), enjoy City Park's Botanical Gardens, golf courses and tennis courts or dine at Cafe Degas just six blocks from Degas House. For reservations call (800) 755-6730. For art, history and ambiance you must visit the Degas House, one of America's premier art bed and breakfast homes.

THE QUEEN'S SOUP

One can only imagine the extravagance of the carnival balls held at the Degas House. It is obvious from this recipe that elegant foods were a major part of these functions. I can envision a large gilded terrine on the Degas table filled with this soup honoring a Queen of Mardi Gras.

INGREDIENTS:

- 4 boneless chicken breasts, skinned
- 1 gallon chicken stock (see recipe)
- 2 bay leaves
- 1 tbsp fresh thyme, chopped
- 1 tbsp fresh sage, chopped
- 1 onion, quartered
- 1 carrot, sliced
- 3 stalks of celery, sliced
- 4 garlic cloves, smashed
- 10 whole peppercorns
- 1/2 cup wild rice
- 1/2 cup long grain converted rice
- 1/4 cup butter
- 1/4 cup flour
- 1/2 cup minced carrots
- 1/2 cup minced yellow bell pepper
- 1 tbsp fresh thyme, chopped
- 1 tbsp fresh sage, chopped
- 1/4 cup chopped chives
- 1 cup heavy whipping cream
- Salt and black pepper to taste

METHOD:

In a large cast iron dutch oven, combine stock with bay leaves, 1 tablespoon of thyme, 1 tablespoon of sage, onion, sliced carrot, celery, garlic and peppercorns. Bring mixture to a rolling boil, reduce to simmer and cook 30 minutes. Strain the flavor ingredients from the stock and discard vegetables. Return approximately 3 1/2 quarts of liquid to the pot and bring to a low boil. Poach chicken breasts in hot stock for 10-15 minutes or until thoroughly cooked. Remove, allow to cool and dice into 1/4-inch cubes. Set aside. Add wild rice to the simmering stock and cook 30 minutes. Add white rice and cook 15 additional minutes or until rice is tender. The rice will act as a thickening agent for the soup. In a separate sauce pan, melt butter over medium-high heat. Add flour and, stirring constantly, cook until white roux is achieved (see roux techniques). Do not brown. Add minced carrots, yellow bell pepper, remaining thyme, sage and chives. Cook 3-5 minutes then add the roux mixture to the stock, stirring constantly to completely incorporate. Add heavy whipping cream, bring to a low boil and season the soup to taste using salt and pepper. Add diced chicken to the soup and cook 2 additional minutes. Additional stock or water may be needed to retain soup-like consistency. Adjust seasonings if necessary. Serve soup in warmed soup bowls over fresh garlic croutons.

PREP TIME: 1 Hour

SERVES: 6

CREOLE POTATO SOUFFLÉ

In the original Creole cookbooks of New Orleans, this dish was referred to as Pommes de Terre Soufflés à la Creole. The English changed the name to Creole Puffed Potatoes. In both cases, the terminology is a bit skewed because the potatoes are not really puffed or souffléd. They are lightened with whipped egg whites. Either way, these potatoes are some of the best tasting!

INGREDIENTS:

- 2 cups mashed potatoes
- 2 tbsps melted butter
- 1/4 cup butter
- 2 eggs, separated
- 1/4 cup cream
- 1 tbsp fresh tarragon, minced
- 1 tbsp minced garlic
- 3 tbsps grated Parmesan cheese
- Salt and black pepper to taste

METHOD:

In order to achieve 2 cups of finished mashed potatoes, use 2 large and 1 small Idaho potato. Peel, cube and boil potatoes in lightly salted water prior to mashing. Once mashed, season generously using salt and pepper. It is imperative that this dish comes out of the oven immediately prior to serving to achieve the best quality and flavor. I suggest prepping all the ingredients in advance and baking the potatoes when the meal is ready to be served. Butter six 6-ounce custard cups using 2 tablespoons of melted butter. Set aside. Preheat oven to 375°F. In a cast iron skillet, melt 1/4 cup butter over medium-high heat. Place the potatoes in the bottom of the skillet and flatten with the back of a cooking spoon. In a mixing bowl, combine egg yolks with cream, tarragon and garlic. Add egg mixture to the skillet and quickly incorporate into the potatoes, stirring until the mixture is thoroughly heated. Blend quickly and be careful not to scramble the eggs. Remove the skillet from heat and blend in Parmesan cheese. In a second mixing bowl, whip egg whites until stiff peaks form. Using a rubber spatula, gently fold egg whites into the potato mixture. Divide the potatoes evenly into each custard cup. Place cups on a cookie sheet and bake until lightly browned, approximately 12-15 minutes.

PREP TIME: 1 Hour

SERVES: 6

MODIFICATIONS:

A Degas print accentuates a guest room on the second floor.

CRÊPES ESTELLE

Degas' uncle, Michel Musson, was head of his New Orleans household at the time the artist was in residence in the late 1800s. Musson's daughter, Estelle, was the subject of at least one Degas painting and obviously the inspiration for this tasty crêpe dish.

INGREDIENTS FOR CRÊPES:

- 4 eggs
- 1 cup flour
- 1 tbsp sugar
- 1 tsp vanilla
- 2 tbsps triple sec
- 2 tbsps melted butter
- 1 1/2 cups milk
- Pinch of salt
- 1/2 cup vegetable oil
- 1/2 cup sugar

METHOD:

In a large mixing bowl, place eggs, flour, sugar, vanilla and triple sec. Using a wire whisk, whip until ingredients are silky smooth. Add butter and milk and continue to blend until batter reaches the consistency of heavy whipping cream. Make sure that all lumps are removed. Season to taste using salt. It is best to make crêpe batter a minimum of 6 hours prior to use and refrigerate. I recommend refrigerating the batter overnight. Place two 6-inch crêpe pans over medium-high heat. Add 2 tablespoons of vegetable oil into one pan and swirl to coat the bottom of the pan. Once hot, pour excess oil into the second crêpe pan. Place approximately 2 ounces of the crêpe batter into the first pan, tilting in a circular motion, until the batter spreads evenly. Cook crêpe until outer edge browns and loosens from the pan. Flip crêpe and cook 1 additional minute. Using a thin spatula, remove crêpe from the pan and sprinkle with sugar. Continue process until all crêpes are done. If you wish to store crêpes overnight or freeze, place plastic wrap between each crêpe to prevent sticking and place in a large Ziploc® bag prior to refrigerating or freezing.

MAKES: 20 Crêpes

INGREDIENTS FOR SAUCE:

- 1/4 pound butter
- 1 tbsp sugar
- Zest of 1 satsuma
- Juice of 2 satsumas
- 1 tsp Grenadine or cherry juice
- 3 tbsps Cointreau or triple sec
- 3 tbsps Kirsch liquor

METHOD:

Juice satsumas by peeling and pressing the segments through a fine sieve or chop in the food processor and then push through a sieve, discarding the pulp. In a cast iron skillet, melt butter over medium-high heat. Add sugar and satsuma zest, stirring until sugar is melted. Add satsuma juice, Grenadine and Cointreau. Continue to stir until ingredients are well incorporated. Remove skillet from heat and add Kirsch. Take caution when returning skillet to the heat as alcohol may ignite for a second or two. Fold each crêpe in half then in half again to create a triangle. Gently simmer the crêpes, 1 or 2 at a time, in the hot sauce and serve immediately. Place 2 crêpes on a 10-inch serving plate and garnish with a few sections of fresh satsumas.

PREP TIME: 1 Hour

SERVES: 6-8

MODIFICATIONS:

OPPOSITE: The patio of Degas House featuring Crêpes Estelle and the original brickwork.

FRICASSÉE OF VEAL & HAM WITH ARTICHOKES

Veal is one ingredient found in many Creole recipes. In fact, veal grillades are much more popular than the original pork version. The addition of ham is a gift from the Germans who saved the Crescent City from starvation, and the artichokes were decorative garden items from the Italian immigrants. This recipe is an excellent example of Creole cuisine.

INGREDIENTS:

- 3 pounds boneless veal stew meat, cubed
- 1 pound diced ham
- 12 artichoke bottoms
- 3/4 cup vegetable oil
- 3/4 cup flour
- 1 cup diced onions
- 1/2 cup diced celery
- 1/2 cup diced red bell pepper
- 1/2 cup diced yellow bell pepper
- 2 tbsps minced garlic
- 1 1/2 quarts beef stock (see recipe)
- 1/2 pound sliced mushrooms
- 2 tbsps fresh thyme, chopped
- 1 tbsp fresh basil, chopped
- 1/2 cup Marsala wine
- 1/4 cup butter
- 1/4 cup chopped parsley
- Salt and black pepper to taste

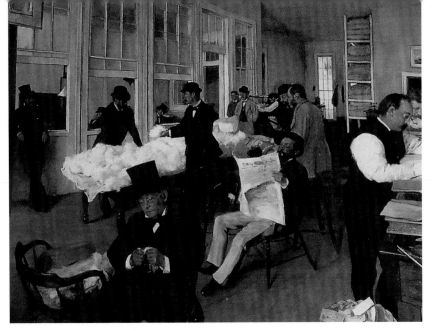

Portraits in an Office: The New Orleans Cotton Exchange, 1873.

METHOD:

In a large cast iron dutch oven, heat oil over medium-high heat. Add flour and, using a wire whisk, stir until dark brown roux is achieved (see roux techniques). Add onions, celery, bell peppers and garlic. Saute 3-5 minutes or until vegetables are wilted. Add veal and diced ham, blend well into the roux mixture and cook an additional 2-3 minutes. Add beef stock, 1 cup at a time, until stew-like consistency is achieved. Bring mixture to a rolling boil and reduce to simmer. Cover and cook 30 minutes. Add mushrooms, thyme, basil and Marsala wine and cook an additional 30 minutes or until veal is tender. Additional stock may be necessary to retain a stew-like consistency. Season to taste using salt and pepper. It is best to cook this dish one day prior to serving and allow it to set overnight in the refrigerator in order for flavors to enhance. When ready to serve, return veal fricassée to a simmer. Rinse artichoke bottoms well under cold running water. In a saute pan, melt butter over medium-high heat. Add artichoke bottoms and saute until thoroughly warmed. Place 2 artichoke bottoms on the bottom of a 10-inch serving plate and top with a ladle of the fricassée. Garnish each dish with fresh parsley. I enjoy serving steamed artichokes with this dish. Not only are the leaves excellent for decorating the plate, but the fricassée becomes a wonderful dipping sauce.

PREP TIME: 1 Hour

SERVES: 6

MODIFICATIONS:

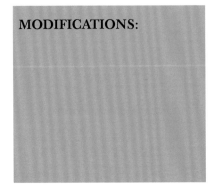

BOUCHE NOIR

The definition of "black mouth," the English translation of Bouche Noir, becomes immediately apparent when you see 12 ounces of dark chocolate as the main ingredient in this recipe. I must caution you however, do not attempt this recipe if you don't consider yourself a chocolate addict! Undecorated layer cakes such as this one were often served in early Creole homes with a topping of fresh fruit and unsweetened whipped cream.

INGREDIENTS:

- 12 ounces Baker's® bittersweet chocolate
- 1 1/2 cups sugar
- 1/2 cup bourbon
- 1 cup butter chips, softened
- 6 eggs (at room temperature)
- 1 1/2 tbsps flour
- 2 cups Louisiana strawberries, sliced (optional)
- 1 cup whipped cream (optional)

METHOD:

Preheat oven to 375°F. Butter a 9-inch springform pan then place a buttered parchment sheet in the bottom of the pan. Cover the outside of the springform pan with aluminum foil to keep water from entering the pan during the cooking process. Place the cake pan into a large roasting pan with 1-inch sides. Set aside. Chop chocolate into 1/4-inch pieces and place into a large stainless steel mixing bowl. Place 1-inch of water in the bottom of a sauce pan and bring to a simmer. Place the bowl of chocolate on top of the sauce pan, stirring occasionally as chocolate melts. In a separate sauce pan, combine 1 cup sugar and bourbon. Bring mixture to a low boil, stirring occasionally. When sugar is fully dissolved, pour the hot mixture over the chocolate, stirring constantly, until chocolate is melted thoroughly. Remove the bowl from the sauce pan to a table or work surface and add the butter chips, a few at a time, melting completely before the next addition. In a separate stainless steel mixing bowl, whip the eggs on high speed with the remaining 1/2 cup sugar and flour until pale yellow and thickened, approximately 5 minutes. Using a rubber spatula, fold the egg mixture into the melted chocolate and blend until well incorporated. Pour the batter into the springform pan and smooth the top with the spatula. Fill roasting pan with hot tap water until it reaches half way up the side of the springform pan. Place cake in oven and bake for 1 hour. The top of the cake should have a thin dried crust when cooked. Do not overbake. Remove cake from oven and allow the cake to cool 1 hour at room temperature. Cover the pan with clear wrap and place the cake in the refrigerator a minimum of 4 hours. When ready to serve, carefully remove the sides of the springform pan. Place a cake plate or cardboard cake circle on top of the cake and invert to remove the bottom of the pan and parchment paper. This cake is extremely rich and truffle-like in consistency. Cut portions into 1 1/2-inch slices and top with fresh fruit and unsweetened whipped cream. Garnish with julienned mint leaves.

PREP TIME: 1 1/2 Hours

SERVES: 8-10

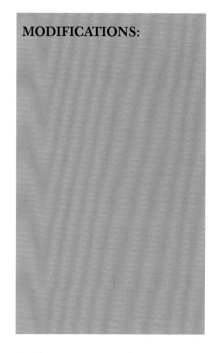

MODIFICATIONS:

Recipe for Romance: Mandarin Slices in Grand Marnier

Annadele's Plantation & Restaurant

COVINGTON

The room is bathed in the amber glow of firelight while the timber cracks and pops in familiar chatter. Empty wine glasses grace the Victorian hearth while blankets lay crumpled near the fireside. Shadows of flames flicker over the faces of lovers who slumber peacefully in each other's arms after hours of pleasure.

Fireplaces often evoke comfortable thoughts and pleasant memories. The history of Annadele's Plantation begins nearly two centuries ago in 1819 when seven police jurors formed the Claiborne Company. These men were searching for a location for the St. Tammany Parish Courthouse and jail. They acquired more than 1,700 acres of land through a sheriff's sale, but the town of Claiborne never flourished. In time the courthouse was abandoned and a new town, Wharton, present-day Covington, became the parish seat. The acreage was divided into parcels and sold.

Colonel Thomas Sully of New Orleans immediately recognized the potential of one particular 24-acre parcel and purchased it. Wasting little time, Colonel Sully began construction on his estate. Although the colonel never intended to use the estate as a plantation, he adopted the West Indian plantation style and named the estate Monrepos. When the one-story home was completed in 1834, it featured 15-foot ceilings, four bedrooms separated by a 54-foot wide hall, a separate outside kitchen and a room containing bathing tubs and laundry pots. An artesian well from a vein in Minnesota that was dug in 1827 still serves as the main water well today.

In 1889, the property became the summer home of New Orleans' mayor Walter C. Flower, his wife Adele and their children. One of his daughters, Corinne Dunbar, became renowned for her Creole restaurant of distinction, Corinne Dunbar's. She opened the restaurant in her 1840s townhome on St. Charles Avenue in New Orleans and took her personal cook, Leona Victor, as a business partner. Guests were greeted by a butler who escorted them to the dining room where Corinne offered a set menu of several courses. Her Oysters Dunbar is still remembered today.

Following the Flower's tenure, the estate passed into the hands of New Orleans' cotton broker Leon Gibert. Gibert elevated the cottage, closed in the first floor as living space, added large wings and brought in a boiler to steam heat the house. After his death, the house passed to his son and grandchildren who sold the property in 1970 to the McEnery trust. In 1976, Linder Schroeder and her parents, Florence and Joseph Pacaccios, purchased the home. They devoted four years to refurbishing the plantation and restoring it to its former splendor.

Annadele's Plantation hosts four elegant rooms, which combine old-world charm with modern conveniences. Whether you are a business traveler seeking lodging near downtown, or a beloved local looking for a getaway close to home, Annadele's eagerly welcomes your arrival. *(Continues on page 86)*

Fireplaces, ever evocative.

OPPOSITE: *Annadele's… for breakfast and dinner.*

(Continued from page 84)

The restaurant on the ground floor continues a long tradition of combining classic Creole and French dishes with an unparalleled dining experience. The executive chef's passion is evident in each of his culinary creations. You might sample his signature dish: Savory Cheesecake St. Tammany. This scrumptious "cheesecake" is served with caramelized onions, smoked shrimp and is then topped with barbecued shrimp. Lunch and dinner are served daily with a weekly Sunday brunch.

This family owned and operated business is located at 71518 Chestnut Street in Covington. For reservations call (985) 809-7669 or visit their web site at www.annadeles.com. While in the Covington area you might enjoy visiting Pontchartrain Vineyards, Heiner Brau Brewery, H.J. Smith's Son General Store and Museum, Brunner Gallery and Insta-Gator Ranch.

Late into the night when a chill fills the air and only glowing embers of the fire remain, slumber well knowing that your lover will be the blanket that keeps you warm.

THE PRUDENT MALLARD OMELETTE

*P*rudent Mallard was a French furniture maker who migrated to New Orleans and became the premier furniture designer of the South. Some say he worked for Duncan Phyfe before moving to the Crescent City and starting his own business on Royal Street. He is credited with introducing the half-tester bed, complete with a silk-lined half canopy and mosquito net, found in many Southern plantations.

INGREDIENTS:

- 2 eggs
- 2 tbsps butter
- 3 oyster mushrooms, sliced
- 2 tbsps milk
- 1/2 tsp Creole seasoning
- 1/4 cup sliced green onions
- 1 tbsp diced red bell pepper
- 1/4 cup shredded cheddar cheese

METHOD:

In a 6-inch crêpe pan, melt 1 tablespoon of butter over medium-high heat. Saute the mushrooms until thoroughly heated and softened, approximately 2-3 minutes. Remove from pan and set aside. In a mixing bowl, combine eggs, milk and Creole seasoning. Using a fork, blend well together but do not over mix. Using a paper towel, wipe out crêpe pan then melt remaining butter over medium-high heat. Pour egg mixture into the pan, decrease heat to medium and cover. When omelette starts to solidify, add mushrooms, green onions, bell pepper and cheese. Fold both sides of the omelet toward the center, cover pan and remove from heat. Allow the omelette to sit approximately 1 minute. Add crumbled bacon or finely diced ham to this recipe for an added twist.

PREP TIME: 15 Minutes

MAKES: 1 Omelette

MODIFICATIONS:

SHRIMP & REDFISH COURTBOUILLON

Although courtbouillon is best known as a flavorful poaching liquid for fish and shellfish, in Louisiana it has evolved into a sumptuous roux-based fish stew. At one time, redfish was the only species used in the courtbouillons of Cajun Country. However, today any firm-fleshed fish may be substituted, but redfish should always be your first choice.

INGREDIENTS:

- 1 pound (21-25 count) shrimp, peeled and deveined
- 3 (8-ounce) redfish fillets
- 3/4 cup vegetable oil
- 3/4 cup flour
- 2 cups diced onions
- 1 cup diced celery
- 1/2 cup diced red bell pepper
- 1/4 cup minced garlic
- 1 (12-ounce) can diced tomatoes
- 1 1/2 quarts fish stock (see recipe)
- 3/4 cup dry red wine
- 2 1/2 tbsps lemon juice
- 3 whole bay leaves
- 1 tbsp fresh thyme, chopped
- 1 tbsp fresh basil, chopped
- 1/4 tsp dried marjoram
- 1/8 tsp allspice
- Salt and black pepper to taste
- Hot sauce to taste
- 1 cup sliced green onions
- 1/2 cup chopped parsley
- 6 lemon slices

METHOD:

Cut each fish fillet into 3 equal slices. Set aside. In a cast iron dutch oven, heat oil over medium-high heat. Add flour and, using a wire whisk, stir constantly until dark brown roux is achieved (see roux techniques). Add onions, celery, bell pepper and garlic. Saute 3-5 minutes or until vegetables are wilted. Add tomatoes with juice and fish stock, one ladle at a time, until sauce-like consistency is achieved. Add red wine, lemon juice, bay leaves, thyme, basil, marjoram and allspice. Bring mixture to a rolling boil, reduce to simmer and cook 45 minutes, stirring occasionally. Additional stock may be necessary to retain sauce-like consistency. The sauce will be slightly thin due to the additional liquid rendered from the seafood. Add shrimp and fish, bring to a low boil and cook 3-5 minutes or until flesh is firm but not falling apart. Season to taste using salt, pepper and hot sauce. Add green onions and parsley and adjust seasonings if necessary. Serve over hot white rice and garnish with lemon slices.

PREP TIME: 1 1/2 Hours

SERVES: 6

Elegant dining.

MODIFICATIONS:

87

PAIN PERDU COUNT PONTCHARTRAIN

Lake Pontchartrain was named by Bienville in honor of the French Count in the court of Louis XVI at the time New Orleans was established. Pain Perdu, or Lost Bread, was a simple breakfast dish made from day-old, stale French bread abundant in the Creole cupboard.

INGREDIENTS:

- 2 (10-inch) loaves day-old French bread
- 3 eggs
- 1/4 cup sugar
- 2 tbsps vanilla
- 1 tsp cinnamon
- 1 tsp nutmeg
- 1 1/2 cups milk
- 3/4 cup melted butter
- 2 cups water
- 1/2 cup dry white wine
- 1/2 cup sugar
- 2 tbsps corn starch
- 2 cups raspberries
- 1 cup blackberries
- 1 cup blueberries
- 1/2 cup strawberries

METHOD:

In a large mixing bowl, combine eggs, sugar, vanilla, cinnamon and nutmeg. Using a wire whisk, whip until well-blended. Slowly blend in milk until well incorporated. Cut the French bread on a bias into 1/2-inch thick croutons and discard ends. Soak the croutons in the egg mixture for 1-2 minutes. In a cast iron skillet, heat butter, 1/4 cup at a time, over medium-high heat. Add more butter as needed during the cooking process. Once hot, saute bread 1-2 minutes on each side or until golden brown. Remove sauteed bread and keep warm. In a separate saute pan, combine water, wine, sugar and corn starch. Using a wire whisk, whip to blend thoroughly. Bring the mixture to a rolling boil, stirring constantly, until reduced to 1/2 volume. This simple syrup should thicken quickly with the corn starch. Remove from heat and add the fruit, coating well in the hot syrup. Allow fruit to sit in syrup until warmed thoroughly and sauce is colored from the natural fruit juices. Place 2 pieces of lost bread in the center of a 10-inch serving plate and top with a tablespoon of the fresh fruit and simple syrup. You may wish to garnish with whipped cream and powdered sugar.

PREP TIME: 30 Minutes

SERVES: 6

OPPOSITE: *The ultimate Louisiana breakfast or dessert dish.*

MODIFICATIONS:

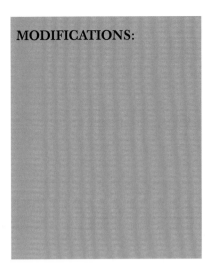

Recipe for Romance: Dry Sack Sherry and a Cozy Fire

Antique bar off main hallway.

OYSTERS CASSEROLE

Most Louisianians would debate at a moment's notice the superior quality of our Gulf oysters over any other American species. They're larger than most and much saltier. Such famous dishes as Oysters Rockefeller and Oyster and Artichoke Soup have been created with these delicacies, but none more flavorful than this simple oysters casserole.

INGREDIENTS:

- 3 dozen oysters, well drained
- 1 cup cracker crumbs, crushed
- 1/2 cup sliced green onions
- 1/2 cup chopped parsley
- 1/4 pound melted butter
- 4 tbsps minced garlic
- 2 tbsps lemon juice
- 1/2 tsp dried mustard
- 2 tbsps fresh tarragon, chopped
- 2 tbsps fresh basil, chopped
- 2 tbsps Worcestershire sauce
- Salt and black pepper to taste

METHOD:

Preheat oven to 450°F. In a saute pan, cook oysters approximately 3-5 minutes to render liquid and until slightly curled. Be careful not to overcook. Drain the oysters well and divide evenly among 6 individual ramekins. Sprinkle 1/2 of the cracker crumbs evenly over the oysters and then layer with green onions and parsley. In a saute pan, melt butter over medium-high heat. Add garlic, lemon juice, dried mustard, tarragon, basil and Worcestershire sauce. Saute seasonings 1-2 minutes and season to taste using salt and pepper. Spoon mixture equally into each ramekin. Place the ramekins on a large cookie sheet and bake until oysters are curled and bubbly, approximately 8 minutes. Add remaining cracker crumbs and cook casserole until golden brown, approximately 5 minutes.

PREP TIME: 30 Minutes

SERVES: 6

"At the Waters Edge" created by artist Wayne Morgan.

MODIFICATIONS:

Entrance to Annadele's.

POT-ROASTED WOOD DUCK IN FRESH FIG GLAZE

The fig tree would be magnificent as an ornamental tree alone. But when fresh figs appear in season, they become the secret ingredient in this much sought after wild duck recipe.

INGREDIENTS:

- 3 wild wood ducks, cleaned
- 2 cups fresh figs
- 1/2 pound bacon, chopped
- 2 cups diced onions
- 1 cup diced celery
- 1/4 cup minced garlic
- 3 sprigs fresh thyme
- 1 sprig fresh sage
- 1 quart chicken stock (see recipe)
- 1 cup sliced green onions
- 1/2 cup chopped parsley
- Salt and black pepper to taste

METHOD:

Preheat oven to 350°F. Rinse ducks well to ensure that they are perfectly clean and blood free. Season the ducks well inside and out using salt and pepper. In a large cast iron dutch oven, cook bacon over medium-high heat. When bacon is crisp, remove and set aside. Place ducks in the hot bacon drippings and slowly sear on all sides until golden brown. Once browned, remove ducks and

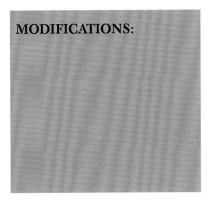
set aside. Into the drippings, add onions, celery and garlic. Saute 3-5 minutes or until vegetables are wilted. Return ducks to the dutch oven, breast side up, and add thyme, sage, figs, bacon pieces and chicken stock. Bring mixture to a rolling boil, reduce to simmer and cover. Place pot in the oven and allow ducks to roast 2 1/2 hours or until tender. Remove pot from oven and transfer ducks to a warming plate. Return pot to the stove and bring sauce to a low simmer over medium-high heat. Add green onions and parsley. Reduce the sauce slightly to intensify the flavor and adjust seasonings if necessary. Strain sauce through a fine sieve and allow to rest 5-10 minutes. Using a spoon or ladle remove all fat that rises to the surface. When ready to serve, cut ducks in 1/2, top with a generous serving of the fig glaze and serve with your favorite rice dressing.

PREP TIME: 3 Hours

SERVES: 6

Michabelle Inn & Restaurant

HAMMOND

*N*othing transforms a quaint dinner like candlelight flickering in the eyes of your lover: tinkling glasses, full-bodied wines swirling languidly in glasses, savory delicacies swimming in resplendent sauces. But then, there is dessert among the fragrant camellias and sweet olive. Walking through the serene moonlit surroundings is even more spectacular when serenaded by a hidden nocturnal chorus. A balmy breeze humming through the knurled arms of the century-old oaks whispers to lovers as they sip sherry and count the stars.

Draped with honeysuckle and scented with azaleas and roses in season, Michabelle Inn & Restaurant is an exquisite bed and breakfast awaiting your arrival. The property on which Michabelle Inn stands was originally the family home of Dr. Edward L. McGehee, Jr. Completed in 1907, this Greek Revival home has four exterior columns and two smaller interior columns. The floors are made of old-growth, edge-grained, long-leaf pine that are five layers thick. There are three working fireplaces in the home with a shared chimney. Accepted on the National Registry of Historic Places in 1982, the house was sold by the McGehee family to Michel and Isabel Marcais in 1998.

Cherubs mean romance.

OPPOSITE:
Exquisite Michabelle.

Chef Michel has traveled around the world delighting people with his culinary skills. He has held positions in his native France along the French Riviera, Switzerland, Portugal, Mexico, Costa Rica and of course, the United States. You are certain to experience Louisiana fare with French flair at the exceptional restaurant.

Michel's wife, Isabel, created the elegance of Michabelle, reupholstering furniture herself as well as designing and sewing all the draperies, window treatments and tablecloths. The rooms are filled with authentic French antiques. The exquisite bed and breakfast offers a superb bar, a stunning library, banquet facilities and conversations in French any time you wish.

Guests will appreciate the unparalleled architecture and grounds as well as the porches and rocking chairs, which are guests' favorites. The Inn has four rooms with private baths in the main house. The Creole Cottage has four suites with king-sized beds and Jacuzzi tubs. All rooms are non-smoking and have internet access. A full breakfast is served to guests daily.

Michabelle Inn is located at 1106 South Holly Street in a quiet neighborhood in Hammond, just a few blocks from Southeastern Louisiana University. Guests can enjoy sporting and cultural events at Southeastern as well as the highly

(Continues on page 94)

(Continued from page 92)

acclaimed *Fanfare* events at the nearby Columbia Theatre. Additional excursions to the Global Wildlife Park and the local Zemurray Park make Hammond a family-oriented town with something for everyone. Your gracious hosts, Chef Michel and Isabel Marcais, can be reached at (985) 419-0550. Please tour their web site at www.michabelle.com.

As you wander the grounds of Michabelle Inn, enjoy a romantic evening nightcap while nature's alfresco symphony entertains you. Allow the universal rhythm of the night to speak to your hearts, and let the celestial splendor lead you where it may.

Come for dinner, then spend the night.

STRAWBERRY PANCAKE EN SURPRISE

*P*ancakes and crêpes can often become mundane when continuously presented in the same fashion time after time. This recipe treats pancake batter with a little respect and there's a surprise in the pan for every guest. Try substituting local, seasonal fruit in the place of Louisiana strawberries.

INGREDIENTS:

- 1/2 cup diced Louisiana strawberries
- 1/2 cup powdered sugar
- 2 tbsps butter
- 2 eggs
- 1/2 cup flour
- 3/4 cup milk
- 1/8 tsp nutmeg
- 2 tbsps rum
- Juice of 1/2 lemon

METHOD:

Preheat oven to 400°F. Dust a 12-inch round platter with 1/4 cup powdered sugar and set aside. In a 10-inch cast iron skillet, melt butter over medium-high heat. Saute strawberries 2-3 minutes, stirring occasionally. In the bowl of an electric mixer, place eggs and beat slightly. Add flour and blend into the egg mixture. Add milk and nutmeg continuing to whip until ingredients are well-blended. It is perfectly fine to leave the batter a bit lumpy in this recipe. When strawberries are tender, pour batter directly into the skillet over the strawberries. Place skillet in the oven and bake 15-20 minutes or until pancake is golden brown. Remove the pan from oven and score the edges of the pan with a paring knife to ensure that pancake will fall easily to the platter. Flip the pancake out onto the sugared-platter and sprinkle with rum and lemon juice. Dust top of pancake with remaining 1/4 cup of powdered sugar and serve.

PREP TIME: 30 Minutes

SERVES: 4-6

MODIFICATIONS:

GARLIC & HERB-STUDDED TENDERLOIN

*P*ork is to the cook what canvas is to the artist. Numerous possibilities arise when this ingredient is present. Because pork is one of the earliest meats to be domesticated, many pork dishes emerged in the early pots of American cuisine. In classical presentations, this fabulous pork tenderloin may be cooked directly on a grill or smoked in your home-style smoker as an alternative to roasting and slicing.

Do I have to go home?

INGREDIENTS:

- 3 pork tenderloins
- 12 garlic cloves, minced
- 1/4 cup fresh basil, chopped
- 1/4 cup fresh thyme, chopped
- 1/4 cup fresh tarragon, chopped
- 3 green onions, finely sliced
- Salt and black pepper to taste
- 1/4 cup olive oil
- 2 tbsps Louisiana cane syrup

METHOD:

Preheat oven to 400°F. Using a paring knife, cut five to six 1/2-inch slits in each tenderloin. In a small bowl, combine garlic, basil, thyme, tarragon, green onions, salt and pepper. Blend these seasoning ingredients until all are incorporated. Stuff each of the tenderloin slits with a generous portion of the garlic/herb mixture. Coat the outside of the tenderloins with olive oil and cane syrup, rubbing gently to distribute the liquids evenly. Season the outside of the tenderloins with the remaining seasoning mixture. Make sure the tenderloins are seasoned perfectly with salt and pepper. Place the tenderloins in a baking pan with 1-inch lip and bake 15-20 minutes or until internal temperature reaches 128°F. Remove from oven, slice into 3/4-inch pieces and serve with your favorite brown sauce such as demi-glace (see recipe). If you wish to make a simple red wine sauce, deglaze baking pan with 2 cups of red wine. Place the pan on a burner over medium-high heat, scrapping the pan and reducing the wine to 1/2 volume. Season to taste using salt and pepper. Place the reduced sauce onto the bottom of a serving platter and top with sliced tenderloin.

PREP TIME: 1 Hour

SERVES: 6

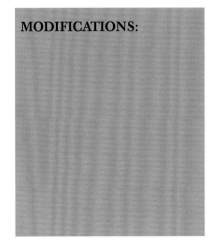

MODIFICATIONS:

ROASTED QUAIL CHARLOTTE

This is just a sample of Chef Michel Marcais' exquisite dishes. The quail, stuffed with candied chestnuts, is roasted and glazed with port wine sauce, then served with a nest of shoestring sweet potatoes and small beignets.

INGREDIENTS:

- 2 whole quail, cleaned
- 2 medium sweet potatoes
- 8 ounces candied chestnuts
- 1/4 cup vegetable oil
- Vegetable oil for deep-frying
- 1/2 cup butter
- 1/2 cup flour
- 1/2 cup milk
- 3 whole eggs
- 2 ounces port wine glaze
- Salt and black pepper to taste
- Granulated garlic to taste

METHOD:

Preheat oven to 375°F. Peel sweet potatoes, cut into shoestring shape and press firmly into the bottom of a small 4-6 inch skillet or form a 4-inch nest of shoestring sweet potatoes onto a baking pan. Place sweet potato "bird nest" into the oven and bake until shoestrings are fully cooked and lightly browned. Remove and keep warm. Season quail thoroughly with salt, pepper and granulated garlic. Stuff equal amount of candied chestnuts into the quail. In a 9-inch saute pan, heat 1/4 cup vegetable oil over medium-high heat. Brown quail on all sides. Place in oven and bake 10-12 minutes or until quail are fully cooked. Remove, set aside and keep warm. In a 1-quart sauce pot, heat 3 inches vegetable oil to 350°F. While oil is heating, in another sauce pot, melt butter over medium-high heat. Sprinkle in flour, using a wire whisk, stir constantly until white roux is achieved (see roux techniques). Do not brown. Add milk and continue to whisk until a thick paste is achieved. Add eggs, one at a time, stirring quickly and constantly to keep from scrambling. When eggs are incorporated, using a mellow baller, scoop out small egg shape pastry from the mix and deep-fry in vegetable oil until golden brown. This will serve as the quail eggs. Remove and keep warm. When ready to serve, cut quail in half and return to saute pan over medium-high heat. Add port wine to deglaze pan and create sauce. Arrange sweet potato "bird nest" in the center of the plate, place 3 birds eggs into the nest and surround with 2 quail halves. Drizzle with port sauce.

PREP TIME: 1 Hour

SERVES: 2

MODIFICATIONS:

OPPOSITE: *A platter of Quail Charlotte.*

BARBECUED SHRIMP TANGIPAHOA

*T*angipahoa, one of Louisiana's 64 parishes, is a Native American Indian word meaning "falling hair"—referring to the moss hanging from the live oak trees in and around the Hammond area. Barbecued shrimp first made its debut at Pascal's Manale Restaurant on Napoleon Street in New Orleans. The original owner of the restaurant served this wonderful garlic and herb infused shrimp to his friends who would visit the restaurant each week to partake in the local poker game. The tradition of "sopping up" the well-seasoned butter with French bread was just a natural evolution because of Louisianians love for the crusty loaf.

Bounty from the Gulf of Mexico.

INGREDIENTS:

- 36 (16-20 count) shrimp, head-on
- 1/2 pound melted butter
- 1/4 cup olive oil
- 1/4 cup minced garlic
- 1/4 cup minced purple shallots
- 1/2 cup sliced green onions
- 3 tbsps fresh basil, chopped
- 3 tbsps fresh oregano, chopped
- 2 tbsps fresh thyme, chopped
- 3 tbsps fresh rosemary, chopped
- 1/2 cup Worcestershire sauce
- 1 cup Amber beer
- Salt and cracked black pepper to taste
- Creole seasoning to taste
- Hot sauce to taste

METHOD:

Preheat oven to 350°F. In a 13" x 9" oven-proof baking dish with 2-inch lip, place head-on shrimp and spread evenly across dish. In a 1-quart sauce pot, heat butter and olive oil over medium-high heat. Add garlic, shallots, green onions, basil, oregano, thyme and rosemary. Saute 3-5 minutes to flavor butter with the herbed mixture. Add Worcestershire sauce and Amber beer then pour the hot mixture over the shrimp. Season to taste using salt, pepper, Creole seasoning and hot sauce. You should over-season with salt, pepper and hot sauce because the shells will protect the meat from absorbing most of the flavor. Place the shrimp in the oven and stir once during the cooking process. Cook shrimp until pink and curled, approximately 15 minutes. Do not overcook, as shrimp will become tough and hard to peel. Remove the shrimp from oven. To serve, place 6 shrimp in each of 6 soup bowls and top with equal portions of the herbed-butter sauce. Serve with crusty, hot French bread.

PREP TIME: 30 Minutes

SERVES: 6

MODIFICATIONS:

BEST DARN PECAN PIE

I don't think anyone knows how many variations there are for this premier Southern dessert. I have seen pecan pies flavored with everything from figs to persimmons and even swirled in chocolate. Personally, I think the old original recipe still outshines them all. So, here we present the traditional Louisiana pecan pie.

INGREDIENTS:

- 1 cup chopped pecans
- 1/4 pound butter
- 1 cup brown sugar
- 3/4 cup corn syrup
- 1/4 cup honey
- Zest of 1 orange, chopped
- 1 tbsp vanilla
- 3 eggs
- 1/8 tsp cinnamon
- 1/8 tsp nutmeg
- 1 (9-inch) deep-dish pie shell, uncooked

METHOD:

Preheat oven to 425°F. In a heavy bottom saute pan, brown butter over medium-high heat. The browning around the edges of the butter gives this pie its unique flavor. Do not burn the butter. Remove butter from heat and allow to cool slightly. In a large mixing bowl, combine brown sugar, corn syrup, honey, orange zest, vanilla, eggs, cinnamon and nutmeg. Using a wire whisk, blend ingredients until all is incorporated. Add the browned butter and pecans, blending well into the egg mixture. Pour contents into the pie shell and bake on center rack of oven for 10 minutes. Reduce temperature to 375° and bake for 35 minutes. Remove pie from oven and allow to cool thoroughly before slicing.

PREP TIME: 1 Hour

MAKES: 1 (9-inch) Pie

MODIFICATIONS:

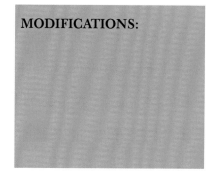

Recipe for Romance: Chocolate-Covered Strawberries and Sparkling Champagne

Pecans…from nuts to dessert.

Hughes House

HAMMOND

For centuries verandas have evoked provocative thoughts and enticed illicit love affairs. Perhaps it is the combined cadence of crickets and gentle creaking of the front porch rocker that arouses lovers. Maybe it is the combined scents of crape myrtle and magnolia that weave the gallery's web of enchantment giving the veranda its allure.

Hughes House boasts a spacious veranda, punctuated by stately columns that complete the flirtatious ambiance. This Queen Anne-style home was built in 1901 by Jefferson Davis Hughes, grandson of Peter Hammond, who founded Hammond, La., in 1820. According to a family member from whom the house was purchased, Hughes promised his children they would each have their own bedroom. He had so many children that he was able to keep his promise as older children moved away and younger children came along.

The kitchen at Hughes House.

During renovations to the house in the early '90s, a wall was opened revealing a tiny pair of leather and linen shoes. These were the shoes of Hughes' youngest child and had been placed in the last finished wall for good luck. Many rooms in the house are named for the children: Opal, Ruby, Pearl, Belle, Coral and naturally, Jefferson Davis.

Hughes' involvement in the lumber business allowed him to use the finest wood and utilize the most talented area craftsmen to build this fantastically solid house. He rode through his timber holdings and marked the trees he intended for his own home and then, only the best were considered.

Hughes House offers four bedrooms for overnight accommodations. The Opal Room located on the main floor features a four-poster queen-sized bed, fine furnishings and private bath. Upstairs the Pearl Room is bathed in light with many windows and a multidirectional view of the neighborhood. There is a four-poster, carved mahogany bed, antique furnishings and private bath with a claw-foot tub and old-fashioned, hand-held shower.

Of course, breakfast is included with your stay. Owner Lee Collins prides herself on using the best ingredients for breakfast. Organic milk is served as well as local produce, and an area family provides farm-fresh eggs. You might begin the morning with coffee in the flower garden, under the gazebo, poolside or on the veranda. Then, enjoy a luscious plantation-style breakfast, including juice and peach Schnapps, in the elegant dining room.

Hammond is a charming university town with Southeastern Louisiana University as a centerpiece. The beautifully renovated Columbia Theatre is within easy walking distance of the bed and breakfast. The Columbia boasts live performances and has many offerings *(Continues on page 102)*

OPPOSITE:
Inviting veranda.

(Continued from page 100)

during the university's *Fanfare* each autumn.

Hughes House is located in historic downtown Hammond just 42 miles from Baton Rouge and 45 miles from New Orleans. Located at 300 North Holly Street in the Adams-Lily historic neighborhood, the area is reminiscent of a time when life was gentler and all neighbors knew each other's names. Complimentary wine or tea is served upon arrival, Southern-style on the veranda. For reservations call (985) 542-0148 or visit the web site at www.hughesbb. com. Just a casual stroll from Hughes House are coffee shops, pubs, cafes and numerous fine restaurants as well as a bookstore, spa, post office, banks and boutique shopping. Also nearby is Global Wildlife Center, home of free-range wild animals that can be fed and enjoyed from motorized wagons.

The rooms of Hughes House have echoed with the laughter of children and played confidant to the hushed conversations of local leaders. After all these years, the veranda of this turn-of-the-century home still lures visitors with the soft glide of its rockers and the gentle breeze playing and swaying along the eaves of the house.

RANOLA

It was Ewell Gibbons, the great forager and author, who first made Americans aware of eating granola. I remember how strange sounding that dish was way back then. Today, healthier eating and the use of greens, grains and organic are just common household terms. Enjoy this healthy taste of granola.

INGREDIENTS:

- 1 tbsp peanut butter
- 2/3 cup honey
- 1/2 cup Canola oil
- 3 cups old fashioned oats
- 1 cup wheat germ
- 1/2 cup sunflower kernels
- 1/2 cup sesame seeds
- 1/2 cup sliced almonds

METHOD:

Preheat oven to 350°F. In a large mixing bowl, combine the peanut butter, honey and oil. Using a wire whisk, whip until peanut butter is liquefied. Add the remaining ingredients and using a large cooking spoon, stir until dried ingredients are well mixed with the coating. Oil a 9" x 13" baking sheet with 1-inch lip. Spread the granola evenly over the sheet and bake for 20 minutes, turning pan once, until granola is golden and toasted. Remove the granola from the oven and allow to cool. Store granola in an air-tight container. If the granola is refrigerated, it will keep for approximately 1 week. You may wish to serve this homemade granola with plain yogurt and a mixture of fresh seasonal fruit.

PREP TIME: 1 Hour

MAKES: 8 Cups

MODIFICATIONS:

FRONT PORCH CARROT BISQUE

The first thing you'll notice as you drive up to Hughes House is the wonderful front gallery of the home. This carrot soup is best when served in coffee cups either hot or cold and enjoyed on the veranda at Hughes House or on your own patio.

INGREDIENTS:

- 1 pound fresh carrots, peeled and sliced
- 2 medium-sized potatoes, peeled and sliced
- 7 cups chicken stock (see recipe)
- 1 cup diced onions
- 1 cup diced celery
- 1/2 cup diced red bell pepper
- 1 tbsp Worcestershire sauce
- Creole seasoning to taste
- Salt and black pepper to taste
- 1/2 cup heavy whipping cream
- 1/8 tsp nutmeg
- 1/4 cup chopped parsley

METHOD:

In a cast iron dutch oven, combine carrots, potatoes, chicken stock, onions, celery, bell pepper and Worcestershire sauce. Bring mixture to a low boil, reduce to simmer and cover. Cook soup until potatoes and carrots are tender, approximately 15-20 minutes. Season to taste using Creole seasoning, salt and pepper. Place the solid ingredients into the bowl of a blender or food processor. Slowly pour the soup in through a strainer. Do not overfill the bowl, because hot liquid will expand and the steam will cause the top to pop up during blending. Place just enough of the hot liquid to cover the vegetables by 1 inch. Take caution. Puree soup until smooth and creamy. Return pureed soup to the dutch oven and bring mixture to a low boil. Add heavy whipping cream, nutmeg and parsley. Adjust seasonings if necessary. The soup may be served hot or cold, garnished with fresh chives and sour cream optional.

PREP TIME: 1 Hour

SERVES: 6

Cali Sbisa enjoys showing guests the property after school.

MODIFICATIONS:

103

CRÈME CARAMEL CUSTARD

I fear to think how many recipes must exist for this simple international dessert. Just about every culture in the world has a variation or two for baked custard. This is yet another version and the addition of pecans makes it truly Louisiana.

INGREDIENTS:

- 1 cup sugar
- 1 tbsp water
- 4 eggs, beaten
- 1/4 tsp salt
- 1 cup milk
- 1 1/2 cups heavy whipping cream
- 2 tbsps vanilla
- 1/4 tsp nutmeg
- 1/4 tsp cinnamon
- 1/4 cup chopped pecans

METHOD:

Preheat oven to 300°F. Butter six 5-ounce custard cups and place on a baking pan with 2-inch lip. Fill the baking pan with water approximately 1/2-inch from the top of the lip. Set aside. In a cast iron skillet, place 1/2 cup sugar and water. Continue to melt sugar and slightly brown the edges to create a caramel, approximately 6 minutes. Do not stir or whisk during this process, just keep the heat low enough to brown the sugar evenly without burning. Pour an equal amount of the caramel into the bottom of each of the custard cups. Be careful as caramel is extremely hot. In a large mixing bowl, whip eggs, remaining 1/2 cup sugar and salt until eggs are thick and lemon-colored. Stir in milk, cream and vanilla. Continue to whisk adding nutmeg and cinnamon. Strain the custard into each cup and allow foam to settle prior to baking. Bake custards for approximately 2 hours or until solid. Remove from the oven and allow to cool overnight. When ready to serve, unmold custards and garnish with pecans.

In search of flavor!

PREP TIME: 2 1/2 Hours

SERVES: 6

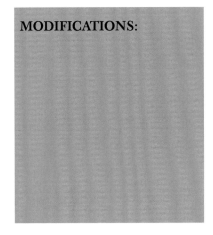

MODIFICATIONS:

Recipe for Romance: Long-Stemmed Cherries in Kahlúa Cream

OPPOSITE: *Fresh seasonal berries enhance this simple dessert.*

SPINACH & RICE CASSEROLE

The "old folks" of Amite, Louisiana, often referred to this simple baked casserole as "green rice." The name becomes apparent once the dish is cooked. What I like most about this recipe is that it can be pulled together quickly when unexpected company arrives. And better yet, it really tastes great.

INGREDIENTS:

- 2 (10-ounce) packages frozen spinach, thawed
- 2 cups long grain rice, cooked
- 1 1/2 cups grated cheddar cheese
- 4 eggs, beaten
- 1/4 cup melted butter
- 2/3 cup milk
- 1/4 cup minced onions
- 1/4 cup minced celery
- 1/4 cup minced red bell pepper
- 1 tbsp minced garlic
- 1 tbsp Worcestershire sauce
- 1 tsp fresh rosemary, chopped
- Salt and black pepper to taste

METHOD:

Preheat oven to 350°F. Using a vegetable spray, coat a 9" x 13" baking dish. Set aside. Squeeze spinach of all excess liquid and drain well. Place the spinach in a large mixing bowl and fold in rice and grated cheddar cheese. Add beaten eggs, butter and milk. Continue to blend until liquid is evenly distributed. Stir in onions, celery, bell pepper, garlic, Worcestershire sauce and rosemary. Continue to blend well and season to taste using salt and pepper. Pour the mixture into the dish and bake approximately 30 minutes, uncovered. This dish is an ideal accompaniment to meat or seafood and is perfect as a stuffing for chicken or Rock Cornish Game Hen.

PREP TIME: 1 Hour

SERVES: 6-8

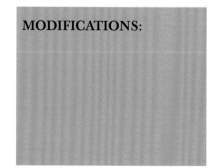

MODIFICATIONS:

Welcome to the enchanted garden.

elegant plate on antique lace.

PECAN-PESTO CHICKEN

Normally, pesto is made with any chopped garden herb, such as basil, blended with pine nuts and olive oil. Here in South Louisiana, we have replaced the pine nuts with pecans to give this pesto that perfect Southern flair. Pesto is ideal as a pasta coating or a topping on pizza or baked garlic bread.

INGREDIENTS:

- 6 boneless breasts of chicken, skin-on
- 1/3 cup pecans
- 1/2 cup freshly grated Parmesan cheese
- 1 tbsp minced garlic
- 2/3 cup fresh basil leaves, loosely packed
- 1/2 cup extra virgin olive oil
- 1/4 cup vegetable oil
- 1/2 cup flour
- 1/4 cup diced shallots
- 1/2 cup sliced oyster mushrooms
- 1 tsp minced garlic
- 1 1/2 tbsps flour
- 1/2 cup dry white wine
- 1 cup chicken stock (see recipe)
- 1 cup heavy whipping cream
- Salt and black pepper to taste

METHOD:

Preheat oven to 200°F. In the bowl of a food processor, place pecans, Parmesan cheese, 1 tablespoon minced garlic and basil leaves. Pulse the processor 1-2 minutes or until mixture is well chopped and blended. With the processor running, add olive oil in a slow steady stream until mixture resembles a paste. Season to taste using salt and pepper. Do not over-process as the basil will darken and appear unappetizing. Set aside. Store the pecan pesto sauce in a glass jar and refrigerate. This sauce will hold for a minimum of 3 weeks. In a saute pan, heat vegetable oil over medium-high heat. Rinse chicken under cold running water and pat dry. Season to taste using salt and pepper. Coat chicken lightly in flour and saute, skin-side down, 3-5 minutes. Turn chicken and continue sauteing until the skin is crispy. Remove chicken from the pan and place on a cookie sheet then set in a warm oven. Into the same saute pan, add shallots, mushrooms and remaining garlic. Saute 2-3 minutes or until vegetables are wilted. Sprinkle in 1 tablespoon flour and blend well. Add white wine and chicken stock. Using a wire whisk, blend liquids into the vegetable mixture. Bring sauce to a low boil and reduce to simmer. Add 2 level tablespoons of prepared pecan-pesto sauce into the pan along with heavy whipping cream. Continue to whisk until pesto is well-blended. Season to taste using salt and pepper. When ready to serve, place a small amount of the sauce on the bottom of a 10-inch plate and top with chicken, skin-side up. Place additional sauce over the edges of the chicken as a garnish. A bouquet of fresh basil leaves may be placed in the center for color. Serve this chicken dish alongside cooked pasta of your choice.

PREP TIME: 1 Hour

SERVES: 6

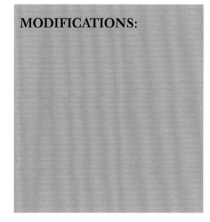

MODIFICATIONS:

Barrow House Inn

ST. FRANCISVILLE

Warm water flows freely as from a geyser, and the cleansing water caresses her body, while you massage her gently in the sweet, soothing scents of lavender and jasmine. Your souls are bathed in splendor as you wash away the sorrows of yesterday and remove the cares of tomorrow.

There is nothing more relaxing than a hot bath after a hard day. Dr. A. Feltus Barrow, a former resident of Barrow House in St. Francisville, relished his baths. He had an enormous tub in a downstairs room situated right next to the window from which he gave instructions for admitting patients to the sanitarium next door. As town mayor he often held court from his bathtub with the accused waiting patiently outside the window for the verdict.

An antique oil lamp in the bedroom window.

Barrow House is one of St. Francisville's oldest structures. The two-story saltbox was built around 1810 by Amos Webb. Webb was a bit egocentric. He owned the local theater, became postmaster, and then he attempted in vain to have the town renamed for himself.

OPPOSITE: *Wrought iron, an elegant architectural feature of Barrow House.*

In 1858 J. Hunter Collins, a local lawyer, purchased the house. He added the cottage extension to the home for his law offices just before the Civil War. In 1866 his partner, William W. Leake, purchased the home in which to raise his 11 children. In 1863, Mr. Leake stopped the War Between the States briefly under flag of truce to bury a fellow Mason, a Union gunboat

commander, in Grace Episcopal Church Cemetery. In later years Leake's daughter, Camilla, lived in the house with her husband, Dr. Barrow, the bath aficionado.

Barrow House Inn features two guest houses–the home itself and The Printer's Cottage across the street. The Printer's Cottage was built in the late 1700s. It was here that the town's newspapers were edited and printed. However, it is believed that the building was originally used by Spanish Capuchin friars who lived across the Mississippi River in the French settlement of Pointe Coupee. They did not want to bury their dead in the low ground of the west bank subject to flooding, so they ferried the bodies across the river to the high bluffs of the east bank, which is now St. Francisville.

Both the Barrow House and The Printer's Cottage are listed on the National Register of Historic Places. The rooms and suites are furnished in 1840-1870s antiques including canopy beds, armoires and claw-foot bathtubs. One suite features a Louisiana Spanish moss mattress, and two rooms have balconies overlooking Royal Street. Guests can choose from a continental breakfast or three New Orleans-style egg breakfasts.

During your stay at Barrow House, enjoy tours of local plantations including Rosedown, Oakley, Butler Greenwood, Greenwood, Afton Villa, The Myrtles and The Cottage. Downtown St. Francisville is filled with quaint shops and art galleries. Also of interest in *(Continues on page 110)*

(Continued from page 108)

the area is the West Feliciana Historical Society Museum. When you get tired of shopping and sight-seeing, enjoy dining at Magnolia Cafe, the Carraige House Restaurant or the Oxbow. The Bluffs, an Arnold Palmer golf course, is just minutes away. West Feliciana Parish is also popular for cycling, hiking, bird-watching and picnicking. If time permits, explore surrounding areas such as East Feliciana Parish, Cajun Country, Port Hudson State Park and Baton Rouge.

Barrow House is located at 9779 Royal Street in the midst of St. Francisville's National Register Historic District. For reservations contact Shirley Dittloff at (225) 635-4791 or online at www.topteninn.com.

Like a warm, relaxing, carefree bath, soak up the comforts of the Felicianas.

Crystal knife rests in multiple patterns.

ROLLIN' FELICIANA BRAN MUFFINS

The Feliciana parishes of Louisiana are quite different from other areas of Bayou Country because of their rolling hills resembling an English countryside. In these rolling hills, one may enjoy the Barrow House creation of bran muffins with a little surprise nestled in the center.

INGREDIENTS:

- 1 (20-ounce) box Raisin Bran cereal
- 4 cups white sugar
- 5 cups all purpose flour
- 1 1/2 tbsps baking soda
- 2 tsps salt
- 1 tbsp cinnamon
- 1 tsp nutmeg
- 4 eggs, beaten
- 1 quart buttermilk
- 1 cup vegetable oil
- 1 cup raisins

METHOD:

Preheat oven to 400°F. Grease muffin tin and dust with flour. In a large mixing bowl, combine all dry ingredients. Using a large spoon, blend until all are well incorporated. Add eggs, buttermilk and vegetable oil. Continue to blend ingredients until muffin batter is achieved. While blending, use the back of a cooking spoon to break the cereal into smaller pieces. Fold in raisins and set aside. Place 1-ounce ladle of the muffin batter into each muffin compartment then top with 1 teaspoon of the cream cheese filling mixture (see recipe). Top cream cheese mixture with remaining 1-ounce ladle of the muffin batter. Bake muffins 20-25 minutes or until golden brown.

PREP TIME: 1 Hour

MAKES: 4 Dozen

CREAM CHEESE FILLING

INGREDIENTS:

- 2 (8-ounce) packages cream cheese
- 2/3 cup sugar
- 4 tbsps flour
- 2 tbsps vanilla

METHOD:

Allow cream cheese to soften at room temperature. In a large mixing bowl, combine cream cheese with sugar and flour. When well-blended, stir in vanilla. This filling may be refrigerated for up to 2 weeks prior to use.

MODIFICATIONS:

MARINATED ZUCCHINI & SUMMER SQUASH SALAD

Romantics say that it's the simple things in life that are best. Well if that's so, then this simple squash salad should set hearts aglow. I recommend serving it in a beautiful cut crystal bowl to enhance its presentation.

INGREDIENTS:

- 3 medium zucchini squash, shredded
- 3 medium summer squash, shredded
- 1 small Bermuda onion, thinly sliced
- 1/2 red bell pepper, julienned
- 1/2 yellow bell pepper, julienned
- 2 tbsps minced garlic
- 1/4 cup sweet pickle relish
- 1/3 cup salad oil
- 1/3 cup red wine vinegar
- 1 tsp dried basil
- 1 tsp dried thyme
- 1 tsp salt
- 1 tsp cracked black pepper

METHOD:

In a large mixing bowl, combine squash, onions, bell peppers, garlic and relish. In a separate mixing bowl, combine salad oil, wine vinegar, basil, thyme, salt and pepper. Using a wire whisk, whip until well-blended. Pour marinade evenly over vegetable mixture, cover and refrigerate salad overnight. Prior to serving, toss and drain off any excess liquid. Place the salad into a decorative serving bowl and garnish with edible flower petals such as pansies, dianthuses or marigolds.

PREP TIME: 1 Hour

SERVES: 6

MODIFICATIONS:

A kaleidoscope of color in a cut crystal bowl.

JUMBO SHRIMP IN CREOLE MUSTARD CREAM

The Germans were probably the first to create a grainy, stone-ground mustard here in Bayou Country. The Gulf of Mexico provided the pantry for jumbo, white shrimp and between the two, this unique dish emerged. Try serving the dish over pasta or simply smothered in Creole cream as an appetizer.

INGREDIENTS:

- 3 dozen (12-15 count) shrimp, head-on
- 2 tbsps Creole mustard
- 1/4 pound butter
- 1/4 cup chopped chives
- 1/2 cup sliced green onions
- 1/4 cup diced red bell pepper
- 1 tsp dried tarragon
- 1/2 cup dry sherry
- 2 tbsps flour
- 1 cup heavy whipping cream
- 1 cup shellfish stock (see recipe)
- Salt and black pepper to taste

METHOD:

Peel the shell from the tail of each shrimp, being careful not to separate the head from the tail. Using a sharp pairing knife, devein the tail and rinse under cold water. Set aside. In a large saute pan, melt 1/2 of the butter over medium-high heat. Do not brown or burn the butter. Saute the shrimp, a few at a time, 1-2 minutes until shrimp are pink and curled. Remove shrimp from saute pan and keep warm. Add chives, green onions, bell pepper and tarragon. Saute 2-3 minutes or until vegetables are wilted. Deglaze pan with sherry and cook until all but 1 tablespoon of the liquid has evaporated. Sprinkle in flour and blend well into the seasoning mixture. Add Creole mustard, whipping cream and shellfish stock. Using a wire whisk, stir until all ingredients are incorporated and sauce thickens. If sauce is too thick, add additional stock or water. Season to taste using salt and pepper. When ready to serve, bring sauce to a low boil and whisk in remaining butter, a few pats at a time, stirring constantly. Add shrimp to the hot sauce and continue cooking until shrimp are heated and ready to serve. Place 6 shrimp on a 10-inch plate as an entree over a nest of spinach or red bell pepper pasta. Top pasta with a generous serving of the mustard cream sauce and garnish with additional chopped chives.

PREP TIME: 30 Minutes

SERVES: 6

OPPOSITE: *Jumbo shrimp nestled in Wedgwood.*

Mosquito netting drapes a four-poster bed.

MODIFICATIONS:

SCALLOPS OF VEAL WITH TASSO & WILD MUSHROOM ESSENCE

*W*ild mushrooms are plentiful in the rolling Felicianas. One may find everything from wild oyster to golden trumpets and morel mushrooms, too. When combined with julienned tasso, that spicy ham from Bayou Country, the flavors explode. What a complement to the subtle taste of veal!

INGREDIENTS:

- 6 (3-ounce) veal loin slices, pounded 1/8-inch thick
- 1/2 cup julienned tasso or ham
- 2 cups sliced wild mushrooms
- 1 tbsp Creole seasoning
- Black pepper to taste
- 1/2 cup seasoned flour
- 1/4 cup olive oil
- 3/4 cup Marsala wine
- 3/4 cup veal stock (see recipe)
- 6 slices Mozzarella cheese

METHOD:

Preheat oven to 375°F. Season the veal to taste with Creole seasoning and pepper and dust lightly in seasoned flour. Set aside. In a 12-inch saute pan, heat olive oil over medium-high heat. Saute veal 1-2 minutes on each side, remove and place on a baking pan. Into

The sun porch through a screen door.

the saute pan drippings, add mushrooms and tasso and stir fry approximately 2 minutes. Deglaze vegetables with wine and veal stock, bring to a rolling boil and reduce liquid to 1/2 volume. The flour left in the saute pan from sauteing the veal should thicken the sauce perfectly. Adjust seasonings if necessary. Remove from heat and keep warm. Place 1 slice of Mozzarella cheese on top of each veal slice. Bake 5-10 minutes until cheese melts and veal is thoroughly heated. To serve, place one portion of veal in the center of a serving plate and top with the tasso and wild mushroom essence.

PREP TIME: 1 Hour

SERVES: 6

MODIFICATIONS:

DOUBLE PRALINE PECAN PARFAIT

Pralines are undoubtedly the most famous candy in the South. Thank God today we have come up with all sorts of praline versions from ice cream to sauce. Here, we unite those two versions into the perfect finish of a Barrow House meal.

INGREDIENTS:

- 6 scoops praline ice cream
- 2 1/2 cups chopped pecans
- 1/4 pound butter
- 1 cup sugar
- 2 cups light brown sugar
- 1/2 cup heavy whipping cream
- 1 cup milk
- 1 tbsp vanilla
- 6 tbsps whipped cream

METHOD:

Place 1 scoop of praline or butter pecan ice cream into each fluted champagne glass and place in freezer. When ready to serve, melt butter in a saute pan over medium-high heat. Add sugars and whipping cream, stirring constantly until sugars are melted and cream is simmering. Add milk, vanilla and 2 cups of the chopped pecans. Reduce heat to simmer and cook 15-20 minutes, stirring occasionally. Remove glasses from freezer and spoon 2 tablespoons of the hot praline sauce on top of the ice cream. Garnish each glass with whipped cream and the remaining chopped pecans. You may wish to decorate with a fresh mint leaf.

PREP TIME: 30 Minutes

SERVES: 6

Recipe for Romance:
Frosty Mint Juleps in a Steaming Hot Tub

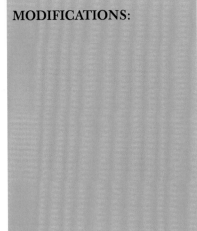
MODIFICATIONS:

Antique wicker furniture on a front veranda.

Butler Greenwood Plantation

ST. FRANCISVILLE

*L*ove letters scrawled on tattered parchment…entries scribbled in journals kept so many years ago…keepsakes and mementos stored as precious heirlooms in rosewood boxes…flowers pressed between book pages preserving fragrant memories of a former time and place. Love that once bloomed still permeates the sunken gardens, peeks around every eave of the house and hides within the walls of the Victorian parlor of this English country home. Butler Greenwood Plantation stands as stoically as its ancient oaks, waiting patiently to whisper love stories to its guests.

Ducks and geese entertain at the Pond House.

Located in St. Francisville, Butler Greenwood was built in 1796 on Spanish land grants received by Dr. Samuel Flower, a Pennsylvania physician. Dr. Flower moved to the area in 1770 and became one of Feliciana's earliest pioneers. The house was inherited by his daughter, Harriet, whose husband, Judge George Mathews, was a justice on the first Louisiana Supreme Court. Court duties often kept Judge Mathews from home, so it was Harriet who ran the plantation. She shipped cotton from her own dock on Bayou Sara, raised sugarcane and extended the family's landholdings. It was she who added the Victorian touches to the home in the 1850s.

The home is listed on the National Register of Historic Places and is built of cypress and blue poplar with laths of sassafras. Slaves made the chimney and well bricks. The plaster of the home was mixed in the English method of combining river silt and white horsehair. Butler Greenwood is adorned with beautiful gardens, which date from the 1840s. The property's live oaks were planted from acorns brought by a planter's family fleeing the 1799 Haiti slave insurrection.

Through eight generations direct descendants of Dr. Flower have owned and cared for the home. Today, eight cottages are available to overnight guests including the 1796 Old Kitchen, Cook's Cottage, Pool Pavilion, Chase's Cottage, Gazebo, Pond House, Treehouse and Dovecote. Each cottage has a unique amenity such as skylights, a hammock or porch swing, while all are furnished with a kitchen, private bath and double Jacuzzi.

During your visit to English plantation country, you will want to visit Oakley Plantation in the Audubon State Commemorative Area, The Cottage Plantation, Afton Villa Gardens and Rosedown Plantation and Gardens. Downtown St. Francisville is listed on the National Register of Historic Places as a Historic District with numerous quaint shops. Tunica Hills is great for hiking and Clark Creek Natural Area has seven scenic waterfalls. Also of *(Continues on page 118)*

OPPOSITE: *An acre of oaks frame Butler Greenwood Plantation.*

(Continued from page 116)

interest in the area is the West Feliciana Historical Society Museum. Enjoy dining at the Oxbow Restaurant and Magnolia Cafe.

Butler Greenwood Plantation is located on Highway 61, just 2 miles north of St. Francisville between Natchez, MS and New Orleans. For reservations contact Anne Butler at (225) 635-6312. A tour of the historic home is available.

Butler Greenwood stands as a reflection of the aristocratic society it once kept, the love it once knew and the family it still nurtures today. Let its Southern charm lull you to sleep each evening with love songs of long ago, a love that still lingers in the oaks, in the gardens and in the quaint cottages of this old hospitable home.

The lumps make 'em real!

WHIPPED POTATO CLOUDS

Only great cooks know how to make great mashed potatoes! If you grew up in the South, chances are pretty good that you've had great mashed potatoes because they are always served on Sunday with Southern Fried Chicken. They are the Confederacy's version of "apple pie and Chevrolet." The secret to good mashed potatoes is to leave a few of the lumps to make sure everyone at the table knows they are made from scratch.

INGREDIENTS:

- 6 large Russet potatoes
- 12 garlic cloves, minced
- 8 tbsps butter
- 1 cup heavy whipping cream
- Salt and white pepper to taste
- Pinch of nutmeg
- 2 pats of butter
- 1/4 cup chopped parsley

METHOD:

Peel the potatoes, removing any discolored spots or "eyes." Cut each potato in half lengthwise and each half into thirds. This will yield six half-moons per potato. Make sure that the pieces are equal in size to guarantee even cooking. In a 1-gallon stock pot, place enough salted water to cover the potatoes by 3 inches. Always use a pot large enough to allow the potatoes room when boiling.

Make sure that you salt the water liberally, being careful not to over salt. Bring water to a rolling boil. Place potatoes and minced garlic in boiling water and when water returns to a full boil, reduce heat to medium. Allow potatoes to boil 15-20 minutes or until the tip of a knife or fork can easily pass through the potato. NOTE: Do not overboil. The result will be mushy, pasty potatoes. When cooked, drain in a colander and toss to remove all cooking liquid. In a heavy bottom saute pan, melt butter over medium-high heat. Add cream, salt, pepper and nutmeg. Bring to a low simmer, stirring occasionally. Place drained potatoes in a large mixing bowl and mash only the major pieces with a fork or potato masher. It is acceptable to have small lumps here and there because this tells the guest the potatoes were made from scratch. Blend in the milk/butter mixture and adjust seasonings to taste. Serve in a warmed bowl and top with a couple pats of butter and a sprinkle of parsley.

PREP TIME: 1 Hour

SERVES: 6

MODIFICATIONS:

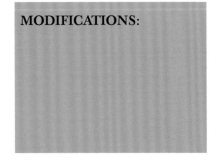

SWEET FARRE DRESSING

Farre is a meat dressing brought to Louisiana, many think by the Germans, that further evolved here in the French kitchens. In many Cajun and German communities of the River Road west of New Orleans, farre was often seen as a sandwich spread at weddings, parties and funerals. This is one of the many variations, which includes sweet potatoes and is undoubtedly from the German Coast of Louisiana.

INGREDIENTS:

- 1 1/2 pounds ground beef
- 1 1/2 pounds ground pork
- 1/2 pound chicken livers
- 1 quart chicken stock (see recipe)
- 2 cups diced onions
- 1 cup diced celery
- 1/2 cup diced green bell pepper
- 1/4 cup diced red bell pepper
- 2 tbsps minced garlic
- 1 cup shredded sweet potatoes
- 1 cup sliced green onions
- 1/2 cup chopped parsley
- Salt and black pepper to taste
- Granulated garlic to taste
- 5 cups cooked rice, optional
- 1/2 cup chopped pecans, optional

METHOD:

In a cast iron skillet, saute ground beef and pork over medium-high heat. Cook meat, chopping with a cooking spoon, until it is golden brown and grains of meat are totally separated, approximately 30 minutes. While meat is browning, poach chicken livers in chicken stock or water for approximately 20 minutes. Drain livers and reserve stock for later use. Chop chicken livers and once meat is browned, add poached livers, onions, celery, bell peppers, garlic and sweet potatoes. Saute 5-10 minutes or until vegetables are wilted. Reduce heat to simmer and add stock as necessary to retain moisture. Simmer, stirring occasionally until meat is extremely tender and sweet potatoes have totally disappeared, approximately 1 to 1 1/2 hours. Additional stock may be needed. Add green onions and parsley and season to taste using salt, pepper and granulated garlic. Farre may be eaten on a sandwich or mixed with cooked rice. Blend well and garnish with pecans.

PREP TIME: 3 Hours

SERVES: 8-10

Sweet Farre Dressing, a delicious accompaniment to Fried Chicken.

MODIFICATIONS:

PORT HUDSON'S SOUTHERN-FRIED CHICKEN

Port Hudson is a small town on the edge of St. Francisville where one of the longest and bloodiest battles of the Civil War ensued. Today, a national cemetery lies on that site and is a unique spot for visitors to this area.

INGREDIENTS:

- 1 (2 - 2 1/2 pound) broiler-fryer chicken, cut into serving pieces
- 3 quarts water
- 1 tbsp salt
- Salt and black pepper to taste
- 1 cup flour
- 2 cups vegetable oil
- 1/4 cup bacon drippings

METHOD:

In a large mixing bowl, combine water and salt. Place chicken pieces into the water, cover and refrigerate for 8 hours. Drain chicken, rinse with cold water and pat dry. NOTE: 2 cups of buttermilk may be substituted for the saltwater solution used to soak the chicken pieces. Season chicken and flour generously using salt and pepper. Do not over season. Place the seasoned flour in a gallon-size Ziploc® bag. Place 2 pieces of chicken in the bag and seal. Shake the bag to coat each piece of chicken completely. Remove chicken and repeat procedure with remaining pieces. Heat vegetable oil and bacon drippings in a cast iron skillet or chicken fryer to 360°F. Add chicken, a few pieces at a time, skin-side down. Once chicken is added, the temperature will drop between 300-325°F, which is the ideal temperature for frying chicken in this recipe. Cover and cook chicken for 6 minutes then uncover and cook an additional 9 minutes. Turn chicken pieces, re-cover and cook 6 minutes then uncover and cook 5-9 minutes. For even browning, turn chicken pieces during the last 3 minutes of cooking. Drain chicken on a plate lined with paper towels placed over a large bowl of hot water.

PREP TIME: 1 Hour

SERVES: 4

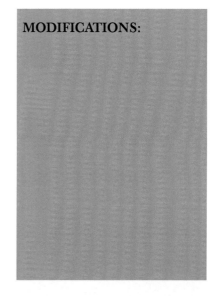

MODIFICATIONS:

OPPOSITE: An elegant setting for any picnic.

A view from the dining room to the corner staircase.

SPICY FRIED CHICKEN PAN GRAVY

I can't begin to tell you how many disputes there are about the technique for making perfect chicken gravy. Fact is, it depends on what kind of chicken gravy you want to make. When herb-roasting a young broiler, I love to simply remove the excess oil and use the natural drippings "as is." In the South, white gravy is preferred with fried chicken, but you better designate the South being everywhere but South Louisiana, where white gravies are despised. The brown roux is preferred in Cajun and Creole Country, but I have to admit even this Bayou Country boy loves this simple milk gravy flavored with pan drippings served alongside our Port Hudson's Southern-Fried Chicken recipe.

INGREDIENTS:

- 1/2 cup flour
- 2 cups milk
- 1/8 tsp nutmeg
- Salt and black pepper to taste

METHOD:

Fry chicken according to Port Hudson's Southern-Fried Chicken recipe. Pour off all but 1/2 cup of oil from the pan drippings and place skillet over medium heat. Add flour to drippings and, using a wire whisk, stir constantly, until lightly browned and almost tan in color. The caramelized particles from the fried chicken should be well incorporated into the flour. Add milk gradually and, stirring constantly, cook until thickened and bubbly about 3-5 minutes. Season to taste using nutmeg, salt and pepper. Serve over or alongside fried chicken.

PREP TIME: 10 Minutes

MAKES: 2 Cups

The formal parlor with original furnishings.

MODIFICATIONS:

Love birds in a cage of climbing roses.

ANNE BUTLER'S SWEET POTATO PIE

The Beauregard yam is one of the sweetest yams in Louisiana and was originally produced at Louisiana State University. My good friend, Irv Daniels, farmed this unique variety and there isn't a better sweet potato available when making this pie. Only use fresh sweet potatoes in this recipe.

INGREDIENTS:

- 6 Beauregard sweet potatoes
- Juice of 1/2 lemon
- 1/4 pound butter
- 1 cup sugar
- 1 tbsp vanilla
- 1 1/2 tbsps flour
- 1/8 tsp allspice
- 1/8 tsp nutmeg
- 3 ounces cream cheese
- 1/4 pound butter
- 1 cup flour

METHOD:

Preheat oven to 350°F. Beauregard sweet potatoes are a smaller variety than normally found in your local grocery stores. The potato is normally 1 1/2 inches in diameter and 4-6 inches in length. If only the larger sweet potato varieties are available, I recommend using 3-4 potatoes instead of the 6 Beauregards. Peel sweet potatoes, split in 1/2 lengthwise and dice into 1/4-inch cubes. Place potatoes in a 4-quart stock pot with lightly salted water. The water should almost cover the potatoes, but not completely. Bring to a rolling boil over medium-high heat and cook until potatoes are tender and water has been absorbed, approximately 15-20 minutes. Remove from heat and allow to cool slightly. During this process, 90% of the water should be absorbed by the potatoes. Discard any remaining liquid. Using a fork, mash potatoes and place in a large mixing bowl. Add lemon juice and 1/4 pound of butter, blending well into the mixture. Add sugar, vanilla, flour, allspice and nutmeg. Continue to blend until all ingredients are incorporated into the potatoes. Set aside. In a separate bowl, blend cream cheese and remaining 1/4 pound of butter. Sprinkle in flour and mix thoroughly. Turn out onto a floured board and knead 3-4 times. Roll pie crust to approximately 1/8-inch thickness. Place crust into a 9-inch pie pan and fill with the sweet potato mixture. Bake approximately 1 hour. Remove and allow pie to chill overnight prior to serving.

PREP TIME: 2 Hours

SERVES: 6-8

MODIFICATIONS:

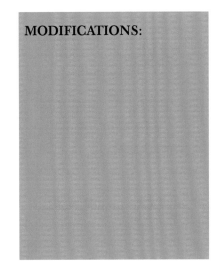

Recipe for Romance: Long-Stemmed Roses and a "Do Not Disturb" Sign

Milbank Historic House

JACKSON

*O*nly on rare occasions do you experience the kind of passion that transcends human existence, transporting body and soul to a surreal dimension. Sacred moments etched forever in memory; sacred events etched forever in time. The small community of Jackson, La., is seemingly shrouded in history and tainted with a mystery and intrigue all of its own.

Time stands still in historic Jackson. According to legend the town was originally called Bear Corners because of the many black bears that crossed nearby Thompson's Creek. Founded in 1815, many believe the town eventually took its name from General Andrew Jackson, who reportedly camped here with his troops sometime after defeating the British at the Battle of New Orleans that same year. Regardless, Jackson was a center for education earning it the title "Athens of the South." The College of Louisiana was located there from 1825 until 1845 and the Methodist-affiliated Centenary College from 1845 until 1908. In the 19th century, Jackson was Feliciana Parish's seat of justice and served as a thriving commerce and transportation center.

It's always nice to curl up with a good book.

Milbank House has been one of the signature structures in historic Jackson for more than 170 years. Standing tall behind its massive Doric columns and peach-colored exterior, this classic Greek Revival mansion was built circa 1836. Over the years it has played a vital role in the Felicianas serving as the banking house for the Clinton and Port Hudson Railroad Company, an apothecary shop, millinery shop, dance hall, ballroom, small hotel and a newspaper publishing house. The home also served as barracks for Union troops during the Civil War. At one point the Miller family purchased the house and converted it into a residence. In the 1980s the Harvey family purchased Milbank, opening it for tours, private functions and as a bed and breakfast in 1984. Milbank House is on the National Register of Historic Places.

Rather than a centrally located entry hall, Milbank's entrance is located on one end of the house. A spiral staircase stands at the end of that hallway. Prominent to Milbank are large rooms with 13-foot ceilings, random width floors, striking woodwork, large fireplaces with spiral flues and unusually wide porches on both floors. Because of its early banking history the house has two-foot-thick walls. The home is furnished with 1800s period antiques and showcases a mostly Victorian style.

Three rooms offer overnight accommodations. The downstairs Queen Room features a beautiful antique four-poster bed and an antique clawfoot tub in the private bath. On the second floor is a two-room Queen Suite furnished with a Mallard half-tester canopy bed, which is part of a matching set. Finally, there is a five-room Gallery Suite on the second floor with private access to the back veranda including a staircase to the ground floor. The master room in this suite has a half-tester Mallard bed while the separate guest room features two Spanish oak twin beds. Additionally, there is a small kitchenette for early morning coffee or tea. A full three-course Southern plantation breakfast is served to guests on fine china. Seasonal fruit

(Continues on page 126)

OPPOSITE:
Time stands still at Milbank Historic House.

(Continued from page 124)

as well as fresh, locally grown products are prepared.

Your stay includes a tour of the historic home, a welcome snack and beverage, snuggly bathrobes, complimentary toiletries, and a massage therapist is available upon request when reservations are made.

Milbank House is located at 3045 Bank Street just off Highway 10 in the heart of downtown Jackson, just 30 minutes north of Baton Rouge. The bed and breakfast has been in operation for 24 years and is within walking distance of The Surrey at Bear Corners Store & Restaurant, Centenary State Historic Site, the Republic of West Florida Museum, Old Hickory Railroad, Southern Belle Station Antiques and Feliciana Cellars Winery and Vineyard, which is open daily for tastings and tours. View Milbank House online at www.milbank.com or call (225) 634-5901 for reservations.

Step back in time in the heart of the Felicianas and share sweet memories of yesterday.

CORN MEAL PECAN WAFFLES

*F*rugal southern women never let a single thing go to waste and often combined leftover fruit with syrups as the perfect topping for waffles. A favorite flavor combination was canned cranberries and maple syrup. Try this recipe sometime!

INGREDIENTS:

- 1 1/2 cups yellow corn meal
- 1/2 cup chopped pecans
- 2 1/4 cups flour
- 1/2 cup sugar
- 3 tbsps baking powder
- 2 1/4 tsps salt
- 1/4 pound melted butter
- 6 large eggs, beaten
- 3 cups milk
- 2 tbsps vegetable oil

METHOD:

Preheat waffle iron to medium heat according to manufacturer's directions. In a large mixing bowl, combine corn meal, flour, sugar, baking powder and salt. Using a wooden spoon, blend well until all ingredients are incorporated. Fold in pecans and coat thoroughly with the waffle mixture. In a separate bowl, combine butter, eggs and milk. Using a wire whisk, whip until well incorporated. Add liquid ingredients alternately to dry ingredients stirring with a wooden spoon. Continue to stir until all of the lumps have been removed. Place a small amount of vegetable oil or spray on the preheated waffle iron. Ladle 3/4 cup of batter onto the hot waffle iron and cook approximately 3-3 1/2 minutes. Once cooked, keep waffles warm until all are done. Serve with cranberry syrup or your favorite fruit-syrup mixture.

PREP TIME: 30 Minutes

MAKES: 8 Waffles

CRANBERRY SYRUP

*C*ranberry sauce blended with maple syrup becomes the perfect topping for Christmas Day waffles.

INGREDIENTS:

- 1 (16-ounce) can whole berry cranberries
- 1 cup maple syrup

METHOD:

In a small sauce pan, combine cranberries and syrup over medium heat. Bring mixture to a low boil and cook, stirring occasionally, for approximately 5 minutes. You may store the cranberry syrup in a glass jar for later use or serve hot over corn meal pecan waffles.

PREP TIME: 10 Minutes

MAKES: 3 Cups

MODIFICATIONS:

FIESTA MAQUE CHOUX SALAD

Maque Choux is an early Louisiana dish that borrows its name from the Creole word for corn—maque and the French word for cabbage—choux. Although cabbage doesn't appear in the dish today, it is believed to have been in the original vegetable casserole, thus the name. Today, maque choux is a corn and shrimp dish enjoyed by the Cajuns of the River Road. It is often cooked as a vegetable by combining corn, tomatoes and shrimp, then baking casserole-style. This fiesta salad is yet another ingenious rendition of this timeless recipe.

INGREDIENTS:

- 2 dozen (16-20 count) shrimp, peeled and deveined
- 1/2 cup lime juice
- 1/4 cup lemon juice
- 1/2 cup Tequila
- 2 tbsps triple sec
- 1 tbsp fresh basil, chopped
- 1 tbsp fresh thyme, chopped
- 1 cup roasted red bell peppers, diced
- 1 cup roasted yellow bell peppers, diced
- 1 cup whole kernel corn
- 1 cup Creole tomatoes, diced
- 1/2 cup diced zucchini
- 1/2 cup canned black beans, rinsed
- 1/2 cup diced Bermuda onions
- 1 tbsp minced jalapenos
- 1/4 cup chopped cilantro
- 1 1/4 cups olive oil
- 1/2 cup white wine vinegar
- 1/4 cup lime juice
- 1/4 cup cilantro leaves
- 1 avocado, diced
- Salt and cayenne pepper to taste

METHOD:

In a large mixing bowl, combine shrimp, 1/2 cup lime juice, lemon juice, Tequila, triple sec, basil, thyme and season to taste using salt and pepper. Toss and marinate shrimp in refrigerator for approximately 30 minutes. While shrimp are marinating, roast the red and yellow bell peppers by placing the whole pepper directly on top of a gas flame on the stove or under the broiler. The skin will blacken totally and when thoroughly blackened and blistered, place the peppers in a sealed Ziploc® bag for 5-10 minutes to steam. Allow to cool then slice peppers lengthwise and rinse under cold running water to remove all of the black parched skin and seeds. Combine the roasted peppers in a separate bowl along with corn, tomatoes, zucchini, black beans, onions, jalapenos and chopped cilantro. Toss all vegetables to incorporate well and set aside. Create a vinaigrette dressing by combining the olive oil, wine vinegar, remaining lime juice and cilantro into the bowl of a food processor. Pulse for 1 minute to blend ingredients. Add avocado and pulse again for 30 second intervals or until blended. Do not over blend. Pour vinaigrette into a bowl and chill. When ready to serve, place a saute pan over medium-high heat. Remove shrimp from marinade and saute 2-3 minutes or until shrimp are pink and curled. Discard marinade. When shrimp are done, remove and combine the roasted red pepper salad with the sauteed shrimp and toss with 1/2 cup of the avocado vinaigrette. I recommend serving this Maque Choux Salad in a large Margarita glass that has the rim garnished by dipping it in lime juice and minced cilantro. Fill the glass or serving bowl with the salad. Garnish with lime slice and serve with tortilla chips.

PREP TIME: 1 Hour

SERVES: 6

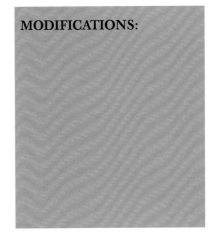

MODIFICATIONS:

BREAKFAST CHEER

In the South, it's considered good manners to serve a breakfast cocktail prior to the first meal of the day. This custom originated back in the plantation days when a mimosa or mint julep was part of a visitor's wake-up call. I've often enjoyed reading about a gathering of gentlemen on the veranda of a beautiful antebellum home at 7 o'clock in the morning, each holding a frosty libation. This combination of fruit and champagne will definitely give you a "kick-start" for the day.

INGREDIENTS:

- 1 (15-ounce) can Bartlett pears
- 1 quart fresh squeezed orange juice
- 1/2 bottle champagne

METHOD:

This delicious breakfast drink should be served in frozen Pilsner glasses. Place glasses in the freezer the day prior to serving this recipe. In the bowl of a blender or food processor, puree pears. Pour pureed mixture into a small pitcher and add orange juice, blending well. Place pitcher in refrigerator until ready to serve. Prior to breakfast, fill the Pilsner glasses 3/4 full of orange juice mixture then top with champagne. (Consider drinking the remaining champagne while preparing breakfast!) Garnish each glass with finely chopped Bartlett pears.

PREP TIME: 1 Hour

SERVES: 6

MODIFICATIONS:

OPPOSITE: *A sparkling welcome to the morning.*

Thomas Jefferson had this bed made for his granddaughter.

FRUIT MEDLEY

Because of our semi-tropical climate, a new crop of fruit ripens on the vine each season. Whether preparing well-known fruit, such as blackberries, strawberries and blueberries, or lesser-known bayou varieties, like mayhaws, muscadines or persimmons, all have the ability to become a unique breakfast addition when combined, chilled and topped with honey/yogurt dressing. This recipe is particularly wonderful on those hot, humid Louisiana summer mornings.

INGREDIENTS:

- 1 pint plain yogurt
- 1/2 cup honey
- 2 tbsps fresh-squeezed orange juice
- 2 tbsps vanilla
- 3 peaches
- 3 plums
- 1 dozen fresh strawberries
- 2 bananas
- 1 cup red seedless grapes
- 1 cup green seedless grapes
- 2 tangerines, peeled and sectioned

METHOD:

In a mixing bowl, combine yogurt, honey, orange juice and vanilla. Using a wire whisk, blend well to create a honey/yogurt dressing. Cover bowl with clear wrap and refrigerate, preferably overnight. Prior to serving,

A medley of fruit in chilled servers.

dice peaches and plums and set aside. Slice strawberries and bananas. In a large mixing bowl, combine diced and sliced fruit with grapes and tangerines. Blend the fruit and place in 6 individual crystal fruit bowls or dessert goblets. Top each with 2 tablespoons of the honey/yogurt dressing. Serve as an appetizer prior to breakfast. I recommend placing the empty fruit bowls or goblets in the freezer overnight for a frosty table presentation.

PREP TIME: 1 Hour

SERVES: 6

MODIFICATIONS:

Recipe for Romance:
Love Potion #9

130

POT-ROASTED GOOSE FALSE RIVER

Nothing makes a better table centerpiece than a specklebelly goose. Geese are nice and juicy because of the fat, but there is enough meat on a goose to serve six hungry hunters. This recipe is a favorite on nearby False River.

INGREDIENTS:

- 1 large specklebelly goose, cleaned
- 1/4 cup vegetable oil
- 2 cups diced onions
- 1 cup diced celery
- 1/4 cup diced garlic
- 1 cup sliced green onions
- 1 quart chicken stock (see recipe)
- 1 cup Merlot wine
- 4 slices bacon
- 2 cups diced turnips
- Creole seasoning to taste
- Salt and cayenne pepper to taste

METHOD:

Rinse goose well using cold water. Season goose inside and out using Creole seasoning, salt and cayenne pepper. In a cast iron dutch oven, heat oil over medium-high heat. Sear the goose well on all sides, turning as needed for even browning. Remove goose from dutch oven and set aside. Into the same oil, add onions, celery, garlic and green onions. Saute 3-5 minutes or until vegetables are wilted. Return goose to the dutch oven and add chicken stock and Merlot wine. Place bacon in a crisscross pattern over the breast of the goose. Bring stock to a rolling boil, reduce to simmer and cover. Cook goose for 2-3 hours or until tender. Depending on the age and size of the goose, this process could take up to 4 hours. Add turnips and cook 30 additional minutes. When ready to serve, place goose on a large serving platter. Surround bird with turnips and vegetable seasonings and a small amount of the cooking juices. I recommend serving the sliced goose over Sweet Farre Dressing (see recipe).

PREP TIME: 4 Hours

SERVES: 6

A good place to savor the scenery.

MODIFICATIONS:

Maison Des Amis

BREAUX BRIDGE

Playing kiss-chase at recess…skinny dipping in Bayou Teche…passing love notes during class…the carving on the old Oak tree in the schoolyard—all subtle reminders that best friends ultimately make best lovers.

Drip pots lined up like sentinels at the café.

Located in historic downtown Breaux Bridge, Maison Des Amis, or the "House of Friends," embraces and epitomizes the "quintessential American dream." The home, located on the National Register of Historic Properties, features porches, wooden floors and a picket fence, plus it is surrounded by beautiful gardens and Bayou Teche.

Scholastique Breaux, the founder of Breaux Bridge, lived directly across the bayou from the house, which was built around 1870. Maison Des Amis was once known as the "Boudier" house and was originally owned by the Domengeaux family. Scholastique married into the Domengeaux family sometime after the death of her husband, Firmin. In the 1890s the home was purchased by the Boudier family, and in the 1960s it was sold to Emile Girard. The house lay abandoned until 1994, when Dickie Breaux, a descendant of Scholastique and Firmin Breaux, bought the home as an anniversary gift for his wife, Cynthia.

The home features Caribbean/Creole architecture, which is unusual to this

OPPOSITE: The front entrance to Maison Des Amis.

area of Louisiana. At the center of the home is a two room bousillage (mud and moss) structure that was built around 1810 and enclosed by the construction of the late 1800s. It could have been used originally as an office or garçonnière for the neighboring Breaux home of which the oldest section is similarly constructed. These two rooms and the Breaux house, later known as "City Hotel," are the oldest structures in the town.

Maison Des Amis was the first bed and breakfast home in historic downtown Breaux Bridge. It has four guest rooms each furnished with period antiques. The home showcases a Queen Anne influenced polygonal bay, Eastlake galleries and a rose trellised garden entrance.

While in the area visit Vermilionville in Lafayette or the Evangeline Oak in nearby St. Martinville. For unique shopping stop by the Jefferson Street Market in downtown Lafayette, The Kitchen Shop in Grand Coteau or Breaux Bridge's Historic District antique stores. For local excursions you will enjoy Rip Van Winkle Gardens, Shadows on the Teche, Atchafalaya Basin Tours, Lake Martin Boat Tours or fishing and canoeing at Lake Fausse' Point. For breakfast enjoy the local flavors at Café Des Amis, located in a renovated store one block from Maison Des Amis. Robin's in Henderson is great for old-time Cajun food. For fine dining try The Fish & Game Grille in Lafayette or Le Rosier in New Iberia. You might also like the Café Jefferson in New Iberia *(Continues on page 134)*

(Continued from page 132)

or Catahoula's in Grand Coteau, or sample Mulate's where Cajun dancing is always on the menu.

Maison Des Amis is conveniently located about two miles from I-10 in Breaux Bridge at 111 Washington Street. For reservations call (337) 507-3399. Visit us online at www.maisondesamis.com.

From rough and tumble beginnings, Breaux Bridge has matured into a mélange of artists and preservationists. Amid it all Maison Des Amis stands as a constant reminder that some friendships become more intimate, more endearing as the years pass.

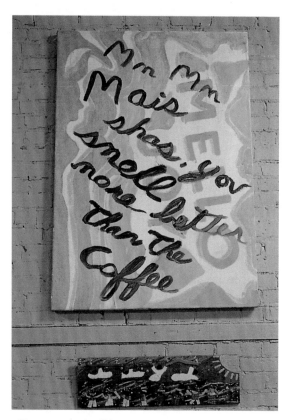

Signage says it all!

SHRIMP & OKRA GUMBO BAYOU TECHE

*B*ayou Teche winds its way through Acadiana and bisects many Cajun villages along the way. If there's one thread of commonality among the people of Cajun country, regardless of what bayou bank they reside on, it's the simple fact that they are all great gumbo cooks. This recipe, or one similar to it, is in the repertoire of most Acadiana households.

INGREDIENTS:

- 3 pounds (35-count) shrimp, peeled and deveined
- 1 (16-ounce) package cut frozen okra
- 1 cup vegetable oil
- 1 1/2 cups flour
- 2 cups diced onions
- 1 cup diced celery
- 1 cup diced green bell pepper
- 1/4 cup minced garlic
- 2 1/2 quarts shellfish stock (see recipe)
- 2 bay leaves
- 2 tbsps fresh thyme, chopped
- 2 tbsps fresh basil, chopped
- 1 cup diced Creole tomatoes
- 1 cup sliced green onions
- 1/2 cup chopped parsley
- Salt and black pepper to taste
- Creole seasoning to taste
- Hot sauce to taste

METHOD:

If you are lucky enough to have head-on shrimp or reserved shrimp shells, I recommend making a shellfish stock according to the recipe. You may wish to purchase clam juice or seafood bouillon cubes from your supermarket or substitute water in this recipe. In a cast iron dutch oven, heat oil over medium-high heat. Add flour and, using a wire whisk, stir constantly until Cajun brown roux is achieved (see roux techniques). Add onions, celery, bell pepper and garlic. Saute 3-5 minutes or until vegetables are wilted. Add stock, a little at a time, until soup-like consistency is achieved. Bring to a rolling boil, whisking constantly, until roux is dissolved and a smooth texture is achieved. Reduce heat to simmer and add bay leaves, thyme, basil, tomatoes and okra. Season lightly using salt, pepper and Creole seasoning. Simmer mixture 30 minutes, stirring occasionally, then add 1/2 of the shrimp. Continue to cook soup 15 additional minutes, adding green onions and parsley. Adjust seasonings if necessary. Remove bay leaves and add remaining shrimp folding gently into the okra gumbo. Cook 3-5 minutes or until shrimp are pink and curled. Serve a generous portion in a soup bowl over steamed white rice with a dash of hot sauce. NOTE: You may wish to sprinkle 1/2 teaspoon of filé powder or ground sassafras leaves over the gumbo prior to serving.

PREP TIME: 1 Hour

SERVES: 6-8

BRAISED RABBIT FUME BLANC

Because of the rich green swamplands of South Louisiana, game has always held a premier spot in the Cajun and Creole pantries. Because of its lean and subtle flavor, rabbit adapts well to most recipes and the early French inhabitants created many unique dishes for this wild game. I often substitute domesticated rabbit in the place of wild. It works perfectly in this recipe as well.

INGREDIENTS:

- 2 rabbits, cut into 6 serving pieces each
- 1/2 bottle Fume Blanc
- 1/4 cup yellow mustard
- 1 cup Italian dressing
- 1/4 cup hot sauce
- 3 bay leaves
- 1/4 cup chopped garlic
- 1/2 cup vegetable oil
- 1/2 cup flour
- 1 1/4 quarts chicken stock (see recipe)
- 2 cups sliced onions
- 2 cups diced carrots
- 12 new red potatoes, skin-on
- 2 sprigs rosemary
- 2 tbsps fresh sage, chopped
- 1 tbsp fresh thyme, chopped
- 1/4 cup olive oil
- Salt and black pepper to taste
- Creole seasoning to taste

METHOD:

Rinse rabbit pieces well under cold running water and drain. Place rabbit pieces in a large mixing bowl. Season rabbit well using salt, pepper and Creole seasoning. Add yellow mustard, Italian dressing, hot sauce, bay leaves and garlic. Blend mixture well and coat rabbit in marinade. Cover bowl with plastic wrap and refrigerate overnight. Prior to cooking, preheat oven to 375°F. Remove rabbit from marinade and place in a large roasting pan. Discard marinade. In a large sauce pot, heat vegetable oil over medium-high heat. Add flour and, using a wire whisk, stir constantly until dark brown roux is achieved (see roux techniques). Add Fume Blanc and chicken stock, blending well into the roux mixture. Bring stock to a rolling boil and reduce to simmer. Add onions, carrots, potatoes, rosemary, sage and thyme. Season sauce to taste using salt, pepper and Creole seasoning. Simmer sauce 10 minutes and keep warm. In a large cast iron skillet, heat olive oil over medium-high heat. Brown rabbit evenly on all sides then return to the roasting pan. When rabbits are browned, top with the wine sauce. Cover pan with aluminum foil and bake 2 hours or until rabbit is fork-tender. Additional stock may be needed to retain consistency. Serve alongside wild rice or Sweet Farre Dressing (see recipe).

PREP TIME: 2 1/2 Hours

SERVES: 6-8

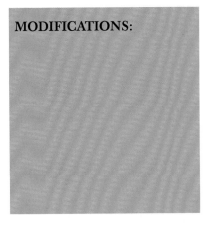

MODIFICATIONS:

Statuary and gardens overlook the gazebo.

STUFFED OREILLE DE COCHON

The translation for this dish is literally "pig's ear." This peculiar name came about because of the appearance of the finished product. Early on in Cajun communities fried triangles of dough would curl during cooking and were often served with cane syrup and powdered sugar as a dessert for children.

INGREDIENTS:

- 2 cups biscuit mix
- 1 1/4 cups pancake mix
- 1 cup milk
- 12 ounces white boudin
- Oil for deep-frying

METHOD:

Preheat oil in a deep fryer to 375°F according to manufacturer's directions. In a large mixing bowl, combine biscuit and pancake mix. Blend well then add milk and stir until dough ball forms. Turn the dough onto a floured work surface and knead 8-10 times, dusting with additional flour if dough becomes too sticky. Divide the dough into 4 equal portions and roll each section into a rectangle-shape approximately 1/4-inch thick.

Using a knife, trim each rectangle into a 6"x 9" triangle. Place 3 ounces of boudin along the 6-inch side and roll the dough in a Crescent-roll fashion, pinching the ends to seal in the boudin. Fry each triangle 3 minutes on each side or until dough is golden brown and floats. Serve with powdered sugar and cane syrup.

PREP TIME: 1 Hour

SERVES: 4

A simple cypress hearth separates these mahogany twin beds.

MODIFICATIONS:

OPPOSITE: *White Boudin wrapped in biscuit dough creates the ultimate surprise package.*

TURTLE CHEESECAKE DES AMIS

Turtle cheesecake gets its name from the pecan and caramel mixture that not only tops the crust in this dessert, but garnishes the finished cake as well. You may wish to substitute almonds or walnuts but we Louisianians prefer pecans.

Chocolate, pecans and caramel dance in the patio garden.

INGREDIENTS:

- 15 Oreo® cookies
- 6 tbsps melted butter
- 1 (14-ounce) bag caramel candy
- 1 (5-ounce) can evaporated milk
- 2 cups chopped pecans
- 1 1/2 pounds cream cheese
- 1/2 cup sour cream
- 4 large eggs
- 1/2 cup sugar
- 2 tbsps vanilla
- 1/2 cup semi-sweet chocolate chips

METHOD:

Preheat oven to 350°F. Spray a 9-inch springform pan with vegetable spray and set aside. In the bowl of a food processor, chop cookies to a fine crumb then coat with the melted butter. Pour the cookie crumbs into the bottom of the pan and, using your fingertips, press evenly to form a crust. Set aside. In a ceramic bowl, combine caramel and evaporated milk. Place mixture in a microwave oven and cook on high at 2 minute intervals stirring until smooth and creamy. Remove and allow caramel topping to cool and thicken slightly, approximately 10 minutes. Pour 1/2 of the caramel mixture over the cookie crust and garnish with 1/2 of the chopped pecans. In a large mixing bowl, combine softened cream cheese and sour cream. Using an electric mixer, cream until well-blended. Add eggs and sugar and continue to blend until smooth batter is achieved. Stir vanilla into cream cheese/sour cream mixture then pour batter into pan. Bake cake 45 minutes to 1 hour or until toothpick inserted into the center comes out clean. Remove and allow the cake to cool for approximately 30 minutes. Top cake with chocolate chips, remaining caramel and garnish with pecans. Place cake in the refrigerator overnight to set.

PREP TIME: 2 Hours

SERVES: 6-8

MODIFICATIONS:

Obviously, a great chef cooks here!

WHITE CHOCOLATE BREAD PUDDING

*B*read pudding is considered the "apple pie" of South Louisiana. Because of our heavy French influence, crusty French bread is in abundance here. Our German population gave us a good supply of milk and eggs and when combined with leftover bread, one of our premier desserts emerged. The addition of white chocolate gussied up this country dish.

INGREDIENTS:

- 9 ounces Bakers® white chocolate
- 3 (10-inch) loaves French bread
- 4 whole eggs
- 6 egg yolks
- 4 1/2 cups heavy whipping cream
- 1 cup milk
- 1 cup sugar

METHOD:

Slice French bread into 1/2-inch thick round croutons and set aside. In a large mixing bowl, combine eggs and egg yolks. Using a wire whisk, whip until well-blended. Set aside. In a large sauce pot, combine whipping cream, milk and sugar. Bring mixture to a low simmer then add white chocolate. Using a wire whisk, stir until chocolate is completely melted. Remove pot from heat and, stirring quickly, add whipped eggs to the cream mixture. Blend thoroughly to keep eggs from scrambling. In a 9" x 13" baking dish, place bread slices in 2-3 layers. Pour 1/2 of the cream mixture over the bread, allowing it to soak up most of the mixture prior to adding the rest. Using your fingertips, press the bread gently allowing the cream mixture to be absorbed evenly into the bread. Pour remaining cream mixture over the bread and repeat process. Cover dish with aluminum foil and allow to soak a minimum of 5 hours or overnight prior to baking. Preheat oven to 300°F. Bake, covered, for approximately 1 hour then remove foil and bake 45 additional minutes or until top is golden brown. This bread pudding is actually better if chilled in the refrigerator overnight, after baking, then cut into squares and heated in individual portions in the microwave. You may wish to create a white chocolate sauce for topping the bread pudding by combining 8 ounces of melted white chocolate and 3 ounces of heavy whipping cream. This may be done in a double boiler or microwave.

PREP TIME: 2 Hours

SERVES: 6-8

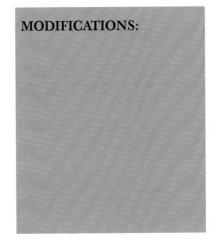

MODIFICATIONS:

Recipe for Romance:
Candy Kisses and French Chablis

Rip Van Winkle Gardens

NEW IBERIA

*Y*ou love her in the autumn when you can snuggle in the briskness of the evening and listen to the serenade of cicadas in the trees. You love her in the winter when you can sip hot mulled cider and toast marshmallows in the fireplace. You love her through the showers of spring and through the picnics of summer. You love her through the seasons, every season of your life.

It does not matter what season you visit Rip Van Winkle Gardens in New Iberia. You will be whisked back in time to a more genteel, gracious style of living. If only for a few days, the lush 25-acre gardens will enrapture the senses, relax the mind and rejuvenate the soul.

Sweet dreams.

Amid the beautiful gardens canopied by stately old oaks, stands the Joseph Jefferson Home. Built in 1870 by acclaimed American actor, Joseph Jefferson, the home is listed on the National Register of Historic Places. Jefferson purchased "Orange Island" in 1869 and built his winter home here. His role as Rip Van Winkle from the legendary Washington Irving tale, gave this place its name.

Jefferson died in 1905 and a little more than a decade later his heirs sold Jefferson Island and the 2,000-acre plantation to John Lyle "Jack" Bayless, Sr. from Kentucky and E.A. McIlhenny of Avery Island. John Bayless, Sr. began the first salt mine on Jefferson Island. In the late 1950s his son, J. Lyle "Jack" Bayless, Jr., diligently developed the gardens around

OPPOSITE: *Only in Louisiana!*

the historic home. He even built a half-acre garden under glass. This conservatory and welcome center featured more than 3,000 species of exotic tropical plants. On the edge of Lake Peigneur, Jack had his home to enjoy in retirement. In time, he donated the home and 800 acres to a private foundation to assure the continued operation of his gardens in perpetuity.

His home, the welcome center and conservatory were precariously situated atop a coastal salt dome, which he never considered an issue until November 20, 1980. On this fateful day a drilling rig pierced one of the giant caverns of the Diamond Crystal Salt Mine. The entire mine flooded with the vortex swallowing the lake, 65 acres of native woodland, destroying the welcome center, his glass conservatory and the new home. Thankfully, just four years later, a rebuilt welcome center, café, theater and restored Joseph Jefferson Mansion were opened to the public.

Today, the property features superior overnight accommodations. Louisiana French antiques subtly complement the furnishings of the three-room cottages. Sleep well in luscious four-poster, king-sized beds handmade from mahogany. Aromatherapy soaps and oils fill each cottage bath, while the refrigerator is stocked with favorite continental breakfast items and coffee, so you can enjoy morning at a leisurely pace. Complimentary wine and cheese is served daily. Also, included with your stay is a complimentary tour of the Joseph Jefferson House. Lunch is available at Café *(Continues on page 142)*

(Continued from page 140)

Jefferson where you can sip Seafood Cream Bisque while savoring the serenity of the gardens and Lake Peigneur from the glass porch.

While visiting the area you might also enjoy a tour of the Jungle Gardens of Avery Island and a factory tour of Louisiana's legendary condiment, TABASCO® Pepper Sauce. While in New Iberia you might also enjoy visiting Shadows-on-the-Teche and Conrad Rice Mill, America's oldest working rice mill and maker of KONRIKO rice products. For dinner you might try Dupuy's Oyster Shop in nearby Abbeville or Prejean's Restaurant in Lafayette.

This semi-tropical paradise is located at 5505 Rip Van Winkle Road in New Iberia. The owners, Mike and Louise Richard, can be reached at (337) 359-8525 for reservations or visit their website at www. ripvanwinklegardens.com.

Rip Van Winkle Gardens offers a glimpse of grandeur in Teche Country where the home and gardens have watched the seasons come and go through moss-veiled eyes for decades. Though some loves are as fickle as the changing leaves of autumn, love on Louisiana's Jefferson Island is as everlasting as evergreen through every season of the year.

HEARTS OF ARTICHOKE FRITTATA

Frittata refers to any baked omelette flavored with a variety of toppings. In this particular recipe one of the main ingredients of Italian Louisiana is combined with Mediterranean flavors to create an interesting breakfast casserole.

INGREDIENTS:

- 1 (9-ounce) package frozen artichoke hearts
- 6 whole eggs, beaten
- 2 tbsps extra virgin olive oil
- 1/2 cup minced onions
- 1/4 cup mince garlic
- 1/2 tsp fresh oregano, chopped
- 3/4 cup grated Parmesan cheese
- 1/2 cup milk
- Salt and black pepper to taste
- 1/8 tsp nutmeg
- 1 cup grated Monterey Jack cheese

METHOD:

Preheat oven to 350°F. Prepare artichokes according to package directions. Set aside. In a cast iron skillet, heat olive oil over medium-high heat. Add onions, garlic, oregano and artichokes. Saute 3-5 minutes or until vegetables are wilted. Remove skillet from heat and set aside. Generously grease a 9" x 13" baking dish and coat the bottom with 1/4 cup Parmesan cheese. Spoon the artichoke mixture evenly over the bottom of the dish. In a mixing bowl, combine beaten eggs, milk, salt, pepper and nutmeg. NOTE: Be careful when adding salt to this recipe since Parmesan cheese normally has a high sodium content. Blend well then add Monterey Jack cheese and 1/4 cup Parmesan cheese. Distribute egg mixture over the artichokes and spread evenly. Bake, uncovered, for 25 minutes. Remove dish from oven, sprinkle evenly with remaining Parmesan cheese and continue baking until Fritatta is puffed and golden brown, approximately 5 minutes.

PREP TIME: 1 Hour

SERVES: 4-6

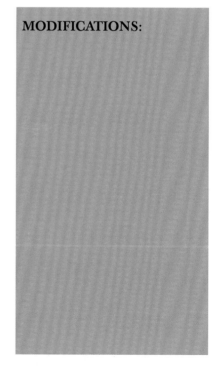

MODIFICATIONS:

SPINACH & LUMP CRABMEAT QUICHE

Quiche is one of those egg-based dishes that fall into the category of breakfast, lunch or dinner. The variations to this dish are too numerous to count, but I'm sure the addition of crabmeat to the recipe is strictly Louisiana in origin.

INGREDIENTS:

- 1 (10-ounce) package frozen spinach, thawed
- 1/2 pound jumbo lump crabmeat
- 1/4 cup melted butter
- 1/2 cup minced onions
- 1/4 cup minced red bell pepper
- 1/4 cup minced yellow bell pepper
- 1 tbsp minced garlic
- 1 cup grated Swiss cheese
- 1 cup grated Colby cheese
- 3 tbsps flour
- 6 eggs, beaten
- 1 cup half and half cream
- Salt and black pepper to taste
- 1/8 tsp nutmeg
- 2 (9-inch) unbaked pie shells

METHOD:

Preheat oven to 350°F. In a heavy bottom saute pan, heat butter over medium-high heat. Add onions, bell peppers and garlic. Saute 3-5 minutes or until vegetables are wilted. Add spinach and blend well

Rockin' life away!

into the vegetable mixture then cook 2 additional minutes. Remove pan from heat and add cheeses and flour. Using a cooking spoon, blend well to incorporate then set aside. In a mixing bowl, combine eggs, cream, salt, pepper and nutmeg. Add the spinach mixture to the eggs and blend well until all is incorporated. Distribute crabmeat evenly over the bottom of the two pie shells and top with the spinach/egg mixture. Bake pies for 45 minutes or until quiche is set and lightly browned.

PREP TIME: 1 Hour

SERVES: 8

MODIFICATIONS:

ROG IN THE HOLE

I'm not quite sure where the name of this recipe originated, but I'm positive that just about every child in Bayou Country has had this dish on occasion. I would imagine that cooking an egg inside of a slice of French bread or toast served a dual purpose. First, the eggs and toast were made at the same time and secondly, the dish seemed to be fun enough that kids would not mind sitting down to eat breakfast. In this recipe, I have elected to use quail eggs which makes the dish perfect as an appetizer or hors d'oeuvre.

INGREDIENTS:

- 2 dozen quail eggs
- 6 slices bread
- 1/2 cup melted butter
- Salt and black pepper to taste
- 1 cup prepared Hollandaise Sauce (see recipe)

METHOD:

Preheat an electric non-stick 11" x 14" flat griddle according to manufacturer's directions. Trim the crust from the bread and cut each slice diagonally into 4 triangles. Using a 3/4-inch pastry cutter, form a hole into the center of each triangle. You may wish to use a 1/2-inch thick French bread crouton in the place of sliced bread in this recipe. Brush each side of the bread slice lightly with melted butter. Place the triangles onto the hot griddle and crack 1 quail egg into the hole of each slice of bread. Cook 2-3 minutes on one side and, using a spatula, turn and cook remaining side until golden brown. The quail egg should be cooked to medium at this point. I recommend serving this quail egg toast garnished with Hollandaise Sauce and often top the sauce with 1/2 teaspoon of caviar.

PREP TIME: 30 Minutes

MAKES: 24

MODIFICATIONS:

OPPOSITE: *Frog in the Hole.*

Farm-raised quail eggs…a breakfast tradition.

EGGPLANT CASSEROLE

Eggplant has certainly worked its way into the kitchens of most Bayou Country homes. Although the eggplant is Middle Eastern in origin, it somehow arrived in New Orleans with the Italians and Spanish and has become a main ingredient in many Louisiana dishes from soups to casseroles. I can't imagine how many different ways I've eaten this vegetable, but this recipe is simple and one of my favorites.

INGREDIENTS:

- 3 medium eggplants, peeled
- 1/4 cup melted butter
- 1/4 cup vegetable oil
- 1 cup diced onions
- 1/4 cup diced green bell pepper
- 2 tbsps chopped garlic
- 3 (8-ounce) cans tomato sauce
- 1 tbsp fresh oregano, chopped
- 1 tbsp fresh thyme, chopped
- 2 tbsps fresh basil, chopped
- 1/4 cup chopped parsley
- 1/2 cup seasoned Italian bread crumbs
- 1 cup cottage cheese
- 2 eggs, beaten
- 1/2 cup grated Parmesan cheese
- Salt and black pepper to taste
- Creole seasoning to taste

METHOD:

Preheat oven to 350°F. Slice eggplants into 1/2-inch thick round slices and place on a cookie sheet. Brush the slices with melted butter and season to taste using salt, pepper and Creole seasoning. Bake eggplant for 10-15 minutes or until golden brown. Turn slices and brown evenly. Remove from oven and set aside.

In a heavy bottom sauce pot, heat oil over medium-high heat. Add onions, bell pepper and garlic. Saute 3-5 minutes or until vegetables are wilted. Add tomato sauce, oregano, thyme, basil and parsley, blending well into the vegetable mixture. Bring to a rolling boil, reduce to simmer and cook 10-15 minutes. Season to taste using salt, pepper and Creole seasoning. In an 8" x 12" casserole dish, place approximately 1/2 cup of tomato sauce. Top sauce with 1 row of eggplant slices and 1/2 of the bread crumbs. In a separate bowl, combine cottage cheese and beaten eggs. Spread cottage cheese/egg mixture over the eggplant then top with the remaining bread crumbs and tomato sauce. Sprinkle top with Parmesan cheese and bake 35-40 minutes or until mixture is bubbly and cheese is melted.

PREP TIME: 1 1/2 Hours

SERVES: 6

MODIFICATIONS:

Jean Lafitte's buried treasure?

FRENCH MARKET FRUIT PIZZA

No matter how old the kids are, eight or eighty, they're sure to love this unique and interesting rendition of pizza. The thing that I like most about it is the simplicity of the dish and the fact that any seasonal fruit will work perfectly.

INGREDIENTS:

- 3 kiwi, peeled and sliced
- 1 banana, sliced
- 1 (11-ounce) can mandarin oranges, drained
- 1/2 cup red grapes, halved
- 1 (18-ounce) package cookie dough
- 1 (8-ounce) package cream cheese, softened
- 1/4 cup confectioner's sugar
- 1 (8-ounce) carton whipped topping
- 1/4 cup sugar
- 1/4 cup orange juice
- 2 tbsps water
- 1 tbsp lemon juice
- 1 1/2 tsps corn starch
- Pinch of salt

METHOD:

Preheat oven to 375°F. Pat cookie dough into an ungreased 14-inch pizza pan. Make sure dough is smooth and evenly distributed. Bake 10-12 minutes or until lightly browned. Remove from oven, cool dough and set aside. In a large mixing bowl, whip cream cheese and confectioner's sugar until smooth. Fold in whipped topping and stir to blend thoroughly. Once the cookie crust has cooled, spread the cheese mixture evenly over the crust. Arrange fruit on top of the crust in a decorative fashion, starting from the outer edge and working toward the center. Place pizza in the refrigerator to chill. In a sauce pan, combine sugar, orange juice, water, lemon juice, corn starch and salt. Using a wire whisk, whip to dissolve the sugar and corn starch into the liquid. Bring mixture to a rolling boil, stirring constantly, for 1-2 minutes or until mixture thickens. Remove from heat and cool slightly. Remove pizza from refrigerator and brush the glaze over the fruit. This glaze will protect the fruit from drying out, flavor the pizza and give a shiny glistening look. Cover pizza and chill until ready to serve. This pizza may be served as a breakfast item or light dessert.

PREP TIME: 1 Hour

SERVES: 16

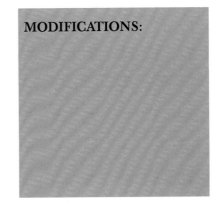

MODIFICATIONS:

Recipe for Romance: Hot Mulled Cider and a Cold Bayou Night

A taste of elegance on Jefferson Island.

Bois des Chênes

LAFAYETTE

The world has known many star-crossed lovers—those unfortunate, tortured souls whose paths crossed, though they were not destined to be together. Romeo and Juliet were Shakespeare's famous ill-fated couple. Evangeline and Gabriel are the tormented souls of Bayou Country. Many believe that if you eavesdrop on the wind, heed the perpetual flow of bayou water or listen intently to the mournful sway of Spanish moss high atop the oak limbs, you can still hear Evangeline's sorrowful cries of long ago as she searched for her Gabriel.

At Bois des Chênes in Lafayette you may well remember your own lost love or discover a new passion amid the tangled oaks. Judge Felix Voorhies, a relative of the present owner, first wrote the Evangeline legend that inspired Longfellow's epic poem.

Bois des Chênes, which means "oak woods," is the name of the bed and breakfast located in the Charles Mouton Plantation. The plantation was built around 1820 by Mouton who was the son of an Acadian settler from Nova Scotia. Mouton's father founded Vermilionville, which is present-day Lafayette. Coerte and Marjorie Voorhies restored the Acadian style plantation home to its original splendor several years ago and transformed it into a bed and breakfast inn.

An antique bottle collection.

OPPOSITE: *A late afternoon at Bois des Chênes.*

There are three suites in the 1890 Carriage House and two in the main house to accommodate guests. The rooms are complete with hardwood floors, antique four-poster and canopy beds and wingback chairs. In the Carriage House guests choose from rooms furnished in country Acadian, Louisiana Empire or Victorian style. Period antiques, primarily of Louisiana French origin are located in the main house, which is listed on the National Register of Historic Places. Guests receive complimentary wine and a plantation tour during their visit.

A delicious Louisiana-style breakfast is served daily on the outdoor patio or in the solarium of the main house. Breakfast items include pain perdu with Louisiana cane syrup, sesame biscuits, herbed eggs, hot boudin and café noir among other fabulous dishes.

You will appreciate the special touches that make the home extraordinary among bed and breakfast inns across the country such as closets containing umbrellas, mini-refrigerators with complimentary bottles of wine, flashlights near the bedside and night-lights in the bathrooms.

Bois des Chênes is located at 338 N. Sterling Street at the corner of Mudd Avenue. It is conveniently situated just a mile and a half from I-10 Exit 103A South and just three blocks off Evangeline Thruway. For reservations call (337) 233-7816. While in *(Continues on page 150)*

(Continued from page 148)

the area, explore Lafayette Museum, Alexandré Mouton House, St. John Cathedral and oak tree, Vermilionville and the Jean Lafitte Cultural Center. You might also enjoy a visit to the Lafayette Nature Station. Shop at Acadiana Mall or the Lafayette Antique Mall. There are many places to enjoy fabulous Louisiana cuisine such as Riverside Inn in Broussard, Prejean's in Lafayette and Catahoula's in Grand Coteau. Coerte, who is a naturalist and consulting geologist, will provide personally guided tours of the Atchafalaya Swamp. You might also be interested in seasonal hunting or fishing trips in the Gulf of Mexico. Do take the time to drive the short distance to St. Martinville, La., to visit the Evangeline Monument and the famous oak tree where Evangeline wept and waited for Gabriel.

Most of us, if we are willing to admit it, have a long lost love…a forbidden passion…an intimacy that never flourished. Some loves were simply never meant to be—frozen forever in memory, treasured indefinitely through time.

NAVAL ORANGE CRISP

*M*any great cooks will tell you that it's not the number of ingredients that make a dish, it's the taste! When I first discovered this simple breakfast "Melba-style" toast, I knew the taste was a winner.

INGREDIENTS:

- 1/2 cup Naval orange zest
- 1 cup sugar
- 1/2 pound butter, softened
- 1 loaf Pepperidge Farm® bread

METHOD:

To remove the zest of the orange, use an orange zester which may be purchased at any specialty store or supermarket or use a paring knife to cut a thin layer of the skin from the orange. Always take care not to cut the white skin below the orange rind since this has a bitter flavor. Place the zest in the bowl of a food processor and pulse to finely chop. Add sugar and butter and continue to process an additional 1-2 minutes to create an orange butter. Remove mixture from processor and set aside. Preheat oven to 350°F. Slice the crust from the bread then cut each slice in 1/2 diagonally. Spread the mixture evenly across the bread and bake 12-15 minutes or until crisp. The orange toast may be made in advance, frozen in Ziploc® freezer bags and reheated as needed. This toast is excellent with coffee!

PREP TIME: 30 Minutes

SERVES: 6

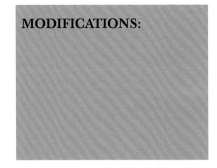

MODIFICATIONS:

The breakfast porch.

OYSTER & ARTICHOKE PATTIES

*O*nce again, the marriage of oysters and artichokes…two of the most frequently used classic ingredients of early New Orleans. Artichokes were grown by the Creoles as decorative garden plants, but the fruit was quickly harvested and blended with oysters to create the now famous New Orleans delicacy.

INGREDIENTS:

- 1 pint fresh shucked oysters in liquid
- 1 (14-ounce) can artichoke hearts
- 12 baked Pepperidge Farm® patty shells
- 1/4 pound butter
- 1/4 cup diced Bermuda onions
- 1/4 cup diced celery
- 1/4 cup diced red bell pepper
- 1/4 cup diced yellow bell pepper
- 2 tbsps minced garlic
- 1 tbsp fresh basil, chopped
- 1 tbsp fresh tarragon, chopped
- 5 tbsps flour
- 1 cup chicken stock (see recipe)
- 1 cup milk
- 1/4 cup chopped parsley
- Salt and cayenne pepper to taste

METHOD:

Preheat oven to 350°F. Rinse artichoke hearts under cold running water and soak for approximately 30 minutes in cold water. Drain well and set aside. In the bowl of a food processor, pulse the artichoke hearts until chopped but not totally pureed. In a sauce pan, melt butter over medium-high heat. Add onions, celery, bell peppers and garlic. Saute 3-5 minutes or until vegetables are wilted. Add basil, tarragon and chopped artichokes, blending well into the vegetables mixture. Sprinkle in flour and stir to incorporate all ingredients. Add chicken stock and milk and, using a wire whisk, blend until creamy white sauce is achieved. Add oyster liquid and season to taste using salt and pepper. Simmer mixture for 10-15 minutes, stirring occasionally to keep the mixture from sticking. When ready to serve, add parsley and oysters. Return mixture to a low simmer and continue to cook until oysters are curled and puffy, approximately 7 minutes. Reheat patty shells in the oven. When hot, place 2 patty shells in the center of 6 serving plates and top with an equal amount of the oyster artichoke sauce. Serve one patty as an appetizer or two as a light luncheon entree.

PREP TIME: 1 Hour

SERVES: 6

The Early Louisiana Acadian bedroom.

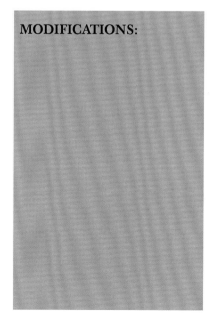

MODIFICATIONS:

WILD BLACKBERRY CRÊPES

The thing I like most about crêpes is their versatility. Not only are they the perfect dessert, but crêpes cross the boundaries of all meal periods. Some of my favorite luncheon items are seafood and chicken dishes wrapped in crêpes. Who among us hasn't longed for yet another crêpes Suzette for dessert? But when it comes to breakfast, nothing makes a more elegant plate presentation than a crêpe.

INGREDIENTS FOR CRÊPES:

- 4 eggs
- 1 cup flour
- 1 tbsp sugar
- 1 tsp vanilla
- 2 tbsps Grand Marnier liqueur
- 2 tbsps melted butter
- 1 1/2 cups milk
- Pinch of salt
- 1/2 cup vegetable oil
- 1/2 cup sugar

METHOD:

In a large mixing bowl, whip eggs, flour, 1 tablespoon of sugar, vanilla and Grand Marnier. Using a wire whisk, whip until ingredients are silky smooth. Add butter and milk and continue to blend until batter reaches the consistency of heavy whipping cream. Make sure that all lumps are

OPPOSITE: *Period antiques and brass coffee servers await the breakfast guest.*

removed. Season to taste using salt. It is best to make the crêpe batter a minimum of 6 hours prior to use and refrigerate. I recommend refrigerating the batter overnight. Place two 6-inch crêpe pans over medium-high heat. Add 2 tablespoons of vegetable oil into one pan and swirl to coat the bottom of the pan. Once hot, pour excess oil into the second crêpe pan. Place approximately 2 ounces of the crêpe batter into the first pan, tilting in a circular motion, until the batter spreads evenly. Cook crêpe until outer edge browns and loosens from the pan. Flip crêpe and cook 1 additional minute. Using a thin spatula, remove crêpe from the pan and sprinkle with remaining sugar. Continue this cooking process in both pans until all crêpes are done. If you wish to store crêpes overnight or freeze, place plastic wrap between each crêpe to prevent sticking and place in a large Ziploc® bag.

MAKES: 20 Crêpes

INGREDIENTS FOR BLACKBERRY FILLING:

- 3 cups wild Louisiana blackberries
- 2 tbsps butter
- 2 tbsps corn starch
- 1 cup water
- 1/2 cup white wine
- 1/2 cup sugar
- 1/8 tsp cinnamon
- 1/8 tsp nutmeg
- 1 cup whipped cream

METHOD:

In a saute pan, melt butter over medium-high heat. Dissolve corn starch in water until thoroughly blended. Pour corn starch mixture, wine and sugar into the saute pan. Bring mixture to a rolling boil, reduce to simmer then add 2 cups of the blackberries. Add cinnamon and nutmeg and continue to cook until sauce thickens, approximately 3 minutes. When ready to serve, divide an equal number of the fresh blackberries into the center of 12 crêpes. Place approximately 1 tablespoon of the cooked sauce over the berries and roll each crêpe into a cigar-shape. Place 2 crêpes in the center of 6 serving plates. Top each crêpe with a generous serving of hot blackberry syrup and 1 tablespoon of whipped cream. Garnish with fresh mint leaves.

PREP TIME: 1 Hour

SERVES: 6

MODIFICATIONS:

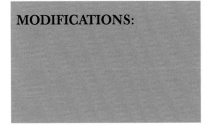

Recipe for Romance: The Cajun Two-Step on a Moonlit Veranda

Maja's Redfish Sauce Piquante

*M*aja, the daughter of Marjorie and Coerte Voorhies who own Bois des Chênes, delights in finding easier ways to create great tasting Creole dishes. She said the mission was simple: cut the time down but never sacrifice quality and flavor. This is one such dish!

INGREDIENTS:

- 6 (6-ounce) redfish fillets
- 3/4 cup vegetable oil
- 1 (8-ounce) can tomato paste
- 1/2 cup flour
- 1 cup diced onions
- 1/2 cup diced celery
- 1/2 cup diced green bell pepper
- 1/4 cup minced garlic
- 2 cups Creole tomatoes, diced
- 1 (6-ounce) can pitted black olives, sliced
- 2 quarts shellfish stock or water (see recipe)
- 6 lemon slices
- 1/2 cup sliced green onions
- 1/4 cup chopped parsley
- Salt and black pepper to taste
- Creole seasoning to taste
- Hot sauce to taste

As fresh as it gets!

METHOD:

Preheat oven to 375°F. This is the perfect dish to cook around a campfire or backyard barbecue grill but for those of you who are less adventurous, a preheated oven will do just fine. Season redfish fillets with Creole seasoning and set aside. In a cast iron skillet, heat 1/4 cup vegetable oil over medium-high heat. Add tomato paste and cook for approximately 15-20 minutes, stirring occasionally, until tomato paste darkens. Set aside. In a cast iron dutch oven, heat remaining 1/2 cup vegetable oil over medium-high heat. Add flour and, using a wire whisk, stir constantly until dark brown roux is achieved (see roux techniques). Add onions, celery, bell pepper and garlic. Saute 3-5 minutes or until vegetables are wilted. Add cooked tomato paste, diced tomatoes and black olives, stirring well into the roux mixture. Add fish stock or water, a little at a time, until stew-like consistency is achieved. Bring mixture to a rolling boil, reduce to simmer and cook 20 minutes to allow flavors to develop. Season to taste using salt, pepper, Creole seasoning and hot sauce. Pour the sauce piquante into a large cast iron oval roaster then add fish fillets. Top each fillet with 1 lemon slice and sprinkle green onions and parsley into the sauce. Cover roaster and simmer over the coals of an outside grill or bake 30 minutes until fish is cooked to your liking. Serve over steamed white rice or pasta.

PREP TIME: 1 Hour

SERVES: 6

MODIFICATIONS:

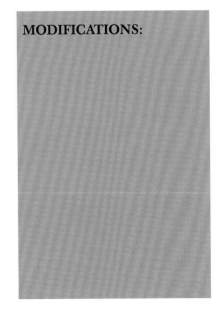

An antique decoy collection at Bois des Chênes.

BRAISED DOVES EVANGELINE

As a young boy growing up in Bayou Country, dove season meant not only good sport shooting but wonderful game birds for the table as well. My grandmother made the best dove and andouille sausage gumbo imaginable. Often when special folks came to visit, she would saute dove breasts in butter, then flame them in sherry and serve each over French bread croutons. Wow, what a breakfast! The dish I remember most often is the braised dove served alongside wild rice or rice dressing.

INGREDIENTS:

- 3 dozen cleaned dove breasts, bone-in
- 1 cup seasoned flour
- 1/2 cup vegetable oil
- 2 tbsps butter
- 1 cup diced onions
- 1/2 cup diced celery
- 1/2 cup diced green bell pepper
- 1/4 cup minced garlic
- 2 quarts chicken stock (see recipe)
- 2 tbsps fresh thyme, chopped
- 2 tbsps fresh basil, chopped
- 1/2 cup sliced green onions
- 1/4 cup chopped parsley
- Salt and cayenne pepper to taste
- Hot sauce to taste

METHOD:

Wash doves well inside and out under cold running water. Drain and season well using salt and pepper. Dust the doves in seasoned flour, shaking off all of the excess. The doves should be lightly coated. In a large cast iron skillet, heat oil and butter over medium-high heat. Brown doves, a few at a time, until all are done. Remove and set aside. Pour off all but 1/2 cup of oil. Add onions, celery, bell pepper and garlic. Saute 3-5 minutes or until vegetables are wilted. Reduce heat and continue to cook the seasonings, stirring occasionally, until well caramelized in the skillet, approximately 10-12 minutes. Do not scorch. Return doves to the skillet. Add chicken stock, thyme and basil. Season to taste using salt, pepper and hot sauce. Bring liquid to a rolling boil, reduce to simmer and cover. Cook doves until extremely tender but not falling apart, approximately 45 minutes. Sprinkle in green onions and parsley prior to serving. I recommend serving the braised doves over your favorite wild rice blend or our Sweet Farre Dressing (see recipe).

PREP TIME: 1 1/2 Hours

SERVES: 6

MODIFICATIONS:

T'Frere's House & Garçonnière

LAFAYETTE

Walking through the arbors of T'Frere's' gazebo is reminiscent of a wedding night, when the groom gently lifts his bride over the threshold and carries her to paradise. Every visitor passes through this gateway to the promised land, which heralds a divine evening and the experience of a nighttime.

In 1880 Oneziphere "T'Frere" Comeaux built this early Acadian colonial home in Attakapas country. (He was nicknamed T'Frere because he was the youngest of seven children.) He hauled red Louisiana cypress from nearby Vermilion Bayou and constructed a house much like those his Cajun ancestors built in Acadie before their exile.

The breakfast place setting.

This "couche et dejeuner," that's Cajun for "bed and breakfast," has a steeply pitched roof adorned with a widow's walk and a porch that wraps around the house on three sides. This extra gallery space was needed when the large family gathered for Mama's Sunday dinner.

A Cajun mystique accents the air as you enter Aaah! T'Frere's House & Garçonnière. The wide entrance hall is softly lit with German crystal chandeliers. Memories of a bygone era become real as you step back in time and see what makes the Cajuns love of life, good food and serving God and their fellowman so

OPPOSITE: *T'Frere's at night.*

contagious. Once inside you will discover the rest of the house including the kitchen, three cypress fireplaces, a parlor, dining room and four bedrooms each with a private bath.

Pat and Maugie Pastor, former restaurateurs and innkeepers extraordinaire and their son John, exemplify the expression, "Notre Maison est Votre Maison," or "Our House is Your House." They unselfishly break bread with guests and offer their hearth and home as a genuine gift from the heart.

Upon arrival guests are served Welcome T'Juleps and Cajun Canapes. Each evening after dinner, drinks are served. Morning finds Maugie dressed in her red silk "retirement" pajamas serving one of her famous Oooh! La La Breakfasts— true Cajun gourmet breakfasts with an international flavoring. Maugie believes that food is a source of inspiration and to cook a meal for someone is truly an act of love.

While in the area you will enjoy a visit to the Acadian Cultural Center, Vermilionville, Rip Van Winkle Gardens, Avery Island, historic St. Martinville, St. John's Cathedral, St. John Oak, Lafayette Museum, Shadows on the Teche, the Alexander Mouton Home and Acadian Village. Shopping is available at Acadiana Mall, and you'll enjoy fine Louisiana cuisine at Randol's, Blue Dog or Don's Seafood & Steak House. *(Continues on page 158)*

(Continued from page 156)

Aaah! T'Frere's House & Garçonnière is located at 1905 Verot School Road in Lafayette, just off Highway 90 East. For reservations call (800) 984-9347 or (337) 984-9347.

When you want a weekend getaway that is "Oooh la la," you can "come pass a good time" at Aaah! T'Frere's House & Garçonnière.

A view of the hallway through beveled glass.

EGGS À LA CRÈME

I've been served many exotic egg dishes in my travels including the thousand-year-old eggs of China. However, I can think of no better egg dish, or one more beautifully presented, than Eggs À La Crème from T'Frere's House in Lafayette. With a cup of hot, black Cajun coffee, nothing more is needed to start the day!

INGREDIENTS:

- 12 eggs
- 1/4 cup melted butter
- 1/8 cup minced onions
- 1/8 cup minced celery
- 1/8 cup minced red bell pepper
- 1/8 cup minced green bell pepper
- 1/2 tbsp flour
- 1/2 cup heavy whipping cream
- 1 tsp fresh thyme, chopped
- 2 tbsps fresh basil, chopped
- 1 tbsp minced garlic
- 2 tbsps chopped parsley
- 2 tbsps sliced green onion tops
- 1/2 cup heavy whipping cream
- 1/4 cup vegetable oil
- 1 cup crawfish tails
- Salt and black pepper to taste
- Creole seasoning to taste

METHOD:

In a cast iron skillet, heat butter over medium-high heat. Add onions, celery and bell peppers. Saute 3-5 minutes or until vegetables are wilted. Add flour, blending well into the vegetable mixture. Add 1/2 cup whipping cream, stirring until thickened white sauce is achieved. Season to taste using salt, pepper and Creole seasoning. Remove from heat and set aside. In a large mixing bowl, combine eggs, thyme, basil, garlic, parsley, green onions, remaining whipping cream and prepared white sauce. Using a wire whisk, blend well to create a whipped egg mixture. Season to taste using salt, pepper and Creole seasoning. In a large cast iron skillet, heat oil over medium-high heat. Add crawfish tails and saute 2-3 minutes or until pink and curled. Add whipped egg mixture and, using a spatula, stir eggs gently until well scrambled but not dry and overcooked. Spoon the eggs into a stemmed champagne goblet and serve with toast. Garnish with chopped parsley and paprika.

PREP TIME: 30 Minutes

SERVES: 6

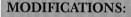

MODIFICATIONS:

$\mathscr{M}$AUGIE'S CRABMEAT VERMILION

$\mathscr{L}$ike all great recipes, this one began in a family-style restaurant. It then evolved over the years into a classic at Chez Pastor's in Lafayette. This dish may be made with any seafood or chicken and can be served as an appetizer or entree, depending on portion size.

Crocheted pillows accent any bedroom.

INGREDIENTS:

- 1/2 pound claw crabmeat
- 1 pound lump crabmeat
- 1/4 cup vegetable oil
- 1 cup diced onions
- 1 cup diced celery
- 1/2 cup diced red bell pepper
- 1/2 cup diced yellow bell pepper
- 1/4 cup chopped garlic
- 1 tsp fresh sage, chopped
- 1 tsp fresh thyme, chopped
- 1 tsp fresh marjoram, chopped
- 2 cups corn flakes
- 2 (12-ounce) cans evaporated milk
- Salt and black pepper to taste
- 1/2 cup chopped parsley
- 14 Ritz® crackers, crushed

METHOD:

Preheat oven to 350°F. Butter 8 individual 6-ounce ramekins and set aside. In a large saute pan, heat oil over medium-high heat. Add onions, celery, bell peppers and garlic. Saute 3-5 minutes or until vegetables are wilted. Add claw crabmeat, sage, thyme and marjoram, continuing to blend well into the vegetable mixture. Sprinkle in corn flakes and, using the back of a large cooking spoon, mash well to absorb the oil and chop into the seasonings. Add evaporated milk, bring to a low boil, reduce to simmer and continue to stir as corn flakes will thicken the milk. Allow sauce to simmer 3-5 minutes then season to taste using salt and pepper. Fold in lump crabmeat, being careful not to break the lumps. Place an equal amount of the Vermilion sauce in each of the ramekins and top with fresh parsley and cracker crumbs. Bake 12-15 minutes or until crabmeat is heated thoroughly. Serve one for an appetizer or two for an entree.

PREP TIME: 1 Hour

SERVES: 8

MODIFICATIONS:

T'FRERE'S TURTLE SOUP

There's been much debate lately as to whether restaurants should feature turtle soup because of the endangered species issue surrounding sea turtles. Of course, here in Louisiana our turtle soups are made with snapper which arguably makes the best and most sought after soup in the world.

INGREDIENTS:

- 2 pounds ground turtle meat
- 3/4 cup vegetable oil
- 1 cup flour
- 2 cups diced onions
- 1 cup diced celery
- 1 cup diced green bell pepper
- 1/4 cup diced garlic
- 2 (8-ounce) cans tomato sauce
- 2 1/2 quarts beef stock (see recipe)
- 1 lemon, sliced
- 1/2 cup sliced green onions
- 1/4 cup chopped parsley
- 1/4 tsp nutmeg
- Salt and cayenne pepper to taste
- Hot sauce to taste
- 3 boiled eggs, grated
- 6 ounces sherry

METHOD:

Season the turtle well using salt and pepper. In a heavy bottom stock pot, heat 1/4 cup vegetable oil over medium-high heat. Pan-fry turtle until water has evaporated from the meat and turtle is caramelized and golden brown. Remove turtle and drain on paper towels. Set aside. Add remaining 1/2 cup vegetable oil and heat over medium-high heat. Add flour and, using a wire whisk, stir constantly until dark brown roux is achieved (see roux techniques). Add onions, celery, bell pepper and garlic. Saute 3-5 minutes or until vegetables are wilted. Add tomato sauce and cook well into the vegetable mixture for 2-3 additional minutes. Slowly add beef stock, a little at a time, until soup-like consistency is achieved. Return meat to the pot along with lemon slices and season lightly using salt, pepper and hot sauce. Bring soup to a rolling boil, reduce to simmer and cook approximately 45 minutes or until turtle is fork-tender. Add green onions, parsley and nutmeg. Cook 2-3 additional minutes and adjust seasonings if necessary. When ready to serve, ladle a generous portion of the soup into a serving bowl and garnish with boiled eggs. Serve this soup with 1-ounce of sherry poured into the bowl at the table.

PREP TIME: 1 Hour

SERVES: 6

OPPOSITE: *Turtle soup…a Creole delicacy from New Orleans.*

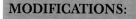

MODIFICATIONS:

A collection of soup spoons tucked for later use.

SWEET & SPICY CHICKEN ETOUFFEE

In many cultures of the world sweet and spicy, like sweet and sour, go hand-in-hand. Here in South Louisiana, where sugar and cayenne pepper are two main ingredients of the Cajun kitchen, it is obvious how this dish evolved.

Tea time at T'Frere's.

INGREDIENTS:

- 1 (3-pound) fryer, cut into 8 serving pieces
- 1/4 cup Worcestershire sauce
- 4 tsps salt
- 3 tsps cayenne pepper
- 1/4 tsp black pepper
- 1 tbsp granulated garlic
- 3/4 cup flour
- 1/2 cup vegetable oil
- 3 cups sliced Bermuda onions
- 1 cup diced celery
- 1 cup sliced red bell pepper
- 1 cup sliced yellow bell pepper
- 2 cups chicken stock (see recipe)
- 1/4 cup brown sugar

METHOD:

In a mixing bowl, combine chicken with Worcestershire sauce, salt, peppers and garlic. Blend thoroughly to coat the chicken in the seasonings. Allow the chicken to sit and marinate in the seasonings for approximately 1 hour at room temperature. NOTE: It is acceptable to leave chicken at room temperature, however, it must be cooked immediately following the marinating process. Remove the chicken to a large cookie sheet and reserve marinating liquid. Dust chicken in flour and set aside. In a cast iron dutch oven, heat oil over medium-high heat. Brown chicken lightly on all sides being careful not to scorch. Remove and set aside. Into the dutch oven, add onions, celery and bell peppers. Saute 2-3 minutes or until vegetables are wilted. Add chicken stock, reserved marinade and brown sugar. Bring mixture to a rolling boil then return chicken to the pot. Reduce heat to simmer, cover and cook until chicken is tender, approximately 45 minutes. Adjust seasonings if necessary. Serve sweet and spicy chicken over steamed white rice.

PREP TIME: 1 1/2 Hours

SERVES: 6

MODIFICATIONS:

BANANAS FOSTER

New Orleans, as a major port city, has always enjoyed fresh bananas shipped in from Latin America. Chef Paul Blangé was asked by Owen E. Brennan of Brennan's Restaurant to create a recipe using this fruit. In 1951, Chef Paul created Bananas Foster naming it for Owen's good friend and fellow member of the New Orleans Crime Commission, Richard Foster. Today, almost 20 tons of bananas are flamed each year at Brennan's in the preparation of this now world-famous dessert.

INGREDIENTS:

- 4 bananas
- 1/4 pound butter
- 1 cup brown sugar
- 1/2 tsp cinnamon
- 1/4 cup banana liqueur
- 1/4 cup dark rum

METHOD:

Cut bananas in half lengthwise then dice into 1-inch cubes. In a heavy bottom saute pan, melt butter over medium-high heat. Add sugar and cinnamon and whisk until bubbly and sugar is melted. Stir in banana liqueur and diced bananas and saute until softened. Remove the pan from the flame. Add rum then return pot to heat, taking care as rum will ignite. Stir constantly and when flames subside, remove from heat and serve as a topping over vanilla ice cream or your favorite cheesecake.

PREP TIME: 30 Minutes

SERVES: 6

MODIFICATIONS:

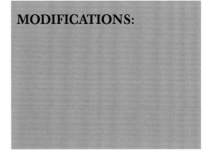

The downstairs suite with antique rocking horse in foreground.

Recipe for Romance: Silk Pajamas and Satin Sheets

Country French

LAFAYETTE

*I*n Louisiana, all roads lead to the country where a mile stretches over three parishes, an hour lasts a day and love lingers in the air eternally. In Louisiana, all roads lead to Country French Bed & Breakfast, a little taste of France tucked into the heart of Lafayette.

Old-world charm…in Lafayette.

Reminiscent of French chateaus scattered throughout the countryside, Country French Bed & Breakfast offers old-world charm amid modern conveniences. The architecture is so uniquely European that guests truly feel as though they've traveled to another place.

Country French was originally built in 1973 by Jane Fleniken as Antiques and Interiors. Her vision then was to have her French antique business on the premises, living and working out of the same location as so many Europeans do. When Jane decided to sell the home, downsizing to her current location in Lafayette, her son Greg Fleniken and daughter-in-law, Susie Aycock Fleniken, decided to buy the chateau and turn it solely into a bed and breakfast business. Susie has thrived now as owner and operator for the past 11 years.

The chalet offers two rooms stylishly furnished with French and Louisiana antiques, art and fixtures. The downstairs suite includes a private bedroom and sitting area. The queen-sized feather tapestry bed is dressed with European linens and comforters, ensuring a good night's sleep after a day of touring Acadiana or a night dancing in the local hangouts. Double French doors lead from the sitting area to the lush gardens where guests relax amid seasonal foliage and flowers. Soothing water fountains and the chatter of songbirds add to the ambience.

The upstairs room features a full-sized antique four-poster bed with a hand-crocheted French tester. A balcony allows guests to sip wine in the moonlight or perhaps start the day with a fresh cup of hot coffee while peering over the gardens and courtyard. On any given day the scent of four o'clocks, gardenias, jasmine and sweet olive linger on the breeze. Each room has a private entrance and bath with continental breakfast served in the privacy of your room.

While only minutes away from museums, cultural sites and fabulous restaurants, the bed and breakfast offers a monastic quality that evokes spiritual renewal. Attractions in the area include Vermilionville, Rip Van Winkle Gardens at Jefferson Island, Jean Lafitte National Acadian Cultural Center, Shadows-on-the-Teche, Evangeline Oak and Acadian Village. You might also enjoy a tour of the Atchafalaya Swamp, a factory tour of Louisiana's legendary condiment, TABASCO® Pepper Sauce, and a tour of the *(Continues on page 166)*

OPPOSITE: *The breathtaking entrance of Country French.*

(Continued from page 164)

Jungle Gardens of Avery Island. Learn to Cajun dance while you're in town or just sit back and listen to any of the fabulous local musicians. Area shopping convenient to Country French includes the downtown Jefferson Street Market, the Oil Center Shopping boutiques and the many specialty shops of River Ranch. For a taste of the local cuisine combined with musical entertainment try I'Monelli featuring live blues and jazz on Fridays, Cafe des Amis for Zydeco Breakfast on Saturday mornings, and Blue Dog Brunch featuring live local music on Sunday mornings. Night time dancing and dining recommendations are Randol's and Prejean's.

Relinquish the cares of the world and enjoy the essence of peace and comfort at Country French Bed & Breakfast, conveniently located at 616 General Mouton near the corner of Taft Street in Lafayette. For reservations call Susie at (337) 234-2866 or visit their web site at www.countryfrench bedandbreakfast.com.

The gracious owners greet your arrival with complimentary wine and are eager to share a slice of French country living that only Acadiana can offer.

UPSIDE-DOWN ORANGE BISCUITS

Although these orange glazed biscuits are made "scratch-style," they're so good I often just create the flavoring and serve it over a can of "whack" biscuits. You may also wish to use this orange syrup as a topping over croissants or French toast.

INGREDIENTS:

- 1/2 cup orange juice concentrate
- 1 tbsp grated orange zest
- 3/4 cup sugar
- 1/4 cup butter
- 2 cups all-purpose flour
- 1/2 tsp salt
- 3 tsps baking powder
- 4 tbsps shortening
- 3/4 cup milk
- 1/2 tsp cinnamon

METHOD:

Preheat oven to 375°F. Butter two 8-compartment muffin tins. In a small sauce pan, combine orange juice, zest, 1/2 cup sugar and butter. Using a wire whisk, stir constantly over medium heat until sugar is dissolved. Distribute mixture evenly between each muffin tin. In a large mixing bowl, sift flour, salt and baking powder. Add shortening and, using a pastry cutter, blend well into the flour mixture. Add milk and stir until dough ball forms. Place dough onto a floured surface and knead

15-20 seconds. Roll dough out to 1/4-inch thickness and sprinkle with remaining sugar and cinnamon. Roll dough jelly roll-style and cut into 1-inch slices. Lay each biscuit, cut-side down, in the muffin tins over the orange mixture and bake 15-20 minutes. Serve hot.

PREP TIME: 1 Hour

MAKES: 10-12

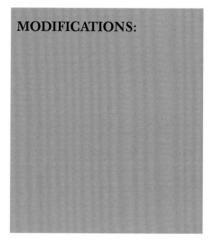

MODIFICATIONS:

The perfect country biscuit, orange glazed and garnished with candied kumquats.

An overnight stay at Country French is as refreshing as the French countryside.

FRENCH-FRIED ASPARAGUS SPEARS

*N*ormally, this dish is seen using fresh garden green beans, but any vegetable, especially asparagus, may be used. The important thing to remember is that asparagus are quite delicate and must not be over-cooked. A few minutes will suffice.

INGREDIENTS:

- 1 pound large asparagus spears
- 3 eggs, beaten
- 2 cups flour
- 2 cups seasoned Italian bread crumbs
- Salt and black pepper to taste
- Granulated garlic to taste
- Oil for deep-frying

METHOD:

Season the beaten eggs and flour with salt, pepper and granulated garlic. In a 3-quart sauce pot, place approximately 2 inches of vegetable oil and heat to 350°F. Dip asparagus in beaten egg, dust in flour, then dip again in egg and into bread crumbs. Deep-fry, a few at a time, until lightly browned and slightly crunchy but not over-cooked, approximately 4-5 minutes.

NOTE: Do not over-crowd the skillet. Remove, drain well on paper towels and serve immediately. Deep-fried vegetables are wonderful accompaniments to grilled steaks or as an appetizer.

PREP TIME: 30 Minutes

SERVES: 6

MODIFICATIONS:

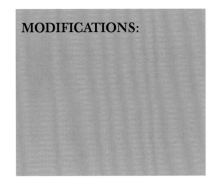

VENISON TENDERLOIN CARENCRO

Carencro is a small Cajun village located directly between the town of Opelousas, the yam capital of the world, and Lafayette, the heart of Acadiana. Most of the early Cajuns used the swamp floor as their pantry, so naturally, venison would have been a main ingredient on their tables. When special company arrived, the back strap or tenderloin was served suggesting the importance of the dinner guests.

INGREDIENTS:

- 6 (6-ounce) venison tenderloin steaks
- 1 cup dry red wine
- 2 tbsps fresh thyme, chopped
- 2 tbsps fresh basil, chopped
- 1 tbsp fresh tarragon, chopped
- 2 tbsps minced garlic
- Salt and cracked black pepper to taste
- 1/4 cup vegetable oil
- 1 tbsp flour
- 3 cups game or veal stock (see recipe)

METHOD:

In a small mixing bowl, combine chopped herbs and garlic. In a large baking pan, place venison steaks and coat each with red wine. Season the steaks evenly with herb/garlic mixture. Using your hands, rub the mixture into the venison steaks. Set aside at room temperature for approximately 2 hours. Reserve marinade for later use. NOTE: The steaks must be cooked immediately upon completion of marinating. The steaks will spoil if they are refrigerated prior to cooking. Preheat oven to 350°F. In a cast iron skillet, heat oil over medium-high heat. Season venison steaks to taste using salt and pepper. Saute steaks, a few at a time, until golden brown on all sides. Return the steaks to the skillet and place in the oven until internal temperature reaches 130°F for medium. Remove steaks and keep warm. Pour all but 1 tablespoon of the reserved drippings from the skillet and place skillet over medium-high heat. Sprinkle in flour and, using a wire whisk, stir constantly until light brown roux is achieved (see roux techniques). Pour the contents of the marinade pan into the skillet along with stock, bring mixture to a rolling boil, stirring constantly, until thickened and reduce to sauce-like consistency. Season to taste using salt and pepper. Place an equal portion of the game sauce in the center of a 10-inch dinner plate and top with a venison steak. You may wish to serve a mixture of fall vegetables such as melon-balled yams, carrots, beets or potatoes as a garnish for this plate.

PREP TIME: 1 1/2 Hours

SERVES: 6

MODIFICATIONS:

Care for a sip?

OPPOSITE: This elegant Venison Tenderloin is fit for royalty.

GIANT MUSHROOMS STUFFED WITH CRAWFISH & TASSO CARDINAL

Normally when you hear of stuffed mushrooms, you immediately have visions of a breaded seafood or vegetable stuffing heavily layered into a mushroom cap. This is an unappetizing thought! This stuffed mushroom is somewhat "smothered" in a rich sauce flavored with crawfish and the smoky, spiced meat of the Cajuns... tasso! This sauce may also be served over chicken, fish or pasta.

INGREDIENTS:

- 24 large mushroom caps, stems removed
- 1 pound crawfish tails, cooked
- 1/2 cup diced tasso ham
- 1/4 cup melted butter
- 1/2 cup minced onions
- 1/4 cup minced celery
- 1/4 cup minced red bell pepper
- 1/4 cup minced garlic
- 1/4 cup diced tomatoes
- 5 tbsps flour
- 1 ounce sherry
- 1/4 cup tomato sauce
- 2 cups fish stock (see recipe)
- 2 cups heavy whipping cream
- 1/4 cup sliced green onions
- Salt and black pepper to taste
- Creole seasoning to taste
- Hot sauce to taste

METHOD:

Preheat oven to 375°F. Brush any dirt or grit from the mushroom caps and place 4 in the center of 6 au gratin-style baking dishes. In a heavy bottom saute pan, heat butter over medium-high heat. Add tasso, onions, celery, bell pepper and garlic. Saute 3-5 minutes or until vegetables are wilted. Add 1/2 of the crawfish tails and tomatoes. Blend well into the vegetable mixture and saute 2-3 additional minutes. Sprinkle in flour and, using a wire whisk, stir to create a white roux (see roux techniques). Add sherry and tomato sauce. Add fish stock and cream and continue stirring until cream-type sauce is achieved. Add green onions and simmer sauce for 5-10 minutes, adding additional liquid as needed to retain consistency. Add remaining crawfish and season to taste using salt, pepper, Creole seasoning and hot sauce. Cook sauce 3 additional minutes then distribute evenly over the mushrooms. Bake until sauce is bubbly and mushrooms are al dente, approximately 15-20 minutes.

PREP TIME: 1 Hour

SERVES: 6

MODIFICATIONS:

French country living in Acadiana.

"Lemon tree very pretty and the lemon flower is sweet, but the fruit of the poor lemon is impossible to eat"... REALLY!

COUNTRY FRENCH LEMON PIE

I wasn't much of a lemon pie aficionado until my first visit to this "house in the country." I don't know what it was about the pie that caught my attention. It may have been the bowl of fresh lemons sitting on the counter next to the pie, or possibly the clouds of perfectly browned meringue crowning it. Later, I discovered that it was not only the look but the incredible taste that made me return as a fan to one of the oldest and simplest country-style desserts.

INGREDIENTS:

- 3 tbsps fresh lemon juice
- 1 tbsp grated lemon zest
- 1/2 cup corn starch
- 4 eggs, separated and beaten
- 2 cups sugar
- 1 1/4 cups cold water
- 2 tbsps butter
- 1 tsp cream of tartar
- 1 (9-inch) baked pie shell

METHOD:

Preheat oven to 375°F. In a bowl, whisk lemon juice, lemon zest, corn starch, egg yolks and 1 3/4 cups sugar. When well-blended, add water and whisk well to incorporate all ingredients. Pour contents of bowl into a sauce pan over medium-high heat and whisk continuously until mixture starts to bubble and thicken. NOTE: Be careful not to over-cook egg mixture. If heat is too high it will cause eggs to scramble and become lumpy. Remove sauce pan from heat and stir in butter. Pour pie filling into pie shell. Set aside to cool slightly. In bowl of an electric mixer, whisk egg whites and cream of tartar on high speed until soft peaks form. Add remaining 1/4 cup sugar and continue to whisk until sugar is dissolved and stiff peaks form. NOTE: It is important to whisk meringue until there are no visible signs of sugar, otherwise the meringue will weep after sitting for a few hours. Using a tablespoon, drop dollops of meringue on top of pie beginning at outer edge of pie and working toward the center. Continue this process until pie is completely covered. If meringue is allowed to adhere to pie crust, it will not shrink during baking. Place pie on center rack of oven and bake 10 minutes or until peaks are lightly browned. Remove from oven, allow to cool and refrigerate until ready to serve. This pie is best when refrigerated overnight.

PREP TIME: 1 Hour

SERVES: 6-8

MODIFICATIONS:

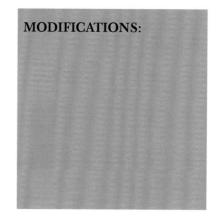

Recipe for Romance: Drunken Figs in Southern Comfort

Tezcuco Plantation

BURNSIDE

There is nothing more haunting than the memory of the woman you could never have. You are still mesmerized by her hourglass shape. You still savor the sweet nectar of her lips and smell the honey scent of her hair. You remember her amorous eyes and the infectious laugh that made you quiver. She comes to you at night in white satin, but you awake to discover an apparition of your tortured thoughts, haunting and taunting you through time.

Haunting, indeed, is the memory of Tezcuco Plantation on River Road in Burnside. Sadly, in 2002 the beautiful historic home burned to the ground. Only the stoic columns remain on the tranquil grounds, guarding the entrance to another time, a distant place of memory.

This Greek Revival-style home was built in 1855 by Benjamin Tureaud, a member of a prominent Creole family, and was raised, unlike most plantations in the area. The home, listed on the National Register of Historic Places, was made of cypress harvested from the original 400 acres and bricks from the plantations kilns. Architecturally, the home featured 16-foot ceilings, pocket doors, original faux bois on window frames and doors, gold frieze work and a cast iron fireplace. The rooms were furnished with period

A cypress privy from the turn of the century.

OPPOSITE:
Apparition of Tezcuco.

antiques and included such pieces as an 1860 rosewood piano, a C. Lee full-tester bed, Meissen porcelains, Limoges china and silver and Charles Eastlake furniture in the child's room.

Tezcuco was named for an ancient Aztec village and meant, ironically, "resting place." This historical home was one of the few offering overnight accommodations. In the manor house guests could rent the General's Suite located at the top of the stairs on the third floor. The room was created in 1982 from attic space and featured a stained glass door entrance, antiques, Empire furnishings, high ceilings and dormer windows. The suite included a kitchen, dining room, living room/library, two bedrooms and two baths.

Nine bed-and-breakfast cottages were available on the Tezcuco grounds. Most of these buildings were restored slave quarters original to the home, though a few were brought from area plantations. The cottages were built of cypress and furnished with some antiques. Most cottages were equipped with a kitchen, fireplace and a porch with rockers. Guests might choose to stay in La Petite Maison honeymoon cottage. This building was listed on the National Register of Historic Places and featured one bedroom, a bath, kitchen and formal parlor. The Pigeonnaire, once home to plantation fowl, was restored *(Continues on page 174)*

(Continued from page 172)

as a cottage with a stained glass entry, high ceilings, two bedrooms, two baths and a large kitchen/dining room with a fireplace. A full country breakfast was delivered to every room and included scrambled eggs, grits, sausage and biscuits.

Other area plantation homes are certainly worth a tour including Oak Alley, Houmas House, Destrehan Plantation, San Francisco Plantation, Laura Plantation and Nottoway. Other attractions include St. Michael's Church, the River Road African-American Museum, the LSU Rural Life Museum, historic Donaldsonville and the Historic Donaldsonville Museum. You will also want to shop at nearby Tanger Outlet Center in Gonzales and Cajun Village in Sorrento. For a taste of local cuisine enjoy dining at The Cabin in Burnside, Captain Anderson's in Gonzales or The Grapevine in Donaldsonville.

Tezcuco was located on Highway 44 (River Road) in Burnside between Baton Rouge and New Orleans.

Haunting, indeed, is the memory of Tezcuco, an apparition veiled in the memory of time.

MADAME TUREAUD CRAWFISH & SHRIMP DIP

*O*ften at the plantation, sweet river shrimp from the Mississippi would be harvested for dips and hors d'oeuvres. This recipe which combined the river shrimp with crawfish seemed to be a favorite in Ascension Parish. Today, gulf shrimp have replaced the hard to find river shrimp.

INGREDIENTS:

- 1/2 pound cooked crawfish tails
- 1/2 pound cooked shrimp, coarsely chopped
- 1/2 cup minced onions
- 1/4 cup minced red bell pepper
- 1/4 cup minced yellow bell pepper
- 1/2 tsp minced garlic
- 1/4 cup sliced green onions
- 1/4 cup chopped parsley
- 4 ounces cream cheese, softened
- 1/4 cup sour cream
- 1/2 cup mayonnaise
- 1/4 cup prepared salsa
- 2 tbsps lemon juice
- 1 tbsp horseradish
- 1 tbsp Worcestershire sauce
- 1 tbsp fresh thyme, chopped
- 1 tbsp fresh basil, chopped
- 1 tbsp fresh tarragon, chopped
- Salt and black pepper to taste
- Creole seasoning to taste

METHOD:

I recommend poaching the shrimp in a Creole-style crab or shrimp boil such as Zatarain's. In a large mixing bowl, combine onions, bell peppers, garlic, green onions and parsley. Using a wooden spoon, blend well. Add cream cheese, sour cream, mayonnaise, salsa and lemon juice. Continue blending mixture until ingredients are well incorporated. Add horseradish, Worcestershire, thyme, basil and tarragon. Continue to blend until cream cheese lumps are dissolved. Fold in crawfish and shrimp, blending well into the mixture. Season to taste using, salt, pepper and Creole seasoning. Cover the bowl with clear wrap and chill overnight. Serve dip cold with chips or garlic bread croutons.

PREP TIME: 30 Minutes

MAKES: 4 Cups

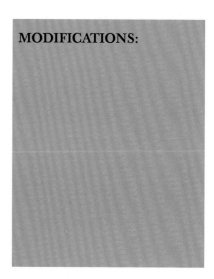

MODIFICATIONS:

Bringer's Nine Bean Soup

Beans have always played an important role in the life of a Southerner. When the Spanish arrived in New Orleans in 1765, they added to the number of beans already available in the area. Kidney, pinto and black were their favorites, while the black-eyed peas were later added by the Africans. This soup is a great example of evolving Creole cuisine.

INGREDIENTS:

- 1/4 cup navy beans
- 1/4 cup red kidney beans
- 1/4 cup lima beans
- 1/2 cup cannellini beans
- 1/4 cup pinto beans
- 1/2 cup black beans
- 1/2 cup sliced green beans
- 1/4 cup black-eyed peas
- 1/2 cup split peas
- 1/4 cup butter
- 1 cup diced onions
- 1/2 cup diced celery
- 1/2 cup chopped red bell pepper
- 1 tbsp chopped garlic
- 1 ham hock
- 2 slices salt pork
- 1 (14-ounce) can diced tomatoes
- 1 gallon beef stock (see recipe)
- 3 bay leaves
- 1 tsp dried thyme, chopped
- 1/2 tsp dried oregano, chopped
- 1/2 tsp cayenne pepper
- 1 cup andouille, sliced 1/4-inch thick
- 1 cup diced ham
- Salt to taste
- Hot sauce to taste

METHOD:

It is always best to rinse the beans once or twice, discarding any discolored beans or those that float to the surface. The beans, with the exception of the green beans, should then be soaked in cold water a minimum of 4 hours or preferably overnight. NOTE: Make sure the black beans are soaked separately. This process will cut the cooking time by 1/3. When ready to cook, discard soaking liquid, rinse beans and set aside. In a large soup pot, heat butter over medium-high heat. Add onions, celery, bell pepper and garlic. Saute 3-5 minutes or until vegetables are wilted. Add ham hock and salt pork and continue to saute 2-3 minutes. Add tomatoes, beef stock and beans except for green beans. Bring mixture to a rolling boil, reduce to simmer and season with bay leaves, thyme, oregano and cayenne pepper. Cover pot and simmer approximately 1 1/2 hours, stirring occasionally. As the beans begin to tenderize, mash a portion of them against the side of the pot using the back of a cooking spoon. This will not only help to thicken the soup, but also create a creamy consistency. Add green beans, andouille sausage and diced ham. Simmer beans an additional 30 minutes and adjust seasonings using salt and hot sauce. NOTE: Additional stock may be needed to retain volume during the cooking process.

PREP TIME: 2 Hours

SERVES: 6-8

A hand-carved mahogany crib that stood in the master bedroom.

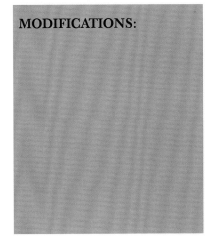

MODIFICATIONS:

CREOLE TOMATO, BASIL & TASSO OMELETTE

Tasso, or spicy Cajun ham, is not only cured but smoked and rubbed in bayou spices. It is often used as a flavoring for vegetables and soups and is also excellent as a breakfast item. You may order tasso from any specialty store or substitute a high-quality, heavy-smoked ham and spice up the dish with a pinch of cayenne pepper.

INGREDIENTS:

- 3 eggs
- 2 Creole tomato slices
- 1 tbsp fresh basil, chopped
- 2 tbsps finely diced tasso
- 2 tbsps unsalted butter
- 2 tbsps chopped red bell pepper
- Salt and black pepper to taste
- Creole seasoning to taste

The planters desk adorned with a unique porcelain piece.

METHOD:

In a 9-inch omelette pan, melt butter over medium-high heat. In a large mixing bowl, whisk eggs thoroughly and season to taste using salt, pepper and Creole seasoning. Set aside. Into the omelette pan, add tasso and bell pepper and saute 1-2 minutes. Pour eggs into the omelette pan and, using a fork, distribute the sauteed ingredients evenly into the omelette. Shake the pan to loosen the eggs, taking care not to scorch the omelette. When edges begin to curl and turn lightly brown, place the tomatoes and basil across the front half of the omelette. When eggs are cooked to your liking, slide the omelette halfway onto a serving plate and turn the top half over the tomatoes to form a half moon. Allow omelette to sit 2-3 minutes prior to serving.

OPPOSITE: *Creole Tomato, Basil & Tasso Omelette.*

PREP TIME: 20 Minutes

MAKES: 1 Omelette

MODIFICATIONS:

CREOLE CHICKEN & BISCUITS

*A*lthough this recipe recommends biscuits as the perfect accompaniment to Creole chicken, you may wish to try serving it over rice or pasta. I often whip up a batch of my cathead biscuits (see recipe) to go along with this dish when company is coming. However, if I just have an urge for this wonderful regional dish, I sometimes use a can of "whack" biscuits.

INGREDIENTS:

- 1 (3-pound) fryer, halved
- 1/2 cup butter
- 1/2 cup diced onions
- 1/4 cup diced celery
- 1/4 cup diced green bell pepper
- 1 tbsp diced garlic
- 1/2 cup flour
- 6 cups chicken stock (see recipe)
- 2 (8-ounce) cans tomato puree
- 1 (8-ounce) can tomato sauce
- 2 tbsps lemon juice
- 1 tbsp horseradish
- 1 tbsp fresh thyme, chopped
- 2 tbsps fresh basil, chopped
- Salt and black pepper to taste
- Creole seasoning to taste
- 1/2 cup sliced green onions
- 1/4 cup chopped parsley

METHOD:

Prepare cathead biscuits according to recipe or use your favorite store-bought variety. Poach chicken by simmering in lightly seasoned water until tender and meat is fallen from the bones. Remove chicken from liquid and reserve 6 cups of stock. Debone meat and set aside. In a cast iron dutch oven, melt butter over medium-high heat. Add onions, celery, bell pepper and garlic. Saute 3-5 minutes or until vegetables are wilted. Sprinkle in flour and, using a wire whisk, stir constantly until white roux is achieved (see roux techniques). Add reserved chicken stock, 1 cup at a time, until stew-like consistency is achieved. Add tomato puree, tomato sauce, lemon juice and horseradish. Bring mixture to a rolling boil, reduce to simmer and cook 20 minutes, stirring occasionally. Add chicken, thyme, basil and season to taste using salt, pepper and Creole seasoning. Cook mixture 10 additional minutes then add green onions and parsley. Should tomato sauce become too acidic, add 1 tablespoon of sugar to this recipe. Serve a generous portion of the Chicken Creole over open-faced biscuits.

PREP TIME: 1 1/2 Hours

SERVES: 8-10

MODIFICATIONS:

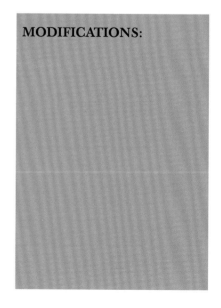

A billboard with directions to a rural coffee house.

CRÈME BRÛLÉE LOST BREAD

*O*ne of the most interesting breakfast dishes came about because of a need to use stale or "lost bread." There are numerous recipes in and around New Orleans for this traditional dish, but Crème Brûlée is one of the most unique.

INGREDIENTS:

- 12 French bread croutons, cut 1-inch thick
- 1/2 cup melted butter
- 1 cup brown sugar, lightly packed
- 2 tbsps cane syrup
- 5 eggs
- 1 cup milk
- 1/2 cup heavy whipping cream
- 1/8 tsp cinnamon
- 1/8 tsp nutmeg
- 1 tbsp vanilla
- 1 tbsp praline liqueur or Frangelico

METHOD:

French bread croutons should be cut out of a baguette-style loaf. These slices should be approximately 2 1/2 to 3 inches in diameter and 1-inch thick. In a cast iron skillet, combine butter, brown sugar and cane syrup over medium-high heat. Cook mixture, stirring constantly, until bubbly and sugar has dissolved. Pour brûlée into the bottom of a 13" x 9" x 2" baking dish. Allow brûlée to cool slightly then top with the French bread croutons. In a large mixing bowl, whisk eggs, milk, whipping cream, cinnamon, nutmeg, vanilla and liqueur. Blend thoroughly then pour evenly over the croutons. Using the tips of your fingers, press bread down gently to force the custard into the croutons without breaking. Cover dish with clear wrap and chill overnight. Preheat oven to 350°F. Allow custard to sit out at room temperature, approximately 1 hour. Bake, uncovered, until French toast is puffed and edges of the croutons are golden brown, approximately 40 minutes. Allow to cool 10 minutes prior to serving. When ready to serve, remove 2 of the Lost Bread Croutons per guest and invert them onto the center of a 10-inch plate. Top with powdered sugar and drizzle with Louisiana cane syrup.

PREP TIME: 1 1/2 Hours

SERVES: 6

A modern convenience in the 1860s.

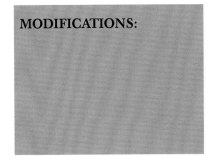

MODIFICATIONS:

Recipe for Romance: Hot Beignets in a Warm Boudoir

Aunt Ruby's

LAKE CHARLES

*H*er tranquil presence seems to linger in time. She bequeaths us a lifetime of devotion: commitment more endearing than cherished heirlooms; purity more perfect than pearls. Mortal beings are still enamored with Aunt Ruby, a retired school teacher and former owner of Lake Charles' first boarding house.

Since 1911, Aunt Ruby's has welcomed guests and provided comfortable beds and hot meals to weary travelers. Today, Aunt Ruby's is a bed and breakfast and is listed on the National Historic Registry.

Lake Charles, the capital of Louisiana's western pinelands, fueled a lumber boom in the 1800s that created much of the city's historic architecture. Experienced lumbermen from the northern United States, known as the "Michigan Men," arrived to buoy Lake Charles' fledgling lumber industry. With their arrival came rapid growth of the city. They brought with them the tall and angular construction style reflective of the Victorian tastes, so popular in America during that period. There was also a variation of the Colonial Revival style, a local sawmill version of antebellum plantations. None of the builders were truly architects; they built what they liked, usually from pattern books. Each house was a combination of styles indicative of the builder's tastes. Though the lumber

Coffee anyone?

OPPOSITE: *Aunt Ruby's… a former boarding house is now a bed and breakfast.*

yards and sawmills are long since gone, their legacy is found in the gorgeous homes of the Charpentier Historic District, which was placed on the National Historic Register in 1990. (Charpentier is the French word for carpenter.) The unique features of these downtown homes have been dubbed "Lake Charles-Style Architecture."

Aunt Ruby's, a craftsman-style house, features two double-decker back porches and a front porch, which is ideal for napping or even sipping refreshing lemonade on hot summer afternoons. It is one of only two houses in the area featuring Lake Charles' columns, square, tapered columns with an inlaid design unique to the area.

Conveniently located in the heart of downtown Lake Charles, Aunt Ruby's offers six luxurious staterooms, all with charming period furnishings. Each room features a large private bath with all the modern amenities of any metropolitan hotel including a phone, cable television and wireless internet access. Aunt Ruby's Poached Eggs is the signature dish of the full gourmet breakfast, which is offered daily in the sitting room. Because so many guests are regular business travelers who make Aunt Ruby's their "home away from home," early-bird breakfasts are available as well.

(Continues on page 182)

(Continued from page 180)

Aunt Ruby's is located two blocks from downtown at 504 Pujo Street. Dan Schaad, the current owner, can be reached at (337) 430-0603. His web site is www.auntrubys.com.

During your overnight stay at Aunt Ruby's Bed & Breakfast, you might like to saunter four blocks to the lake front where there is a picturesque boardwalk surrounding beautiful Lake Charles. Also nearby are casinos, Pujo Street Café, La Truffe Sauvage restaurant, the Children's Museum and Lake Charles' Mardi Gras Museum of Imperial Calcasieu.

Guests at Aunt Ruby's seem to feel right at home, probably because they are.

Ruby-red chair nestled by the fireplace.

SPICY CORN BREAD SKILLET CAKE

There are many recipes in the South that have obviously evolved from simple corn bread batters. After the Civil War, there were so little food ingredients for one to create great dishes that simple dishes emerged with added twists to "fancy 'em up." This skillet cake is one such corn bread variation that I think you'll find interesting and useful.

INGREDIENTS:

- 1 cup yellow corn meal
- 1/2 cup flour
- 1 tbsp sugar
- 1/2 tsp salt
- 1/8 tsp cayenne pepper
- 2 tsps baking soda
- 1/2 cup milk
- 1 egg, beaten
- 1 tbsp melted butter
- 1/2 cup creamed corn
- 1 jalapeno, diced
- 1/2 cup minced onions
- 1/4 cup sliced green onions
- 1/2 cup crushed bacon
- 2 tbsps bacon drippings

METHOD:

Preheat oven to 350°F. Lightly grease a 10-inch cast iron skillet and set aside. In a large mixing bowl, combine corn meal, flour, sugar, salt, cayenne pepper, baking soda, milk and egg. Using a wire whisk, blend well. Add melted butter, corn, jalapenos, onions and green onions.

Continue to whisk until all ingredients are blended and lumps are removed from the corn meal batter. Add bacon pieces and bacon drippings and blend thoroughly into the batter. Pour the batter into the greased skillet and bake 20-25 minutes or until golden brown. Serve with flavored butters or cream cheese.

PREP TIME: 1 Hour

SERVES: 6

MODIFICATIONS:

Apple Pancake with Strawberry Whipped Cream.

MICHIGAN MAN'S APPLE PANCAKE

"Michigan Man" was the name given to the early lumbermen and carpenters arriving in Lake Charles after the Civil War seeking their fortune in lumber. This recipe was found in an old family cookbook but has been altered to create a new version. One must prepare this recipe to appreciate the final product, which is truly spectacular. However, any local fruit may be substituted as a filling.

INGREDIENTS:

- 1 red apple, cored and diced
- 1 green apple, cored and diced
- 1/4 cup melted butter
- 1/4 cup brown sugar
- 1 tbsp lemon juice
- 1/4 cup golden raisins
- 1/8 tsp cinnamon
- 1/8 tsp nutmeg
- 4 eggs
- 1/2 cup flour
- 1/4 cup sugar
- 1/2 tsp salt
- 1/2 cup milk
- 1 tbsp vanilla
- 1/2 cup whipped cream
- Powdered sugar (optional)

METHOD:

Preheat oven to 375°F. Grease a 9-inch non-stick oven-proof frying pan with approximately 1 tablespoon butter. Set aside. NOTE: It is imperative that a non-stick frying pan be used in this recipe, otherwise this pancake will stick to the pan and the presentation will be impossible. In a separate saute pan, heat melted butter over medium-high heat. Add red and green apples. Saute apples until tender but not overcooked, approximately 10-12 minutes. Add brown sugar, lemon juice, raisins, cinnamon and nutmeg. Continue to stir until brown sugar is melted and apples are coated with the spices. Remove from heat and set aside. In a large mixing bowl, combine eggs, flour, sugar and salt. Add milk and continue blending until ingredients are well incorporated. Using a wire whisk, whip to blend thoroughly dissolving any lumps of flour which may appear in the batter. Add vanilla and whisk for 1 additional minute. Pour batter into the greased frying pan and place on the center shelf of the oven. Bake pancake for 20-25 minutes or until golden brown around the edges. During the cooking process, the pancake will rise approximately 2 inches out of the pan in a souffle-style fashion. When pancake is done, remove from oven and fill with apple mixture. Slide the pancake onto a large serving platter, folding the top half over the apple filling in a half-moon fashion. Cut pancake into 4 equal slices and gently place on serving plates. Top each pancake with an equal portion of whipped cream and powdered sugar.

PREP TIME: 1 Hour

SERVES: 4

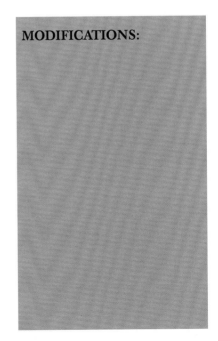

MODIFICATIONS:

183

MULLED CIDER WITH AROMATIC SPICES

Well, there's no doubt that apple cider was one of the warm drinks cherished by the Michigan lumbermen after leaving their homes in the North for a new life in Bayou Country. However, it didn't take long for apple cider to make its way across the Mason-Dixon line and for interesting variations to appear in the Lake Charles area. This is a favorite during the Christmas season.

INGREDIENTS:

- 4 quarts apple cider
- 1 cup orange juice
- 1/2 cup sugar
- 1 tsp allspice
- 1/2 tsp mace
- 1 tsp coriander seeds
- 2 tbsps whole cloves
- 4 cinnamon sticks
- 2 tbsps orange zest
- 1/4 tsp salt

METHOD:

In a large ceramic sauce pan, combine apple cider and orange juice over medium-high heat. Blend well then add sugar and stir until dissolved. Add allspice, mace, coriander seeds, cloves, cinnamon, orange zest and salt. Using a wire whisk, blend spices well into the juices. Bring mixture to a rolling boil, reduce to simmer, cover and cook 30 minutes. Strain cider and serve hot. For an interesting option, chill cider and serve as a festive cold punch.

OPPOSITE: *Mulled Cider with Aromatic Spices.*

Come…sit for a while!

PREP TIME: 1 Hour

MAKES: 20 (6-ounce) Servings

 *Recipe for Romance:* Red Velvet Cake and Black Velvet Bourbon

MODIFICATIONS:

LUMBERMAN'S MEAT LOAF & GRAVY

As the great lumber barons began to arrive in the Lake Charles area after the Civil War, the lumber industry boomed here in Louisiana. Soon, lumber mills and great lumber yards exploded in the region. The men employed in this industry were hearty eaters. This meat loaf recipe is typical of their daily fare.

INGREDIENTS:

- 2 pounds ground beef
- 1 egg, beaten
- 3/4 cup minced onions
- 1/2 cup minced celery
- 1/4 cup minced green bell pepper
- 2 tbsps minced garlic
- 1/4 cup milk
- 1/2 cup seasoned Italian bread crumbs
- 1/4 cup melted butter
- 1/2 cup diced onions
- 1/4 cup diced celery
- 1/4 cup diced green bell pepper
- 1 tbsp diced garlic
- 2 tbsps flour
- 2 (8-ounce) cans tomato sauce
- 1 (15-ounce) can Rotel® tomatoes
- Salt and black pepper to taste
- Creole seasoning to taste

METHOD:

Preheat oven to 375°F. In a large mixing bowl, combine ground beef with egg, minced onions, celery, bell pepper and garlic. Using your fingers, blend the ingredients well into the ground beef. Add milk and season to taste using salt, pepper and Creole seasoning. Sprinkle in bread crumbs and blend well into the mixture. Form ground beef into a loaf and place in a casserole dish. Set aside. In a sauce pot, heat butter over medium-high heat. Add diced onions, celery, bell pepper and garlic. Saute 3-5 minutes or until vegetables are wilted. Sprinkle in flour and, using a wire whisk, blend until white roux is achieved (see roux techniques). Add tomato sauce and Rotel® tomatoes, blending well into the vegetable mixture. Season to taste using salt, pepper and Creole seasoning. NOTE: Do not over-season the sauce due to the level of seasoning in the meatloaf. Bring mixture to a rolling boil, reduce to simmer and cook 10 minutes. Pour the tomato sauce over the meatloaf and bake, uncovered, for approximately 1 hour.

PREP TIME: 1 1/2 Hours

SERVES: 6

Slumber comfortably at Aunt Ruby's.

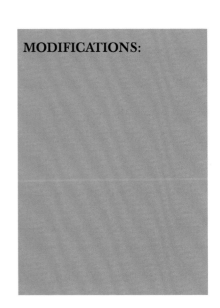

MODIFICATIONS:

Mom's bread hot from the oven.

Mom's HOLIDAY BREAD

This soft-centered bread served hot out of the oven is perfect for the holidays. It's amazing how simple the technique is to create such a masterful loaf. I'm sure the recipe will continue to be handed down in families.

INGREDIENTS:

- 6 cups bread flour
- 2 packages quick acting yeast
- 1 tsp sugar
- 1/2 cup warm water
- 1 1/2 tsps baking powder
- 2 tbsps shortening
- 2 tbsps sugar
- 1 tsp salt
- 1 1/2 cups warm water
- 1/4 cup melted butter

METHOD:

Dissolve yeast and 1 teaspoon of sugar in 1/2 cup warm water and set aside to blossom for approximately 10 minutes. Grease 2 loaf pans and set aside. In a large mixing bowl, combine flour, baking powder and shortening. Using a pastry cutter, cut the shortening into the flour. Add 2 tablespoons of sugar, salt, 1 1/2 cups warm water and yeast mixture. Blend well to create a dough ball then turn out onto a lightly floured surface. Knead dough approximately 5-8 minutes then place dough in a lightly greased bowl. Cover bowl with a dry cloth and set in a warm place to rise for approximately 1 hour. Once dough has doubled in size, punch it down, re-cover and allow it to rise again for approximately 1 additional hour. Punch down dough again then separate into 2 halves. Form each ball into a loaf and place into pans. Cover each pan and allow to double in size again. Preheat oven to 375°F. Bake bread 1 hour to 1 hour 15 minutes or until golden brown. Remove from oven and brush each loaf with melted butter. When ready to serve, slice and top with additional butter or honey.

PREP TIME: 3 Hours

MAKES: 2 Loaves

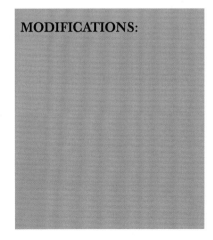

MODIFICATIONS:

C.A.'s House

LAKE CHARLES

Since primitive man first gathered around campfires to scrawl muddy drawings on cave walls, there has been a wild fascination, a primal instinct, a basic animal desire to hunt. Perhaps it is the thrill of the chase or knowing that your captor lurks just beyond the darkness. Perhaps, it is the sense of danger and smell of dampness that stalk the wilderness and chill the shadows. Ultimately, it is desire that drives this savage quest. He is the hunter. You are his prey.

Located in Lake Charles' Charpentier Historic District, C.A.'s House Bed and Breakfast offers anything but rustic accommodations befitting the huntsman. Built in 1900 by Walter and Annie Goos, the grand, three-story colonial revival home graciously sits amid the majestic section of Lake Charles beckoning visitors to its wide veranda and comfortable rockers. Walter and Annie resided in the home with its distinctive square columns until about 1922. The home's subsequent owner, T.L. Huber who was president of the Huber Motor Company and Quality Oil, lived in the home until his death in 1941. It was not until 1975 that C.A. King II purchased the home and refurbished the weathered boards and time-worn floors. King returned the home to its original splendor, then resided in its comfortable interior until he passed from this life in 1991. Today, his niece Tanis is the owner and innkeeper.

Ready in the dining room.

OPPOSITE: *A quiet afternoon at C.A.'s House.*

Two large doors stand in the foyer, one leading to the living room with its mantled fireplace and the other providing passage into the extensive dining room containing the original canvas on the walls. Now known as King's Kitchen, a full gourmet breakfast is served on weekends in the exclusive dining room.

Guest rooms are located atop the mahogany staircase on the second and third floors. Superb accommodations are available in one of four luxury suites. You might choose to stay in the Carriage House, a separate facility with a king and queen bed, living area, kitchen and washer and dryer. Pets and children are welcome to stay. Little C.A.'s House is 1800 square feet of fine living with two bedrooms as well as a family area and kitchen. Just outside the mansion in a serene hideaway, a private hot tub awaits your arrival.

When staying at C.A.'s House Bed & Breakfast, you are minutes from virtually everything in Lake Charles. Nearby are casinos, Pujo Street Café, La Truffe Sauvage restaurant, the Children's Museum, Lake Charles' Mardi Gras Museum of Imperial Calcasieu and the boardwalk surrounding beautiful Lake Charles. And, if world-class hunting and fishing are what you desire, the delights of Louisiana's sportsman's paradise are in close proximity.

Located a few minutes east of downtown Lake Charles, C.A.'s House stands sentinel at 624 Ford Street on the corner of Division Street. Tanis can be reached at (337) 439-6672 or toll free at (866) 439-6672. Information about C.A.'s House Bed & Breakfast can be found at www.cas-house.com.

SILVER QUEEN CORN & TARRAGON EGGROLL WITH CREOLE TOMATO SAUCE

Silver Queen corn is the sweetest and most sought after corn in South Louisiana. Tarragon has always been associated with egg dishes from omelettes to sauces. This interesting dish is not only beautifully presented but is further garnished with a bright yellow coulis.

INGREDIENTS:

- 1 1/2 cups cooked Silver Queen corn
- 2 tbsps fresh tarragon, chopped
- 8 eggs
- 2 cups heavy whipping cream
- 2 cups diced Creole tomatoes
- 2 tsps white wine vinegar
- 1 tbsp olive oil
- 1/4 cup melted butter
- 2 tbsps chopped chives
- 1/4 cup cream cheese, cubed
- Salt and black pepper to taste
- Creole seasoning to taste
- 1 large piece parchment paper

METHOD:

Preheat oven to 325°F. Butter a 15 1/2" x 11" x 1" jelly-roll pan and line with parchment paper. Spray parchment paper well with vegetable spray. Set aside. In a large mixing bowl, combine tarragon, eggs, whipping cream and season to taste using salt, pepper and Creole seasoning. Pour egg custard into the jelly-roll pan and bake for 8 minutes, then rotate pan and bake 8 additional minutes. In the bowl of a blender, place tomatoes, vinegar and olive oil. Puree mixture until smooth. Season lightly with salt, pepper and Creole seasoning. Set aside. In a cast iron skillet, melt butter over medium-high heat. Add chives and cook 1-2 minutes. Add cream cheese and corn, blending well into the chives. Stir constantly until cream cheese is melted, approximately 2-3 minutes. When eggs are cooked, remove from oven and spread corn mixture evenly on top, leaving a 1-inch border on all sides. With the long side of the pan facing you and using the parchment paper as an aid, roll the omelette jelly-roll fashion then carefully transfer it to a warm platter. Cut omelette into 12 equal slices, approximately 1-inch thick. Serve omelette with Creole Tomato Sauce.

PREP TIME: 1 Hour

SERVES: 6

Sideboard in King's Kitchen.

BREAST OF CHICKEN HOLLY BEACH

Holly Beach, often called the Cajun Riviera, is one of the best areas for duck and goose hunting in Southwest Louisiana. Hunters from all over the world converge on this area during the season. One Italian cook left behind this recipe.

INGREDIENTS:

- 6 (4-ounce) boneless, skinless chicken breasts
- 24 poached spinach leaves, chilled
- 6 ounces tasso, thinly sliced
- 7 ounces goat cheese
- 18 whole fresh basil leaves
- 1 cup seasoned flour
- 1/4 cup olive oil
- Salt and black pepper to taste
- Creole seasoning to taste
- 3 cups Marinara Sauce (see recipe)

Copper kitchen tools.

METHOD:

Allow goat cheese to set at room temperature for 30 minutes. Preheat oven to 350°F. Place chicken breast between clear wrap and, using a meat mallet, pound each breast lightly. Season breasts thoroughly on each side using salt, pepper and Creole seasoning. Cover each breast with an equal portion of spinach leaves, tasso, goat cheese and basil leaves. Roll breast in a jelly-roll fashion and secure with toothpicks.

Coat the chicken lightly in seasoned flour, shaking off all excess. In a large cast iron skillet, heat olive oil over medium-high heat. Saute breasts, a few at a time, until golden brown on all sides. Remove skillet from heat, top chicken with Marinara Sauce and bake in oven for 20 minutes. Remove from oven, discard toothpicks and serve with rice or pasta.

PREP TIME: 1 Hour

SERVES: 6

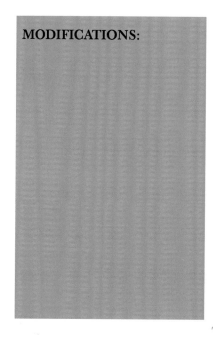

MODIFICATIONS:

SMOKED WOOD DUCK & ANDOUILLE GUMBO

Almost every species of wild game in Louisiana has been used in the creation of gumbo. Since most Cajun men were hunters and trappers, it is not surprising that wild duck and smoked andouille were often used. Many times wood ducks from the morning hunt are combined with smoked andouille to create a magnificent gumbo for the evening meal.

INGREDIENTS:

- 3 smoked wood ducks, halved
- 1 pound sliced andouille
- 1 gallon cold water
- 1 cup vegetable oil
- 1 1/4 cups flour
- 2 cups chopped onions
- 2 cups chopped celery
- 1/2 cup chopped green bell pepper
- 1/2 cup chopped red bell pepper
- 1/2 cup chopped yellow bell pepper
- 1/4 cup minced garlic
- 3 quarts reserved stock
- Salt and black pepper to taste
- Creole seasoning to taste
- 2 cups sliced green onions
- 1 cup chopped parsley
- 2 tbsps filé powder

METHOD:

Smoke the wood ducks in a homestyle smoker according to manufacturer's directions. It is not necessary to smoke the ducks beyond rare since the flavor of smoke and not cooking temperature is important here. In a 2-gallon stock pot, place duck halves and andouille in water over medium-high heat. Bring to a rolling boil, reduce to simmer and cook until wood ducks are tender, approximately 30-45 minutes. Remove ducks and andouille from the pot and reserve 3 quarts of the duck/andouille stock. Bone the duck once it has cooled. In a large cast iron dutch oven, heat oil over medium-high heat. Add flour and using a wire whisk, stir constantly until dark brown roux is achieved (see roux techniques). Add onions, celery, bell peppers and garlic. Saute 3-5 minutes or until vegetables are wilted. Add duck and andouille, blending well into the vegetable mixture. Add reserved stock, one ladle at a time, stirring constantly until soup-like consistency is achieved. Bring mixture to a rolling boil, reduce to simmer and allow to cook 45 minutes. During the cooking process, season the gumbo at 20 minute intervals, using salt, pepper and Creole seasoning. Add green onions, parsley and filé powder. Blend well into the gumbo and cook 5 additional minutes. Serve gumbo over steamed rice.

PREP TIME: 2 1/2 Hours

SERVES: 6

MODIFICATIONS:

Guarding a secret hideaway.

OPPOSITE: *Smoked Wood Duck & Andouille…ready for the gumbo.*

MALLARD DUCK SASUAGE

Though I am using mallard duck in this recipe, this sausage has been made at Lafitte's Landing using all types of wild game including rabbit, venison and alligator. It continues to be a novelty whenever it is served.

INGREDIENTS:

- 2 1/2 pounds wild mallard duck, boned
- 2 1/2 pounds pork
- 1/2 pound pork fat
- 1/2 pound bacon
- 1/4 pound butter
- 2 cups diced onions
- 1 cup diced celery
- 1/2 cup chopped green onions
- 2 tbsps diced garlic
- 1/2 cup port wine
- 1/4 cup cognac
- 1 tbsp dried thyme
- 1 tbsp cracked black pepper
- 1/2 cup chopped parsley
- Salt and cayenne pepper to taste
- 10-12 feet sausage casing

METHOD:

Grind duck, pork, pork fat and bacon using the fine cutting blade of a meat grinder. Once ground, place in a mixing bowl and remove all visible sinew or bone which may have passed through the cutting blade. Set aside. In a heavy bottom saute pan, melt butter over medium-high heat.

Superb accommodations await weary guests.

Add onions, celery, green onions and garlic. Saute 3-5 minutes or until vegetables are wilted. Remove from flame and add port wine and cognac. Return to stove top, being careful as cognac will ignite on open flame. If using an electric range, ignite saute pan using a kitchen match. Cognac will burn approximately 2 minutes. Reduce liquid to 1/2 volume. Add thyme and cracked black pepper, blending well into mixture. Remove from heat and cool to room temperature. Add sauteed seasonings to ground meat mixture and blend well to incorporate all seasonings into sausage. Add parsley for color and season to taste using salt and cayenne pepper. To check for proper seasoning, form a small patty and saute in hot oil for a few minutes. Taste and adjust seasonings if necessary. You may stuff into casing, using the sausage attachment on your grinder or take the mixture to your local butcher

for stuffing. This mixture will stuff approximately 10-feet of sausage. You may wish to link the sausage into 6-inch links. Once stuffed, poach links in simmering water for 10-15 minutes. Slice sausage into 1-inch serving pieces and serve with Creole mustard as an hors d'oeuvre, or serve a 6-inch link as an appetizer. You may wish to create one of the Cajun or Creole butter sauces to accompany this sausage (see recipe).

HINT: Domestic or Long Island Duck may be substituted in this recipe.

PREP TIME: 1 Hour

MAKES: 20 (6-inch) Sausage Links

MODIFICATIONS:

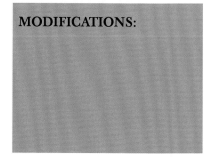

CHOCOLATE CHESS PIE

Almost every cook raised in the South certainly has had their fill of chess pie. This dessert was developed in the 1700s because of the volume of butter, eggs and molasses available on the plantations. Today there are many variations to the chess pie, most including buttermilk, raisins, nuts and even chocolate. No one really knows where the name chess pie comes from but some think it's a corruption of the word cheese from the English curd cheese pie. Others say it's derived from the chest or pie safe where these desserts were often stored.

tique European wood carvings used to identify d on the buffet.

INGREDIENTS:

- 6 tbsps cold butter
- 1 1/4 cups all-purpose flour
- 2 tbsps shortening
- 1/4 tsp salt
- 3 tbsps iced water
- 3 ounces Bakers® bittersweet chocolate
- 3/4 stick unsalted butter
- 1 1/3 cups sugar
- 2 tbsps flour
- 4 eggs
- 3 tbsps heavy whipping cream
- 2 tbsps rum
- 1 tbsp vanilla

METHOD:

In a large mixing bowl, combine cold butter, 1 1/4 cups flour, shortening and salt. Using your fingertips or a pastry cutter, blend until flour resembles coarse meal. Drizzle in ice water evenly over the mixture and continue to blend until dough is formed. Gently squeeze the dough to make sure the texture holds together without crumbling. Additional water may be added if necessary. Turn dough onto a floured work surface and, using the heel of your hand, knead dough 8-9 times. Cover dough with clear wrap and refrigerate 1 hour. Remove and roll out approximately 1/8-inch thick and form into a 9-inch pie pan. Preheat oven to 425°F. Line the pie shell with aluminum foil and weight the dough down with a cup of raw rice. Place pie on center shelf of the oven and bake for 15 minutes. Remove foil and rice and bake 5 additional minutes or until golden brown. Remove and set aside to cool. Reduce oven temperature to 325°F. Chop chocolate into small pieces. In a large mixing bowl, combine chocolate and unsalted butter. Place the bowl over a pot of simmering water, making sure the bottom of the bowl does not touch the water. Using a wire whisk, stir occasionally until chocolate and butter are melted and smooth. Remove the bowl and allow the chocolate to cool slightly. In a separate mixing bowl, combine sugar and flour. Add eggs and, using a wire whisk, blend well into the dry mix. Add chocolate/butter mixture, cream, rum and vanilla. Whisk thoroughly and pour mixture into the cooked pie shell. Place on center shelf of the oven and bake for 40 minutes or until pie is set. Cool completely and chill overnight.

PREP TIME: 2 Hours

SERVES: 6

MODIFICATIONS:

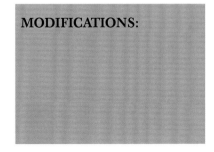

Recipe for Romance: Wild Berries and Tangled Sheets

Judge Porter House

NATCHITOCHES

She is a star in the heavens, and you are the astronomer. You gaze upon her celestial splendor from dusk to dawn and are drawn to her luminous form by a force that defies gravity. In universal resplendence, you eclipse her like the Earth overshadowing the moon, and wake with stardust in your eyes.

The splendor of the heavens is matched by a small taste of heaven on Earth at the Judge Porter House in Natchitoches. Located in the heart of the National Historic District, the home was built in 1912 and is surrounded by beautiful live oak trees planted by the original owners, "Judge" Thomas Fitzgerald Porter and his wife, Wilhemenia. It took only three months and $1,500 to construct the home, and it was built using materials from the dismantled Blunt Lodge Hall, which once stood on the grounds.

The dining room with fruit motif wallpaper.

The architectural style of the house constitutes an eclectic mix of turn-of-the-century tastes. A two-story gallery wraps around two sides of the home suggesting a Queen Anne influence. Many of the windows surrounding this gallery measure more than eight feet in height and were once used as passageways to the porch. The home features high ceilings, five fireplaces and heart of pine floors original to the house. Colonial Revival-style architecture is seen in the colossal columns that rest on brick pillars.

OPPOSITE: *A Second Street view of Judge Porter House.*

The home was introduced as a bed and breakfast establishment in 1996 after years of renovation and landscaping. There are four rooms and a guest house available. Each room features a private, spacious bath and is decorated in American and Louisiana antiques. A full breakfast is served each morning during your stay.

While visiting central Louisiana be sure to visit Fort St. Jean Baptiste Commemorative Area, which features a reproduction of the French colonial fort built here in the 1730s. This became the first permanent European settlement in the territory later known as the Louisiana Purchase. You will also enjoy a visit to the Cane River Creole National Historic Park, which consists of portions of Oakland and Magnolia Plantations south of Natchitoches. Melrose Plantation, circa 1796, is a National Historic Landmark and was once owned by a freed woman of color. Included on the grounds is a Clementine Hunter gallery of primitive folk art. Day-trips to Kisatchie National Forest and Briarwood are a must for nature and outdoors enthusiasts. You will want to visit Kaffie Fredrick Inc.–a general mercantile founded in 1863 and the city's oldest business. A variety of antique stores are located in the Historic District including Ann's Antique Mall, Carriage House Market, Days Gone By, Granny's Antiques and Madeleine's House of Antiques. Take a break from sightseeing to dine at Lasyone's Meat Pie Kitchen where the Natchitoches Meat Pie originated. Other dining establishments *(Continues on page 198)*

(Continued from page 196)

include Mariners, The Landing, Crawfish Hole and Almost Home.

Judge Porter House is located at 321 Second Street in Natchitoches on the corner of Second and Rue Poete. From I-49 take the Natchitoches/Many Exit. Follow Highway 6 to Natchitoches (about 5 miles), and turn left on Second Street. For reservations contact the innkeeper at (318) 352-9206 or (800) 441-8343.

Come experience turn-of-the-century elegance in an ethereal setting where the nights are never long enough for stargazing.

"Mile-high" Apple Pie!

WILHEMENIA'S 4TH OF JULY APPLE PIE

Thomas Fitzgerald Porter and his wife, Wilhemenia, built their home on Second Street in Natchitoches in 1912. The Queen Anne-style home was often the site of holiday events since it was near Bayou Amulet. This apple pie was a favorite of the family and it was Wilhemenia's job to prepare it for any holiday.

INGREDIENTS:

- 2 quarts or 12 small tart apples, peeled
- 1 cup light brown sugar, tightly packed
- 2 tsps lemon juice
- 3 tbsps water
- 1 tsp nutmeg
- 1 tbsp grated lemon zest
- 2 large eggs, beaten
- 2 (9-inch) pie shells, uncooked

METHOD:

Slice apples approximately 1/8-inch thick on a slicer or mandoline. Place 1 1/2 quarts of apple slices in a sauce pan with 1/2 cup brown sugar, lemon juice and water over medium-high heat. Cover and cook until apples are steamed and tender, approximately 10 minutes. When done, remove the lid and continue to cook, stirring occasionally, until chunky marmalade is achieved. Remove from heat and allow mixture to cool thoroughly. Preheat oven to 325°F. To apple marmalade, add nutmeg, lemon zest and eggs. Pour mixture into one pie shell and, using the back of a cooking spoon, smooth down the filling. Arrange remaining apple slices over the marmalade and sprinkle with remaining 1/2 cup brown sugar. Cover pie with the second crust or cut crust into a lattice pattern. Bake for 1 hour 50 minutes or until apples are tender and crust is golden brown. NOTE: Oven temperatures vary dramatically, so check pie after 1 1/2 hours of cooking time has elapsed.

PREP TIME: 1 1/2 Hours

SERVES: 6-8

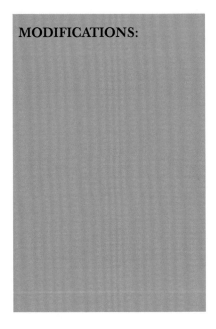

MODIFICATIONS:

Recipe for Romance: Angel Food Cake with Whipped Cream Clouds

CHEESE & OLIVE ROULADES

According to Tod Working, owner of Judge Porter House, this recipe was first encountered on a visit to the home. As he walked up the entrance sidewalk to the front door of the home, guests were sipping ice-cold martinis and eating bright orange truffle-shaped hors d'oeuvres. After tasting one, Tod knew that this simple recipe should be shared with visitors stopping at the Judge Porter House.

INGREDIENTS:

- 12 ounces grated Sharp cheddar cheese, softened
- 1 (10-ounce) jar small stuffed olives
- 2 cups sifted flour
- 1/2 tsp cayenne pepper
- 1 tsp granulated garlic
- 1 1/2 sticks butter, melted
- 1 tsp Worcestershire sauce
- Creole seasoning to taste

METHOD:

Preheat oven to 400°F. In a large mixing bowl, combine flour, cayenne pepper, garlic and Creole seasoning. Blend well then add cheese, melted butter and Worcestershire sauce. Using a wooden spoon, stir ingredients until a dough consistency is created. Pinch off enough of the dough to flatten into a 2-inch round patty in the palm of your hand. Place

The Judge Porter Suite.

1 olive in the center of the dough and encase the olive with the cheese mixture. Place the stuffed olive balls on a cookie sheet and bake for approximately 10 minutes. Serve hot.

PREP TIME: 30 Minutes

MAKES: 3 Dozen

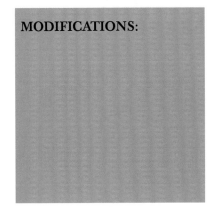

MODIFICATIONS:

JUDGE PORTER'S CANE RIVER FISH SOUP

Typical fish soups in this part of the country often begin with a brown roux and are flavored with tomatoes and spices such as our redfish courtbouillon. This recipe is a much needed twist from the original because it's easier to make and definitely unique in flavor.

INGREDIENTS:

- 12 (21-25 count) shrimp, head-on
- 2 pounds redfish, cut into 1-inch cubes
- 1 dozen clams
- 1 dozen mussels
- 1 dozen oysters
- 6 whole crawfish
- 1/4 cup butter
- 1 cup diced onions
- 1 cup diced celery
- 1/2 cup diced red bell pepper
- 1 tbsp minced garlic
- 1 cup diced carrots
- 3 tbsps flour
- 2 quarts (8 8-ounce bottles) clam juice
- 1/2 cup diced tomatoes
- 1 cup sliced mushrooms
- 2 (8-ounce) cans tomato sauce
- 1 bay leaf
- 1 tbsp fresh thyme, chopped
- 1 tsp fresh tarragon, chopped
- 1/4 cup sliced green onions
- 1/4 cup chopped parsley
- Salt and black pepper to taste
- Hot sauce to taste

METHOD:

In a cast iron dutch oven, melt butter over medium-high heat. Add onions, celery, bell pepper, garlic and carrots. Saute 3-5 minutes or until vegetables are wilted. Sprinkle in flour and, using a wire whisk, stir constantly until white roux is achieved (see roux techniques). Add clam juice, bring to a rolling boil and reduce to simmer. Cook soup 10-12 minutes or until carrots are al dente. Add tomatoes, mushrooms, tomato sauce, bay leaf, thyme and tarragon. Continue to cook 5 additional minutes, stirring occasionally. Add shrimp and cook for 2 minutes then add fish. Take care when stirring the soup since the tender fish will break apart easily. Add clams, mussels, oysters and crawfish. Cook an additional 2 minutes or until clams and mussels open. Add green onions and parsley and season to taste using salt, pepper and hot sauce. To serve, place an equal portion of the seafoods in each bowl and top with broth. Serve with French bread or garlic croutons. I recommend serving a Pinot Noir or Beaujolais wine with this soup.

OPPOSITE: *Judge Porter's Cane River Fish Soup.*

PREP TIME: 45 Minutes

SERVES: 6

MODIFICATIONS:

And all that Jazz!

EGGPLANT FARCIES

Other than okra and chayote squash, eggplant is certainly the most often seen vegetable on a Louisiana table. No spring garden in the Bayou State is planted without a few rows of Black Beauty Eggplant. Here is one of the many eggplant recipes favored by Louisianians.

INGREDIENTS:

- 3 medium eggplants
- 8 slices bacon
- 1/4 cup melted butter
- 1 1/2 cups diced onions
- 1/2 cup diced celery
- 1/2 cup diced red bell pepper
- 1/4 cup minced garlic
- 1 cup sliced green onions
- 1/4 cup chopped parsley
- 1 tbsp fresh thyme, chopped
- 2 tbsps fresh basil, chopped
- 1 cup (70-90 count) shrimp, peeled and deveined
- 1 cup chicken stock (see recipe)
- Salt and black pepper to taste
- Creole seasoning to taste
- 3/4 cup seasoned Italian bread crumbs
- 6 bay leaves
- 1 cup diced carrots
- 2 1/2 cups Marinara Sauce (see recipe)

METHOD:

Preheat oven to 350°F. In a cast iron skillet, saute bacon over medium-high heat until crisp. Remove bacon, drain and crush. Set aside. Reserve bacon drippings. Split the eggplant in half lengthwise and, using a paring knife and spoon, scoop out the center to form a shell. Finely chop eggplant and set aside. Cover the shells with clear wrap and refrigerate. Into the same skillet, combine reserved bacon drippings and butter over medium-high heat. Add onions, celery, bell pepper, garlic and green onions. Saute 3-5 minutes or until vegetables are wilted. Add chopped eggplant and continue to saute until eggplant is fork-tender, approximately 10-15 minutes. Add parsley, thyme, basil, shrimp and chicken stock. Bring mixture to a rolling boil, reduce heat to simmer and season to taste using salt, pepper and Creole seasoning. Remove skillet from heat and add crushed bacon and bread crumbs. Stir mixture until bread crumbs have absorbed the liquid and a stuffing consistency has been achieved. Stuff each shell with the eggplant mixture and top with 1 bay leaf. Place stuffed eggplants into a 9" x 13" baking dish. Surround eggplants with carrots and Marinara Sauce. Cover dish with aluminum foil and place on the center shelf of the oven. Bake for 45 minutes, uncover and continue baking 10 additional minutes to slightly brown the eggplant. Remove bay leaves and serve 1 eggplant as an entree with a generous portion of Marinara Sauce.

PREP TIME: 1 1/2 Hours

SERVES: 6

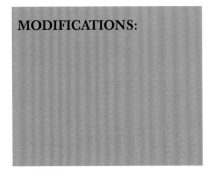

MODIFICATIONS:

The inviting parlor with period antiques.

 REAST OF QUAIL LA COLOMBE

*O*n the Cane River in Natchitoches, Louisiana, wild game dishes were often served as hors d'oeuvres and in interesting breakfast presentations. This boneless breast of quail on toast is one such rendition. You may also wish to present this dish as an interesting starter course for a formal dinner.

INGREDIENTS:

- 12 whole quail breasts
- 1/2 cup flour
- 1/2 cup melted butter
- 1/2 cup minced onions
- 1/4 cup minced celery
- 1/4 cup minced red bell pepper
- 3/4 cup sliced oyster mushrooms
- 1/4 cup sherry
- 2 cups beef stock (see recipe)
- 1 (8-ounce) can tomato sauce
- 1/2 cup sliced green onions
- 1/4 cup chopped parsley
- Salt and black pepper to taste
- Creole seasoning to taste
- 12 French bread croutons, toasted

METHOD:

Bone quail breasts and remove wing bone and any small pin bones. Rinse quail under cold running water and cut each breast into 1/2-inch slices. Season the meat generously with salt, pepper and Creole seasoning. Dust each breast in flour and set aside. In a cast iron skillet, heat butter over medium-high heat. Saute breasts, stirring constantly, until golden brown, approximately 2-3 minutes. Be careful not to overbrown or burn the butter. Remove breasts and set aside. Add onions, celery, bell pepper and oyster mushrooms. Saute 3-5 minutes or until vegetables are wilted. Return quail to skillet and deglaze with sherry. Add beef stock and tomato sauce. Bring mixture to a rolling boil, reduce to simmer and cook until quail are fork-tender. Add green onions and parsley and adjust seasonings if necessary. When ready to serve, place 2 of the French bread croutons in the center of a 10-inch plate and divide the breast evenly across the croutons.

PREP TIME: 1 Hour

SERVES: 6

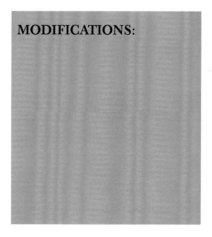

MODIFICATIONS:

A simple fountain is magic in the garden.

Fleur de Lis

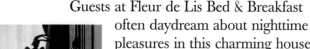

*I*n your mind you caress her often. You trace the gentle curve of her neck with your lips, run your fingers through her long mane of hair, follow the sleekness of her legs from her ankles to euphoria. Through the morning and afternoon you anticipate the evening hours, when you make her unmistakably yours.

Guests at Fleur de Lis Bed & Breakfast often daydream about nighttime pleasures in this charming house in Natchitoches. The Fleur de Lis, named after the royal emblem of France, was established as Natchitoches' first bed-and-breakfast home in 1983. The Queen Anne Victorian home is adorned with beautiful woodwork, massive cypress doors, ornamental molding and a grand old-fashioned wraparound porch with rockers and a swing. It also has bay windows, a steeply pitched roof and a dominant front-facing gable. The home is located in the National Historic Landmark District and is the only remaining home with a pressed tin roof. This "painted lady" has traditionally flaunted shades of soft mauve, burgundy, Williamsburg blue and oyster shell.

Victorian furnishings and turtle-top tables welcome visitors!

The home was built in 1903 by James Madison Hall McCook and his wife, Anna Belle Templeton McCook. They settled in Robeline from Cusseta, Ga., then built this home and moved to Natchitoches to benefit their children's higher education at the Normal College (present-day Northwestern State University). Mr. McCook and

OPPOSITE: *Fleur de Lis… a "painted lady" in Victorian elegance!*

two brothers operated general stores in Robeline and Natchitoches and were also partners in the Stephens and McCook Lumber Company.

Fleur de Lis offers five spacious guest rooms decorated with antiques and Victorian accents. Each room has a private bath. A full breakfast is served daily at a 12-foot Louisiana cypress table where guests from around the world can visit.

Located along Cane River Lake, Natchitoches is the oldest settlement of the Louisiana Purchase. While in the area you will enjoy a visit to Melrose Plantation, Fort St. Jean Baptiste, the Caroline Dorman Nature Preserve, Hodges Gardens, the Louisiana Sports Writers Hall of Fame, Kisatchie National Forest, Bayou Pierre Alligator Farm, Toledo Bend and Black Lake. There is also a variety of charming shops in the Downtown Historic District within walking distance of the inn. When dining out sample Lasyone's Meat Pie Kitchen, The Landing, Mariner's or Just Friends.

For reservations at Fleur de Lis contact Harriette and Tom Palmer at (800) 489-6621 or (318) 352-6621 or visit them on the Internet at www.fleurdelisbandb.com. Fleur de Lis is located at 336 Second Street. From I-49 take the Natchitoches/Many exit. Follow Highway 6 to Natchitoches and turn left onto Second Street.

For historic ambiance and an atmosphere reminiscent of days gone by, remember Fleur de Lis.

SHRIMP & SPINACH MOLD

Here in the South, greens of all varieties were seen on the dinner table. Greens were so often associated with poverty or casual dining that it was necessary to create interesting recipes if they were to be served in the finer dining rooms of New Orleans. Here is one such example.

INGREDIENTS:

* 1 cup (70-90 count) cooked shrimp, peeled and deveined
* 4 (10-ounce) packages chopped frozen spinach
* 4 eggs, separated
* 8 ounces shredded Sharp cheddar cheese
* 3 tbsps flour
* 3 tbsps melted butter
* 1/4 cup minced onions
* 1/4 cup minced red bell pepper
* 1 tbsp lemon juice
* Salt and black pepper to taste
* Creole seasoning to taste

METHOD:

Preheat oven to 350°F. Line the bottom of a bundt pan with strips of aluminum foil then coat with a non-stick vegetable spray. Set aside. Cook spinach according to package directions, drain thoroughly and allow to cool. Using your hands, squeeze out all of the excess water. In a large mixing bowl, whip egg yolks and combine with cheese, flour, butter, onions, bell pepper and lemon juice. Blend well to thoroughly incorporate all ingredients. Using a hand mixer, beat egg whites until stiff peaks form. Fold the spinach into the cheese mixture then gently stir in the shrimp and egg whites. Season the mixture to taste using salt, pepper and Creole seasoning. Spoon the spinach mixture into the mold and position the mold in the center of a large baking pan with 1-inch lip. Place mold on the center shelf of the oven and add approximately 1/2 inch hot water to the baking pan. Bake mold for 40-50 minutes or until toothpick or knife comes out clean. Remove bundt pan from the oven and allow to sit for 5 minutes. Place a serving platter on top of the bundt pan and invert mold quickly. The spinach mold should slide out of the bundt pan. Remove the aluminum strips and garnish appropriately. I enjoy serving glazed carrots or sweet potatoes around the base of the mold for a beautiful color contrast.

PREP TIME: 1 1/2 Hours

SERVES: 6-8

Serve this party dip at your next gathering.

MODIFICATIONS:

CELERY & POTATO SALAD WITH LEMON MAYONNAISE

The Germans who settled the River Road of Louisiana developed many variations for potato salad. Potatoes were one of the staple crops found in most Bayou gardens. This celery-enhanced potato salad was created as a perfect side dish to seafood soups and stews.

INGREDIENTS:

- 1 1/2 cups diced celery
- 1 pound new potatoes, skin-on
- 1 tbsp grated lemon peel
- 3/4 cup heavy duty mayonnaise
- 1/2 cup minced onions
- 1/4 cup minced red bell pepper
- 1/4 cup sweet pickle relish
- Salt and black pepper to taste

METHOD:

Quarter the potatoes and boil in lightly salted water until tender but not falling apart. Drain and rinse potatoes under cold water. In a large mixing bowl, combine celery, lemon peel, mayonnaise, onions, bell pepper and relish. Using a wooden spoon, mix until ingredients are well blended. Drain potatoes thoroughly and add to dressing mixture. Stir until all ingredients are incorporated. Be careful not to break the potatoes. Season to taste using salt and pepper. Cover, refrigerate and allow potatoes to marinate in the lemon dressing a minimum of 4 hours prior to serving.

PREP TIME: 1 Hour

SERVES: 6

MODIFICATIONS:

This four-poster French bed enhances this suite.

ℱLEUR DE LIS SEAFOOD PASTALAYA

Jambalaya is one of the oldest rice dishes in Louisiana. The dish traces its roots back to paella, that great Mediterranean rice dish. With the heavy Italian influence in South Louisiana, it is quite easy to understand how the ingredients of seafood jambalaya made their way onto the pasta platter.

INGREDIENTS:

- 2 dozen (21-25 count) shrimp, peeled and deveined
- 1 pound cooked crawfish tails
- 1 pound jumbo lump crabmeat
- 12 ounces Penne pasta
- 1/4 cup olive oil
- 1/2 cup diced onions
- 1/4 cup diced red bell pepper
- 1/4 cup diced yellow bell pepper
- 1/4 cup minced garlic
- 3/4 cup julienned andouille sausage
- 1/2 cup diced Creole tomatoes
- 2 tbsps flour
- 1 quart shellfish stock (see recipe)
- 1 tbsp fresh thyme, chopped
- 2 tbsps fresh basil, chopped
- 1/4 cup sliced green onions
- Salt and black pepper to taste

OPPOSITE: *Simplistic elegance!*

- Creole seasoning to taste
- 12 whole mussels
- 6 (21-25 count) shrimp, head-on

METHOD:

In a large cast iron dutch oven, heat olive oil over medium-high heat. Add onions, bell peppers, garlic and andouille sausage. Saute 3-5 minutes or until vegetables are wilted. Add tomatoes and blend well into the vegetable mixture. Sprinkle in flour and, using a wire whisk, stir constantly until white roux is achieved (see roux techniques). Add shellfish stock, 1 ladle at a time, until all has been incorporated. Add thyme, basil and season to taste using salt, pepper and Creole seasoning. Bring mixture to a rolling boil, reduce to simmer and cook 5 minutes. Add peeled shrimp, crawfish and lump crabmeat. Gently blend seafoods into the simmering liquid. Add green onions then fold in raw pasta. Reduce heat to low, cover and cook pastalaya 20-25 minutes or until pasta is al dente and liquid has been absorbed. Prior to serving, line mussels and head-on shrimp across the top of the pasta, cover pot and cook until mussels open and shrimp are pink and curled, approximately 7-10 minutes. When ready to serve, transfer pasta to a decorative platter and arrange mussels and large shrimp across the top as garnishes.

PREP TIME: 45 Minutes

SERVES: 6

MODIFICATIONS:

Nature's chandelier.

Sausage, Egg & Green Chilies Gratin

Although there are many breakfast casseroles using sausage as a main ingredient, this one has the added ingredient of a "spicy kick." In addition, the Monterey Jack and Parmesan give the dish a nice gratin look which is treasured in Cajun Country.

INGREDIENTS:

- 1/2 pound breakfast sausage
- 3 eggs, separated
- 1 (4-ounce) can chopped green chilies, drained
- 1 tsp fresh sage, chopped
- 1/2 tsp fresh thyme, chopped

Garden conversationalist.

- 1 cup minced onions
- 1 fresh jalapeno pepper, minced
- 1/4 cup minced red bell pepper
- 2/3 cup grated Monterey Jack cheese
- 1 tbsp unsalted butter
- 1 tbsp all-purpose flour
- 1/2 cup milk
- 1/3 cup freshly grated Parmesan cheese
- Salt and black pepper to taste
- 1 tsp cream of tartar

METHOD:

Preheat oven to 375°F. Butter a 2-quart au gratin dish and set aside. In a large cast iron skillet, cook sausage over medium heat. Using the back of a metal spoon, chop meat and stir occasionally until meat is golden brown and grain for grain, approximately 10-15 minutes. Add chilies, sage, thyme, onions, jalapeno and red bell pepper. Saute 3-5 minutes or until vegetables are wilted. Remove from heat and allow to cool. Blend in Monterey Jack cheese and set aside. In a small sauce pan, melt butter over medium-high heat. Sprinkle in flour and, using a wire whisk, stir until flour is dissolved into the butter. Add milk in a slow and steady stream, whisking constantly, until white sauce is achieved. Remove sauce pan from heat and add egg yolks, one at a time, whisking constantly until incorporated.

Sprinkle in Parmesan cheese and season to taste using salt and pepper. Continue whisking until cheese is blended. Pour sauce into the cooked sausage mixture, blend thoroughly and set aside. In a large mixing bowl, combine egg whites and cream of tartar. Using an electric mixer, whip on high speed until stiff peaks form. Stir 1/4 of the egg whites into the sausage mixture, blend well then fold the sausage mixture into the remaining egg whites, stirring gently. Pour the mixture into a 2-quart au gratin dish and bake for 25 minutes.

PREP TIME: 1 Hour

SERVES: 6

MODIFICATIONS:

JACK DANIELS®
CHOCOLATE ICE
CREAM

Liquor and liqueurs are often used to flavor ice creams and sorbets. In the south, sour mash whiskeys provide the southern flavor that adds the perfect finish to chocolate ice cream.

INGREDIENTS:

- 2/3 cup Jack Daniels® Whiskey
- 1 (5 1/3-ounce) package semi-sweet chocolate, chopped
- 1 2/3 cups unsweetened cocoa powder
- 1 1/3 cups sugar
- 1 quart heavy whipping cram
- 1 quart half and half
- 12 large eggs, room temperature

METHOD:

In a heavy bottom sauce pan, sift together the cocoa powder and sugar. Add heavy whipping cream and half and half and, using a wire whisk, stir until well-blended. Add the semi-sweet chocolate and cook over medium-high heat, stirring constantly until chocolate is melted. Remove sauce pan from heat and set aside. In a large mixing bowl, whisk eggs until frothy. Add 1/4 of the hot chocolate mixture into the eggs, whisking constantly. Add remaining egg mixture into the hot chocolate, whisking until

The cozy warmth of a window seat.

well-blended. Stir mixture over medium-high heat for 4-5 minutes until chocolate coats the back of the spoon. Do not allow mixture to boil as eggs will scramble. Pour the chocolate into a metal bowl and place it into a larger bowl of ice cold water to help chill the mixture. While chocolate is cooling, place the Jack Daniels® in a small sauce pan over medium-high heat. Heat until liquor ignites. NOTE: Take care as flame will flare up and extinguish itself quickly. Stir the Jack Daniels® into the chocolate mixture and allow to cool. Once chocolate custard is completely cooled, place into a homestyle ice cream machine and freeze according to manufacturer's directions.

PREP TIME: 1 Hour

MAKES: 4 Quarts

MODIFICATIONS:

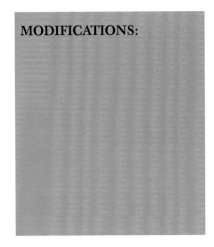

Recipe for Romance: Devil's Food Cake and Graham's Port

Levy-East House

NATCHITOCHES

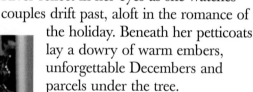

Silver water pitcher and an antique Victorian coffee cup.

OPPOSITE: *Wrought iron complements this home's entrance.*

Bedecked in Christmas finery, her white gown cascades about her like lace draping a crystal chandelier. A veil of evergreen wraps its fragrant scent about her gentle frame, the subtle aroma wishing "Seasons Greetings" to every caroler on the street. Twinkling lights from Cane River reflect in her eyes as she watches couples drift past, aloft in the romance of the holiday. Beneath her petticoats lay a dowry of warm embers, unforgettable Decembers and parcels under the tree.

The warmth of Christmas lingers about the Levy-East House in Natchitoches where glad tidings are celebrated all-year long. The home, built in 1838 by Trizzini and Soldini, was once the office and residence of Dr. Nicholas Michel Friedelezy, a French Canadian. Dr. Friedelezy practiced medicine for 20 years until it was discovered that his medical certificates were forgeries, and he was run out of town.

The three-story, French-influenced Greek Revival structure with gabled roof and twin brick chimneys is located in the heart of the Natchitoches National Historic Landmark District. A wooden upper story was added to the original one-story red brick home prior to the Civil War. Iron lace encircles the second-floor balcony, which is of the same design as the Old New Orleans Mint. An iron-grilled door leads to a century-old garden just off the front porch where you can relax beneath the sprawling branches of magnolia and gingko trees. Bayou Amulet, a ravine located on the south side of the home, flows as a reminder of Natchitoches' early days as the United States westernmost outpost. The water was once called "Bayou a Mule" because of the traders' mules tied to trees along its banks as they waited for wagons to be loaded with supplies from boats that came up the Red River and into Bayou Amulet.

Avery and Judy East purchased this Louisiana Landmark in 1994 and began restoring both the house and its furnishings. The four guest rooms feature period antiques, family heirlooms, queen-size beds and whirlpool baths. Special sitting areas are located on the second and third floors, or guests may choose to relax on the front and back balconies. Louisiana armoires adorn the hallways and the parlor holds a walnut parlor set created in finger mold design. The dining room, where home-cooked gourmet breakfasts are served, features a late Victorian table and a set of Queen Anne Revival chairs.

While in Natchitoches, the oldest settlement in the Louisiana Purchase, you will want to visit the Natchitoches Parish Old Courthouse Museum, Melrose Plantation, Hodges Gardens, the Natchitoches Art Center and Fort St. Jean Baptiste. If you visit the area during the Christmas season, you must experience the Natchitoches Christmas Festival of *(Continues on page 214)*

(Continued from page 212)

Lights held annually the first weekend in December. Boat and trolley tours of the town are also available. A multitude of unique antique stores and craft shops adorn the streets of the historic district. Local dining includes The Landing, Mariner's Seafood and Steak House, Merci Beaucoup, Just Friends and Lasyone's Meat Pie Kitchen.

To arrive at the Levy-East House travel I-49 to the Natchitoches/Many exit. Follow Highway 6 into Natchitoches, approximately four miles, and turn left on Jefferson Street. The home is located at 358 Jefferson Street. For reservations contact Judy and Avery East at (318) 352-0662 or (800) 840-0662.

Enjoy a wonderland of history and hospitality at the Levy-East House, one of the most luxurious bed and breakfast homes in the South.

An antique platter of Cornish Hens.

CREOLE MUSTARD-GLAZED CORNISH HENS

I love roasted chicken, especially the French-roasted kind! The great thing about this type of dish is the many variations and flavors that are achieved when the cook gets creative. You may wish to use this recipe on boneless breast of chicken for the grill or on a large roasting capon for your next holiday table.

INGREDIENTS:

- 4 tbsps Creole mustard
- 6 (2-pound) Cornish hens
- 1/4 cup lemon juice
- 1/4 cup melted butter
- 3 tbsps fresh basil, chopped
- 3 tbsps fresh thyme, chopped
- 3 tbsps fresh tarragon, chopped
- 4 tbsps minced garlic
- 1 1/2 tbsps honey
- Salt and black pepper to taste
- Creole seasoning to taste

METHOD:

Preheat oven to 400°F. Rinse Cornish hens inside and out under cold running water. Drain hens well and place on a large roasting pan with 1-inch lip. Top the chicken evenly with lemon juice and melted butter. Rub the liquids over the chicken including between the breast skin and meat. In a large mixing bowl, combine basil, thyme, tarragon and garlic. Place a small amount of the herbed mixture under the breast skin and rub remaining seasoning inside and out of each Cornish hen. Season the hens generously using salt, pepper and Creole seasoning. Roast chicken, uncovered, 30-40 minutes or until Cornish hens are golden brown and completely cooked. Create a glaze by combining the mustard and honey. Using a pastry brush, paint the mustard/honey mixture over the breast and legs of the hens and bake 5-10 additional minutes or until glaze is golden brown.

PREP TIME: 1 Hour

SERVES: 6

MODIFICATIONS:

HOT & SPICY BLACK-EYED PEAS

Black-eyed peas are one of those ingredients that seem to pop up everywhere from rice dishes and soups to vegetable casseroles. Most people would never consider sitting at the New Year's Day table without a bowl of black-eyed peas to bring good luck during the upcoming year. This recipe is a simple way to "jazz up" that good luck and create pizzazz in an otherwise simple dish.

INGREDIENTS:

- 2 (16-ounce) cans black-eyed peas
- 1/4 cup melted butter
- 1/2 cup minced onions
- 1/2 cup minced celery
- 1/2 cup minced red bell pepper
- 1 fresh jalapeno pepper, seeded and diced
- 2 tbsps minced garlic
- 1/2 pound diced andouille sausage
- Salt and black pepper to taste
- Creole seasoning to taste
- 1 tsp hot sauce

METHOD:

In a large cast iron dutch oven, heat butter over medium-high heat. Add onions, celery, bell pepper, jalapeno pepper and garlic. Saute 3-5 minutes or until vegetables are wilted. Add andouille and continue to saute 2-3 minutes, stirring occasionally. Add black-eyed peas with liquid and season to taste using salt, pepper, Creole seasoning and hot sauce. Bring mixture to a rolling boil, reduce to simmer and cook 15-20 minutes, stirring occasionally. Additional water may be needed to retain liquid.

PREP TIME: 1 Hour

SERVES: 6

MODIFICATIONS:

LUSCIOUS LEMON SOUP

I'm not quite sure if this recipe should fall into the category of soup or "luscious lemon malt!" Either way though I have to say that not only is the flavor unique, it is the perfect beginning or ending to any meal—especially during our hot Louisiana summers.

INGREDIENTS:

- 3 tbsps lemon juice
- 2 tbsps grated lemon peel
- 2 eggs
- 1/2 cup sugar
- 1 tbsp vanilla
- 1 quart buttermilk
- 1 cup vanilla ice cream

METHOD:

I recommend using only fresh squeezed lemon juice in this recipe. When grating the lemon peel, be careful to remove only the peel and not the white skin of the lemon. In a large bowl, whisk eggs, sugar and vanilla. Add lemon juice, lemon peel and buttermilk, continuing to whisk constantly until well-blended. Pour mixture into the bowl of a 9-cup food processor. Add 1/2 cup ice cream and blend mixture until ice cream is blended into the soup and liquid has become frothy, approximately

1-2 minutes. If you do not have a 9-cup processor, blend the soup in equal batches. Transfer soup into a large crystal pitcher, cover and chill for a minimum of 4 hours. Serve soup in champagne glasses and garnish with remaining ice cream, mint and additional zest if desired.

PREP TIME: 1 Hour

SERVES: 6-8

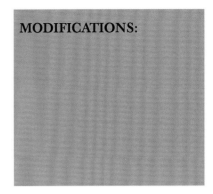

MODIFICATIONS:

Recipe for Romance:
Spicy Eggnog and Mistletoe

OPPOSITE: *Luscious Lemon Soup in a bouquet of memories.*

An antique coffee service displayed in the parlor.

HERB-ROASTED NEW POTATOES

There are as many potato varieties available to the cook today as there are colors in the rainbow. I still consider the tiny, new red potatoes to be the best variety when it comes to simple roasting or as an accompanying starch to roasted meats. This seasoning procedure allows the cook to prepare the dish well ahead of roasting and simply cook it as needed.

INGREDIENTS:

- 2 pounds new potatoes, quartered
- 1/2 cup diced onions
- 1/2 cup diced red bell pepper
- 1/2 cup diced yellow bell pepper
- 2 tbsps minced garlic
- 2 tbsps fresh rosemary, chopped
- 2 tbsps fresh thyme, chopped
- 1/4 cup olive oil
- 1/4 cup melted butter
- 2 tbsps red wine vinegar
- Salt and black pepper to taste
- 2 tsps Creole seasoning

METHOD:

Place the quartered potatoes in a large Ziploc® bag. Add onions, bell peppers, garlic and herbs. Pour in olive oil, butter and vinegar. Season to taste using salt, pepper and Creole seasoning. Seal the bag and shake vigorously to completely season the potatoes. Place bag in the refrigerator until ready to bake. Preheat oven to 400°F. Pour contents of bag onto a large baking sheet and roast 45 minutes to 1 hour, stirring occasionally, until potatoes are tender and golden brown. These potatoes are excellent when served as a garnish around Creole Mustard-Glazed Cornish Hens (see recipe).

PREP TIME: 1 Hour

SERVES: 6

MODIFICATIONS:

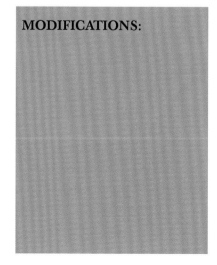

An elegant dinner table set for that special event.

An interesting canopy designed especially for the Eastlake furnishings.

ALMOND CREAM PIE

Almonds have a long and interesting history in the pastry kitchen. However, here in Louisiana pecans are most often seen in our dessert recipes. When the Ursuline nuns arrived in Louisiana, they brought with them a love of almonds and hazelnuts as the main ingredients in praline candy. Upon finding an ample supply of pecans in this area, they were immediately substituted for the other nuts. You may wish to try any of the above combinations in this pie.

INGREDIENTS:

- 1/2 cup almond slices
- 3/4 cup sugar
- 1/3 cup flour
- 1 tbsp corn starch
- Dash of salt
- 2 cups milk
- 5 eggs, separated
- 2 tbsps butter
- 1/2 tsp almond extract
- 1/2 tsp cream of tartar
- 1/2 cup sugar
- 1 (9-inch) cooked pie shell

METHOD:

In a large mixing bowl, combine 3/4 cup sugar, flour, corn starch and salt. Using a wire whisk, blend in the milk and egg yolks. Pour mixture into a 1-quart sauce pan and bring to a rolling boil, stirring constantly, until thickened. Remove from heat and fold in butter and 1/4 teaspoon almond extract. Cover sauce pan and cool mixture to room temperature. Pour custard into the pie shell and set aside. Preheat oven to 350°F. In the bowl of an electric mixer, combine egg whites and cream of tartar. Whip whites at high speed until foamy. Gradually add 1/2 cup of sugar, a little at a time, until stiff peaks form and sugar is totally dissolved, approximately 3 minutes. Add remaining almond extract and continue beating 5-10 additional seconds. Spread the meringue over the top of the pie, making sure that the meringue touches the pie crust on all edges. Sprinkle almonds over the meringue and bake 12-15 minutes or until golden brown at peaks. Chill thoroughly prior to serving.

PREP TIME: 2 Hours

SERVES: 6-8

MODIFICATIONS:

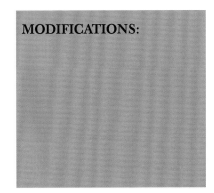

219

JuJu's Cabin

MANY

The campfire penetrates the lake front darkness like a candelabra shining through a dining room window. After a late-night swim and sips of champagne, you watch the fireflies dance upon the waters, imagining that each iridescent flame reflects a lifetime together. As the locusts compose a lake front lullaby and waves gently lap upon the shore, you slumber peacefully beneath a blanket of stars and share your dreams.

Let your wilderness visions become reality amid the rolling hills and pine forests of Toledo Bend Lake. JuJu's bed and breakfast, built in 1992 as a guest home, is an ideal Louisiana cottage for outdoors enthusiasts. The two-bedroom, two-bath cabin has a fully functional kitchen and large sitting area dressed in an outdoors motif. Swings and rocking chairs grace the porch and a lake side deck is perfect for enjoying afternoon cocktails or the day's catch.

Toledo Bend Lake is a haven for bass fishermen. JuJu's caters to recreational sportsmen with a fishing pier, boat house and commercial ice maker. The private cottage is ideal for families and offers adequate parking space for boats and trailers. If you enjoy water sports, the lake is perfect for skiing, jet skiing, boating or swimming. Nature lovers will enjoy the cypress trees surrounding the area where white pelicans land during their winter migration. Ducks and water fowl can be found on the lake year-round. Guests might also enjoy canoeing on Toro Creek or hiking in Stoker Hills.

Though ideal for the outdoorsman, JuJu's is also a pleasant haven for anniversary and honeymoon couples. A continental breakfast is served daily and full breakfasts are provided upon request.

While in the area you will enjoy a visit to Fort Jessup. Established in 1822 by Zachary Taylor, the fort protected the western boundary of the United States. The village of Fisher, established in 1899, is listed on the National Historic Register and is a typical turn-of-the-century sawmill town. Hodges Gardens is another "must see" in the area. Cypress Bend Golf Course and Resort and Wildwood Resort, both of which are on Toledo Bend Lake, are just minutes from JuJu's Cottage. Area golfing also includes Emerald Hills in nearby Florien. Sabine Parish is home to many annual festivals including the Zwolle Tamale Festival in October, the Free State Festival in November, the Battle of Pleasant Hill in April and Fisher Sawmill Days in May. JuJu's is centrally located between Natchitoches, La., and Nacogdoches, Texas—both great areas for antique shopping. Within 45 minutes of JuJu's are 17 antique and collectible shops. While in the area enjoy dining *(Continues on page 222)*

Anticipation!

OPPOSITE: *JuJu's...a view of nature at its best on Toledo Bend!*

(Continued from page 220)

at Fisherman's Galley, El Giro Mexican Restaurant and Country Boys.

JuJu's is located on Highway 191, just off Highway 6 west of Many and about 35 miles from I-49. For reservations contact Judy Cathey at (318) 256-5952 or (318) 256-9844.

For a relaxing romp in the remote outdoors, rendezvous at JuJu's.

A hearty country breakfast with a Spanish twist.

CANTINO TOLEDO BREAKFAST

*O*f course it makes sense! After all, the Spanish came by the thousands from Mexico and Texas to settle the banks of the Sabine River in and around Many, Louisiana. They brought with them not only their herbs and spices, but many of their favorite dishes as well. In fact, just 10 miles away from Toledo Bend is the town of Zwolle, the tamale capital of the world.

INGREDIENTS:

- 1/2 pound bulk breakfast sausage
- 3 tbsps melted butter
- 1 cup diced onions
- 1 cup diced green bell pepper
- 1 tbsp minced garlic
- 3/4 cup sliced Monterey Jack cheese
- 6 eggs
- 1/4 cup milk
- Salt and black pepper to taste
- Creole seasoning to taste
- 1/2 cup grated cheddar cheese
- 1/2 cup prepared Picante sauce
- 1/2 cup sour cream
- 1/4 cup sliced jalapeno peppers
- 12 (6-inch) flour tortillas

METHOD:

Flour tortillas may be purchased fully-prepared and ready-to-use in the Mexican section of any grocery store. In a large saute pan, heat butter over medium-high heat. Add sausage and, using the back of a cooking spoon, chop and stir often until meat is browned and grain for grain. Drain off all excess oil, reserving approximately 2 tablespoons. Add onions, bell pepper and garlic. Saute 3-5 minutes or until vegetables are wilted. Add Monterey Jack cheese, reduce heat to low and stir until cheese is melted. In a small mixing bowl, whisk eggs and milk. Season to taste using salt, pepper and Creole seasoning. Pour egg/milk mixture into the sausage and blend well, stirring constantly, until eggs are scrambled. Remove from heat and keep warm. Wrap 12 flour tortillas in a damp kitchen towel and microwave 1-2 minutes to steam. Place the hot shells along with condiments on a decorative Southwest platter. When ready to serve, place a spoon of egg/meat mixture into the center of each tortilla, top with a mixture of condiments and roll fajita-style. To serve this dish as a brunch item, I recommend filling each shell ahead of time with egg/meat mixture and condiments and place in a large baking dish. Top tortillas with salsa and cheese and bake until thoroughly heated and cheese is melted.

PREP TIME: 1 Hour

SERVES: 6

PEPPER-MARINATED GRILLED FLANK STEAK

For those people visiting the lake who cannot eat seafood or shellfish, I recommend throwing a sweet and spicy flank steak onto the grill. After all, at JuJu's the grill is hot and there's ample tortilla shells to make a unique and interesting fajita wrap. The only thing missing is a perfectly cooked London broil, so here's the recipe!

Now, this is roughin' it!

INGREDIENTS:

- 1 (2-pound) flank steak, trimmed
- 1/4 cup vegetable oil
- 1/4 cup balsamic vinegar
- 1 tbsp hot sauce
- 1 tbsp cane syrup
- 1/4 cup minced garlic
- 1/2 tsp dried red pepper flakes
- 1/4 tsp fresh cracked black pepper
- 2 tbsps fresh thyme, chopped
- 2 tbsps fresh basil, chopped
- 1/8 tsp ground cloves
- 2 tbsps firmly packed brown sugar
- Salt to taste
- Creole seasoning to taste

METHOD:

Place the steak in a large baking pan and, using a sharp paring knife, cut 1/4-inch slits at 1-inch intervals across the top of the flank. Top the meat with oil, vinegar, hot sauce and cane syrup. Using the tips of your fingers, rub the liquid generously around the steak. In a small mixing bowl, combine garlic, red pepper, black pepper, thyme, basil, cloves and sugar. Continue to season the meat by rubbing the herbed mixture over the flank steak. Season to taste using salt and Creole seasoning. Cover pan and allow the meat to sit at room temperature a minimum of 4 hours. Meanwhile, heat a homestyle grill such as the Lodge Outpost Grill or Cajun Grill according to manufacturer's directions. I recommend adding more flavor to the steak by soaking pecan wood chips in root beer and tossing them onto the pit during the grilling process. When ready to cook, place the steak directly over the hottest part of the coals and cook 5 minutes on each side, turning once, for medium-rare or 8-10 minutes on each side for medium. When done, place the flank steak on a wooden cutting board and thinly slice on a 45 degree angle prior to serving.

PREP TIME: 30 Minutes

SERVES: 6-8

MODIFICATIONS:

GRILLED BASS WITH HERBED GARLIC MARINADE

Toledo Bend Lake in Many, Louisiana is known as a fisherman's paradise because of the volume of largemouth and striped bass as well as crappie and catfish. As one motors around the lake, a common site is the outdoor fish fry complete with hush puppies and ice-cold beer. Every now and again, when a three to four pound bass is brought ashore, it is simply scaled, cleaned, rubbed in garlic and herbs and placed head-on over a hot grill.

INGREDIENTS:

- 1 (3-4 pound) bass, cleaned
- 1/4 cup olive oil
- 1/4 cup white wine
- Juice of 1 lemon
- 1/2 tsp hot sauce
- 1 tbsp Worcestershire sauce
- 1/4 cup fresh thyme, chopped
- 1/4 cup fresh basil, chopped
- 1/4 cup fresh dill, chopped
- 1/4 cup fresh tarragon, chopped
- 1/4 cup minced garlic
- Salt and black pepper to taste
- Creole seasoning to taste

OPPOSITE: *Cleaned, scaled and on the grill!*

METHOD:

Light charcoal in a homestyle grill such as the Lodge Outpost Grill or another of my favorites the Cajun Grill. While coals are heating, prepare fish by removing the gills and rinsing thoroughly under cold running water. Place the fish in a large baking pan and top with olive oil, wine, lemon juice, hot sauce and Worcestershire sauce. Using your fingertips, rub the liquids completely over the fish, inside and out. In a small mixing bowl, combine herbs and garlic. Using a sharp paring knife, cut slits at 2-inch intervals down each side of the fish. Place a generous portion of the herbed mixture into each of the slits and then completely over the fish. Place remainder of herbed mixture into the belly cavity. Season fish generously with salt, pepper and Creole seasoning. Spray the grill with a non-stick vegetable spray. Place fish over the hot coals, 2-3 minutes on each side, turning occasionally, until meat is flaky and cooked to the bone. Using a pastry brush, baste the fish with any remaining seasoning liquid from the pan. Take extreme care when turning the fish to keep it from falling apart during the cooking process. You may choose to place the fish in a grill basket designed for that purpose, prior to cooking. I recommend serving grilled fish with a melange of roasted vegetables flavored in the same fashion as the fish and grilled alongside.

PREP TIME: 1 Hour

SERVES: 4-6

MODIFICATIONS:

225

ROASTED LOIN OF PORK WITH NATURAL JUICES

I really do think that pork is the most flavorful of all meats but often a little tricky, especially the loin. Many cuts of pork are layered with fat and marbling whereas the loin tends to be rather dry. Ample seasoning and quick pan-searing prior to roasting are the key to a successful pork loin entree.

INGREDIENTS:

- 1 (2 1/2-pound) deboned pork loin
- 1 tbsp vegetable oil
- 1 tbsp fresh rosemary, crushed
- 1 tbsp minced garlic
- 1 tbsp rubbed sage
- Salt and black pepper to taste
- 1/4 cup olive oil
- 1 tbsp softened butter
- 2 tbsps flour
- 2 cups chicken stock (see recipe)

METHOD:

Preheat oven to 450°F. Place the pork loin in a large baking pan and top with vegetable oil. Rub the oil over the entire loin. Season to taste using rosemary, garlic, sage, salt and pepper. In a large cast iron dutch oven or skillet, heat olive oil over medium-high heat. Add pork loin and brown well on all sides,

Knick Knacks of Judy's pastime…

turning occasionally. Place the pan on the center shelf of the oven and cook 35 minutes or until internal temperature reaches 150°F. Remove pan from the oven, place loin on a platter and keep warm. Pour off all but 1 tablespoon of the drippings from the roasting pan. Add softened butter to the pan and melt over medium-high heat. Using a wire whisk, blend in flour to create a white roux (see roux techniques). Add chicken stock and blend into the roux mixture. Place the pan over medium-high heat and bring mixture to a low boil, whisking until juices thicken to a sauce consistency. Adjust

seasonings if necessary. Strain the sauce through a fine sieve into a sauce boat and serve with sliced loin.

PREP TIME: 1 Hour

SERVES: 6

MODIFICATIONS:

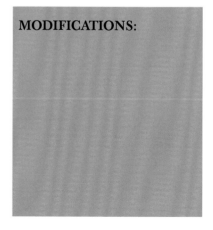

226

QUICK STRAWBERRY MOUSSE

Desserts are one of those dishes that a cook seems to spend all day preparing. Often this is impossible when unannounced company appears on the door-step or an "emergency" dessert is needed in a short time. This quick strawberry mousse is the perfect answer to your dilemma.

INGREDIENTS:

- 1 (10-ounce) package frozen sweetened strawberries
- 1/2 pint sour cream
- 1/2 cup sugar
- 1 tbsp vanilla
- 1 cup prepared whipped topping
- 6 sugar cookies

METHOD:

In the bowl of a blender or food processor, combine strawberries and sour cream. Blend mixture on high for 30 seconds. Add sugar and vanilla and continue to blend until sugar is dissolved and mixture is smooth and textured. Pour the strawberry mousse into fluted-champagne glasses and place in the freezer approximately 3-4 hours. When frozen and ready to serve, garnish with a dollop of whipped topping and 1 sugar cookie. You may wish to formalize the dish with the addition of 1 or 2 chocolate-covered strawberries and fresh mint.

PREP TIME: 2 Hours

SERVES: 6

MODIFICATIONS:

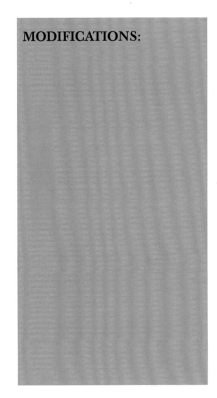

Recipe for Romance:
Roasted Marshmallows and a Sleeping Bag

The best tamales north of the Rio Grande!

Matt's Cabin

ALEXANDRIA

Rainwater tap dances on the tin roof above you, while lightning streaks the sky in playful patterns. The echoing thunder is chased by the wind across cotton fields, its hollow voice ricocheting off the walls of the sharecropper's cabin.

Wildflowers grow where rain cools the thirsty ground.

Matt's Cabin, situated on the banks of Bayou Robert, is the perfect cottage in which to spend a rainy summer night. Built around the turn of the century, this sharecropper's bungalow is located in a stately pecan grove on Inglewood Plantation near Alexandria. Inglewood, one of the few plantation homes to have survived the Civil War in central Louisiana, has been a working plantation since the 1820s. Crops such as cotton, soybeans, corn and wheat are still grown in the fields today. Inglewood Plantation has been designated as a National Historic District.

Matt's Cabin, a rustic yet elegant one-room bed and breakfast, features a porch, fishing dock, barbecue pit and wood burning fireplace. The kitchen is fully equipped with a variety of breakfast items that guests can prepare at their leisure. The cabin is furnished with a queen-sized bed, child's trundle bed and a private bath. Oil paintings by Kathryn Keller adorn the walls and depict a variety of plantation scenes.

OPPOSITE: *Matt's Cabin…a secluded getaway for two.*

During your stay at Matt's Cabin you can enjoy ventures to historic homes such as Kent House, Frogmore Plantation or Loyd's Hall near Cheneyville. While in the area enjoy shopping at the Alexandria Antique Mall, Saxon Guild or Odyssey. Visit such cultural attractions as the Alexandria Museum of Art, Southern Heritage Museum or River Oaks Square. Outdoors enthusiasts will enjoy hiking at Kisatchie National Forest, boating on Kincaid Lake or at Indian Creek Campground, fishing on Saline Lake and duck hunting on Catahoula Lake. A visit to the area is not complete without dining at Lea's Lunchroom in Lecompte, even if it's only for coffee and a slice of their famous pies. Other area restaurants include Bistro on the Bayou, Tunk's for catfish and Suburban Garden for Italian cuisine.

Matt's Cabin at Inglewood Plantation is located three miles south of Alexandria, just off Highway 71 and I-49. For reservations call Susan at (318) 487-8340 or (888) 575-6288. Your visit includes a tour of the private Inglewood Plantation home and access to its swimming pool and tennis court.

There is nothing more electrifying than a lover's touch on a stormy night. At Matt's Cabin time seems to stand still making a rainy night that much more intense.

Matt would be proud.

LUMP CRABMEAT INGLEWOOD

Inglewood Plantation, located on the outskirts of Alexandria, Louisiana, is the home of Matt's Cabin and is three hours away from the best blue crab waters in Louisiana. Imagine what a delicacy this dish must have been considered on the plantation table.

INGREDIENTS:

- 1 pound jumbo lump crabmeat
- 1/4 cup heavy duty mayonnaise
- 1/3 cup plain yogurt
- 1/2 cup thinly sliced green onions
- 1 tsp capers
- 1 tbsp fresh thyme leaves, chopped
- 1 tbsp fresh basil, chopped
- 2 tbsps fresh tarragon, chopped
- 1 tbsp chopped parsley
- 1 tbsp fresh jalapenos, chopped
- 1/4 cup minced red bell pepper
- 1 tbsp minced garlic
- Salt and black pepper to taste
- Creole seasoning to taste
- Juice of 1/2 lemon

METHOD:

Gently pick through the jumbo lump crabmeat, removing all shells and cartilage. Cover and place in the refrigerator. In a stainless steel bowl, combine mayonnaise and yogurt. Add green onions, capers, thyme leaves, basil, tarragon, parsley and jalapenos. Using a wire whisk, blend well to incorporate all seasonings. Add red bell pepper and garlic, continuing to blend until well mixed. Season to taste using salt, pepper, Creole seasoning and lemon juice. Add crabmeat and fold gently into the sauce mixture to keep from breaking the lumps. When crabmeat is well coated, cover and refrigerate a minimum of 4-6 hours to allow flavors to develop. When ready to serve, place an equal portion in 6 champagne glasses or crab shells and serve with crackers or garlic croutons. You may wish to present this appetizer garnished with a fresh basil leaf or in a decorative mold for an hors d'oeuvre party.

PREP TIME: 1 Hour

SERVES: 6

MODIFICATIONS:

FRIED PARMESAN EGGPLANT STRIPS

As you already know, eggplant is one of our premier vegetables. I think the main reason that we love it so much is because of its versatility. Although I enjoy eggplant more in a casserole than any other method of preparation, I often fry them in sticks or medallions flavored with Parmesan cheese as an interesting appetizer.

INGREDIENTS:

- 3 small purple eggplants
- 1/2 cup Parmesan cheese
- 2 cups buttermilk
- 3 cups seasoned fish fry
- 1/2 cup fresh basil, chopped
- 1/4 cup fresh oregano, chopped
- Cracked black pepper to taste
- Oil for deep-frying

METHOD:

Preheat oil in a Fry Daddy or homestyle fryer to 350°F according to manufacturer's directions. If using a cast iron skillet, make sure there is enough oil for deep-frying. In a paper bag, combine fish fry, Parmesan cheese, basil and oregano. Season the fish fry with enough black pepper to give the breading a "kick." Close the bag and shake vigorously to combine the seasonings. The reason I like to use a small eggplant is because the skin is tender enough to eat and there is no need to peel the vegetable. Cut the eggplants into 1/2-inch strips and place in the buttermilk. When ready to fry, drain the eggplant strips well and place 6-8 at a time into the paper bag. Close bag completely and shake vigorously to coat all eggplant pieces with the fish fry mixture. Deep-fry, a few at a time, until golden brown and eggplant floats to the surface. Drain well on paper towels and sprinkle with salt, if desired. Continue frying process until all eggplants are cooked. Serve plain or with your favorite homemade salsa.

PREP TIME: 30 Minutes

SERVES: 6-8

Cotton…Central Louisiana's main crop.

MODIFICATIONS:

WILD DEWBERRY ICE CREAM

Whenever the end of April or beginning of May rolls around in Bayou Country, the kids hit the fields in search of wild dewberries or blackberries. Not only are they delicious off the vine, but they are perfect for jams and jellies. In those years when the dewberries were plentiful, mama would bring out the ice cream maker and whip up a batch of this unbelievable dessert.

INGREDIENTS:

- 1 quart dewberries or blackberries
- 2 cups milk
- 1 pint heavy whipping cream
- 3 cups sugar
- 2 eggs
- 1/4 cup Grand Marnier®
- 1 pint dewberries for garnish

METHOD:

Wash dewberries 2-3 times under cold running water and drain. Mash 1 quart of the dewberries and chill. In a small sauce pot, combine milk and whipping cream over medium-high heat. Bring mixture to a low simmer, approximately 190°F. NOTE: Do not boil. While cream is heating, combine sugar, eggs and Grand Marnier® in a large mixing bowl. Using a wire whisk, whip until ingredients are well incorporated. When milk has scalded, slowly pour the milk into the egg mixture, whipping constantly to keep eggs from scrambling. Continue to whisk until sugar is dissolved in the hot cream. Chill mixture or place bowl over another bowl of ice cubes and stir constantly for a rapid chill. Prepare a homestyle electric ice cream maker according to manufacturer's directions. Combine crushed dewberries with the cream mixture and pour into the drum of the ice cream maker. Once ice cream is frozen, allow it to temper in the freezer approximately 1 hour prior to serving. Garnish with whole dewberries.

PREP TIME: 2 Hours

MAKES: 2 1/2 Quarts

OPPOSITE: *Sugar and spice make all things nice!*

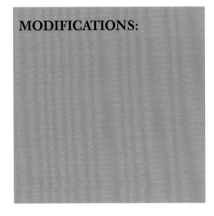

MODIFICATIONS:

Recipe for Romance: Melted Ice Cream and Lady Fingers

Quittin' time!

MATT'S CHARBROILED LEG OF LAMB

Although fresh leg of pork is most often considered the meat of choice over an open fire in Louisiana, exotic meats such as game or lamb are often substituted. In this recipe, the leg is boned and marinated prior to grilling. It is definitely one of the tastiest grilled entrees you will ever prepare.

INGREDIENTS:

- 1 (5-pound) leg of lamb, boned and butterflied
- 1 cup olive oil
- 2/3 cup lemon juice
- 1/4 cup minced garlic
- 4 fresh bay leaves
- 2 tbsps rubbed sage
- 2 tbsps fresh rosemary, chopped
- 2 tbsps fresh thyme leaves
- 2 cups lamb stock (see recipe)
- 1/2 cup dry red wine
- 2 tbsps sliced green onions
- 1 tsp rubbed sage
- 1 tsp fresh rosemary, chopped
- 1 tsp fresh thyme leaves
- 2 tbsps butter
- Salt and black pepper to taste
- Creole seasoning to taste

METHOD:

Have your butcher bone the lamb and remove all visible fat from the meat. Place the lamb in a large baking pan and top with olive oil, lemon juice, garlic, bay leaves, 2 tablespoons sage, 2 tablespoons rosemary and 2 tablespoons thyme leaves. Rub the seasoning mixture thoroughly over the lamb, cover and refrigerate overnight. When ready to prepare, drain and reserve marinade. Preheat outdoor grill according to manufacturer's directions.

When pit is ready, season the lamb inside and out using salt, pepper and Creole seasoning. I prefer to tie the leg into a round roast and cook on the rotisserie, however, you may wish to lay the lamb flat on the grill. If using a rotisserie, cook the lamb approximately 45 minutes, brushing occasionally with the marinade. When internal temperature reaches 130°F, remove from the rotisserie and allow to rest 20 minutes prior to slicing. Before serving, place lamb stock, red wine, green onions and remaining herbs in the bottom of a sauce pot over medium-high heat. Bring sauce to a rolling boil and reduce the liquid to approximately 3/4 cup. Slice lamb and shingle it on a large serving platter. Immediately prior to serving, whisk the butter into the lamb stock. Once butter has thoroughly been incorporated, season to taste using salt, pepper and Creole seasoning. Ladle sauce over lamb and garnish with a large sprig of fresh rosemary.

PREP TIME: 2 Hours

SERVES: 6-8

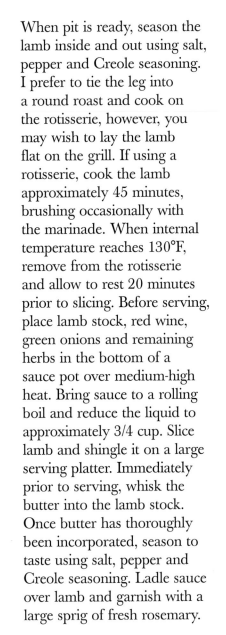

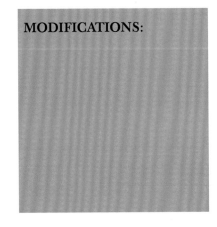

MODIFICATIONS:

Flavor develops over the coals of The Cajun Grill.

Room for two!

PORTOBELLO PIZZAS

*I*t seems that whenever one fires up the barbecue grill, we know exactly what entree is destined for the pit, yet we still look for the perfect "something to munch on." Normally in the South, we enjoy grilled, spicy pork sausage as an easy solution, however, why not get creative at your next cookout and prepare some unique, flavorful pizzas.

INGREDIENTS:

- 3 large portobello mushrooms
- 1/4 cup extra virgin olive oil
- 1/2 cup Marinara Sauce (see recipe)
- 1/2 cup shredded Mozzarella cheese
- 1/2 cup crawfish tails
- 6 slices Louisiana smoked sausage
- 1/4 cup fresh basil, chopped
- Salt and black pepper to taste
- Creole seasoning to taste

METHOD:

Preheat grill according to manufacturer's directions or oven to 350°F. Brush mushrooms well to remove any sand or grit especially from the gill area. You should never rinse a mushroom under water as they are extremely porous and will pick up excess liquid. Place mushrooms, gill side up, on a large baking sheet and paint evenly with olive oil on both sides then season to taste using salt, pepper and Creole seasoning. Top each mushroom with a generous portion of prepared Marinara Sauce and sprinkle with 1/2 of the Mozzarella. Top each with crawfish tails and smoked sausage then top again with remaining Mozzarella. Garnish each mushroom with basil and place directly on the grill. Close cover and allow mushrooms to cook until cheese is melted and mushrooms are tender on the inside and crispy on the outside, approximately 20-30 minutes. If cooking in oven, place baking sheet on center shelf and allow to cook for 20-30 minutes. When ready to serve, cut each mushroom in half and serve as an appetizer.

PREP TIME: 1 Hour

SERVES: 6

NOTE: Many people question whether a mushroom should be washed or not. According to Harold McGee in his book, *The Curious Cook*, mushrooms are 80% water and do not absorb any more liquid in a quick rinsing process. In fact, 6 ounces of mushrooms placed in a bowl of water for 5 minutes and then dried of any surface water, will gain approximately 1/4 ounce of water weight. So, rinse them if you will, but only immediately prior to cooking.

MODIFICATIONS:

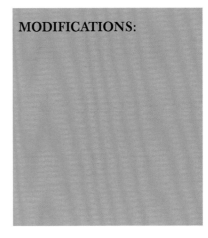

Fairfield Place

SHREVEPORT

*T*ogether you watch the sunrise, capturing that moment of truth evident only in the dawn of a new day. As sunlight streams forth over the horizon in outstretched arms of passion, you realize he is your beacon of the day, just as the moon is your beacon of night. Dew glistens in the sunshine, christening the morning like moisture on would-be lovers. Slowly, the sun rises to warm the day the way he waits to warm your night.

Warm thoughts and a parasol of sunshine greet every guest at Fairfield Place Bed & Breakfast in Shreveport where it is always easy to experience the brighter, lighter side of life. Fairfield Place, a restored 1870s mansion, is located in Shreveport's Highland Historic District on one of the city's most beautiful residential streets. Listed on the National Register of Historic Places, Fairfield Place was originally constructed for the family of Judge David Land who lived there until his death. In the early 1900s it was moved from its original location four doors away to its present site at 2221 Fairfield. In 1983 the classical Victorian house was restored to its former splendor.

Today, the home features two downstairs suites and four rooms upstairs, each with a private bath, robes, complimentary

The painted ceiling of the entrance foyer.

OPPOSITE: *2221 Fairfield Avenue.*

toiletries and wireless internet. The rooms brim with antiques as well as fine American and European paintings. A spiral staircase winds from the second-story front balcony to a manicured lawn and secluded garden. Fireplaces are located throughout the home. Bricks from the original kitchen fireplace, which was removed during the renovation, were used to pave one of the front walkways. Brass light fixtures and copper door hardware original to the home can be found throughout the inn.

Adjacent to the inn is Bed and Breakfast on Boulevard. In 1995 this turn-of-the-century home, formerly the Boldridge Home, was added to the Fairfield Place estate. This property provides two additional luxurious suites with whirlpool tubs, a parlor, dining room and garden room and makes an excellent facility for special events, meetings and weddings.

Gourmet breakfasts are provided daily with menus that include baked apples, French toast, caramelized bacon and banana praline scones.

The city of Shreveport dates back to the 1830s. Along the riverfront, historic Shreve Square is reminiscent of New Orleans' French Quarter with many restaurants, boutiques and the restored Strand Theater. Fairfield Place is near the Barnwell Memorial Garden and Art Center, Pioneer Heritage Center at LSU-Shreveport, Barksdale Air Force *(Continues on page 238)*

(Continued from page 236)

Base Museum, as well as the Louisiana Boardwalk and downtown night life. Nearby, explore the German community of Minden and the plantation country surrounding Natchitoches. Nature lovers and sportsmen can enjoy fishing, hunting and water sports. Annual festivals include Holiday in Dixie in April and the Louisiana State Fair in October. While in Shreveport, enjoy dining at the Mabry House, Village Grille, Olive Street Bistro and Ernest's Orleans.

Fairfield Place Bed & Breakfast, Shreveport's largest bed-and-breakfast inn, is located at 2221 Fairfield Avenue. From I-20 Westbound, take the Fairfield Avenue Exit, turning left onto Fairfield. The inn is located about 11 blocks on the left. For reservations contact Pat or Mark Faser at (318) 222-0048 or visit their website at www. fairfieldplace.com.

Fairfield Place Bed & Breakfast—where days last forever and nights vanish as quickly as the morning mist.

FAIRFIELD EGG CASEROLE

I believe this is the ultimate omelette casserole. What makes it special, in addition to the great taste, is the fact that one may consume vegetables, meat and dairy all in one dish. Save this casserole for a holiday when the house is full of guests, because it definitely feeds a crowd. Feel free to cut the recipe in half.

INGREDIENTS:

- 18 eggs
- 3 (10-ounce) packages frozen chopped spinach
- 1/4 pound butter, halved
- 1 cup cubed ham
- 1/2 cup minced onions
- 1 cup flour
- 4 cups milk
- 1 cup heavy whipping cream
- 12 strips bacon, cooked and drained
- Salt and black pepper to taste
- Creole seasoning to taste
- 1/2 cup canned fried onion rings, crushed
- 1 cup grated Monterey Jack cheese

METHOD:

Butter a 9" x 13" baking dish and set aside. Cook spinach according to package directions, drain completely and chop once more. In a large saute pan, melt 1/2 of the butter over medium-high heat. Pan-fry ham for 3-4 minutes, remove and set aside. In the same skillet, add onions and saute 2-3 minutes or until wilted. Add flour, a little at a time, and using a wire whisk, stir constantly until white roux is achieved (see roux techniques). Add milk, 1 cup at a time, stirring into the roux mixture. Bring to a low boil and continue stirring until mixture is smooth. Remove from heat and gently fold in the chopped spinach. Season to taste using salt, pepper and Creole seasoning. Keep warm. In a large saute pan, melt remaining butter over medium-high heat. In a large mixing bowl, whisk eggs with whipping cream and season lightly using salt and pepper. Pour mixture into saute pan and soft scramble the eggs until lightly set. Do not overcook. Spread 1/2 of the eggs in the bottom of the baking dish. Layer alternately with 1/2 of the ham, bacon and spinach mixture. Repeat with remaining layers and then top with onion rings and Monterey Jack cheese. This casserole MUST be covered and refrigerated overnight prior to baking and may also be frozen for later. When ready to cook, preheat oven to 275°F and bake, uncovered, for 1 hour.

PREP TIME: 2 Hours

SERVES: 10

ORANGE MARMALADE MUFFINS

These muffins are extremely interesting because of the additional flavor brought about by the marmalade. They are simple to make and if you are not fond of orange, please experiment with your favorite marmalade or preserve.

INGREDIENTS:

- 1/2 cup orange marmalade
- 2 cups all-purpose flour
- 1/2 cup sugar
- 1 tbsp baking powder
- 1 large egg
- 1 cup plain yogurt or buttermilk
- 1/4 cup melted butter
- 1 tsp vanilla
- 3/4 cup chopped pecans

METHOD:

Preheat oven to 375°F. Grease 8 muffin cups or use foil baking cups. In a large mixing bowl, combine flour, sugar and baking powder. Using a wire whisk, blend well. In a separate bowl, combine egg, yogurt or buttermilk, butter, vanilla and pecans. Whisk thoroughly until smooth. Pour the egg mixture into the flour and fold 2-3 times until the dry ingredients are moistened. Do not overmix. Spoon 1 heaping tablespoon of batter into each muffin tin. Using the back of a teaspoon, press a small dimple into the batter.

Pampered and spoiled rotten!

Place approximately 1 teaspoon of marmalade into the dimple of the batter tin and top with approximately 2 tablespoons of muffin batter. Bake 25-30 minutes or until muffins are golden brown. Allow muffins to cool 5 minutes prior to removing from the oven. Serve warm after muffins have cooled for an additional 5 minutes. Serve with softened butter.

PREP TIME: 1 Hour

MAKES: 8 Muffins

MODIFICATIONS:

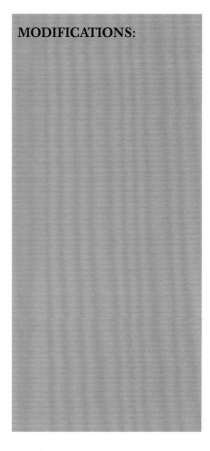

POACHED PEARS ST. VALENTINE

This poached pear dish is absolutely the most fitting dessert for Valentine's Day. Not only is the pear colored to a rich burgundy by the wine, it is subtly sweet and the perfect light finish to a romantic meal.

INGREDIENTS:

- 8 Bartlett pears, stem in tact
- 1 bottle dry red wine
- 2 cups sugar
- 1 bay leaf
- 1 tsp black whole peppercorns
- 1 sprig fresh thyme
- 1 sprig fresh rosemary
- 1 cinnamon stick
- 2 vanilla beans

METHOD:

Using a paring knife, slice off approximately 1/4 inch from the bottom of the pear so it will sit flat on a plate. Peel and core the pear without puncturing the outer surface. If you should choose not to core the pear, you should instruct your guests that seeds are present in the center. Store the pears in water until ready to cook to keep from turning brown. In a 1-gallon sauce pot, combine wine and sugar. Using a wire whisk, stir constantly until sugar is dissolved. Add bay leaf, peppercorns, thyme, rosemary and cinnamon stick. Using a paring knife, split the vanilla beans in half and scrape the black inside into the liquid. Place the remaining bean hulls into the pot as well. Add pears and enough water to cover by 1/4 inch, if necessary. Place the pot over medium-high heat and bring mixture to a low boil. Reduce heat to simmer and cook until pears are slightly tender but not overcooked, approximately 45 minutes. NOTE: Check the texture often after 30 minutes. Remove the pot from the heat and allow the pears to cool in the liquid. Cover and place in the refrigerator a minimum of 1 day to marinate and pick up the color of the wine. When ready to serve, place a pear in the center of a 10-inch serving plate and top with 1-ounce of the poaching liquid. You may wish to garnish with candied orange peel, whipped cream or mint leaves.

PREP TIME: 1 Hour

SERVES: 8

Sit and see a garden grow.

MODIFICATIONS:

Recipe for Romance: Chocolate Truffles and Hot Cocoa

OPPOSITE: *Cupid Cuisine!*

241

HOMEMADE-STYLE CORNED BEEF BRISKET

There is no dish more suited for dining in front of the fire than corned beef brisket. Most people consider it for St. Patrick's Day, but try eating it with friends around the open hearth on the coldest day of the year, and I think you'll experience it in a different light.

INGREDIENTS:

- 1 (5-pound) beef brisket, trimmed
- 1/2 cup Kosher salt
- 1 tbsp ground allspice
- 1 tbsp dried thyme
- 3/4 tbsp paprika
- 2 tbsps black whole peppercorns
- 3 bay leaves, crushed
- 1 pound carrots, peeled and sliced
- 1 pound turnips, peeled and quartered
- 2 pounds new potatoes, halved
- 1 small cabbage

METHOD:

Place the trimmed brisket in a large pan and, using a skewer or meat fork, pierce the meat 25-30 times on each side. Rub each side of the brisket evenly with salt. Continue this process with allspice, thyme and paprika. Place brisket in a 2-gallon Ziploc® bag and add peppercorns and bay leaves. Squeeze bag to remove

The dining room complete with family heirlooms.

as much air as possible. Place the bag on a baking sheet and place a second sheet weighted down with 2 bricks or a similar object on top. Refrigerate brisket a minimum of 7 days, turning once each day, When ready to cook, preheat oven to 200°F. Remove the brisket from the bag and drain thoroughly. Place the brisket in a 2-gallon stock pot and cover by 1-inch with cold water. Bring brisket to a low boil, skimming any impurities that rise to the surface. Cover pot and allow brisket to boil for 2 1/2 hours or until brisket is tender at the thickest part. The meat is fully-cooked when the muscle fibers begin to loosen and a fork can be inserted easily. Remove the brisket from the pot allowing the poaching liquid to continue simmering and place brisket in a large baking pan with 1-2 cups of the cooking liquid. Cover pan with aluminum foil and place in oven to keep warm. Add carrots, turnips and potatoes to the simmering poaching liquid. Simmer 10-

12 minutes. Cut cabbage into 6 wedges, core and add to the pot. Continue to poach until cabbage is fork-tender. When ready to serve, remove the brisket from the oven and slice across the grain into 1/4-inch serving pieces. Transfer the sliced meat to a large serving platter and surround with poached vegetables and a generous serving of the cooking liquid.

PREP TIME: 3 Hours

SERVES: 8

MODIFICATIONS:

STEAMED BROCCOLI WITH ORANGE GINGER PECAN DRESSING

Broccoli is one of those great "stand-by" vegetables. It's always ready to be cooked in a hundred different recipes at a moment's notice. Additionally, broccoli is available all year long so there can never be too many ways to prepare this delicacy.

INGREDIENTS:

- 2 bunches broccoli
- Juice of 1 orange
- 1 tbsp chopped ginger
- 1/4 cup chopped pecans
- 1/2 tsp salt
- 2 tbsps peanut oil
- 1 tbsp Louisiana cane syrup
- 1 tbsp soy sauce
- 1 tbsp grated orange zest
- 1 tsp minced garlic
- Salt and black pepper to taste

METHOD:

Separate florets from the stalk using a paring knife, and cut away the thick woody bottom. You may wish to peel the stems if you think the skin is a bit tough. Place 3 inches of water into a 1-gallon pot, season with 1/2 teaspoon salt and bring to a rolling boil. Add broccoli and cook until fork-tender, approximately 5 minutes. Do not overcook. While broccoli is boiling, combine peanut oil, cane syrup and soy sauce in a blender or food processor. Add the orange zest, orange juice, garlic and ginger. Process 2-3 times, scrapping down the sides as needed. Season to taste using salt and pepper. When ready to serve, remove the broccoli from the boiling liquid, place in a serving bowl and top with the dressing and chopped pecans. Toss gently to combine the dressing with the steamed broccoli. Season to taste using salt and pepper. Serve hot as a vegetable or cold as a salad.

Amber glow through etched glass.

PREP TIME: 30 Minutes

SERVES: 6

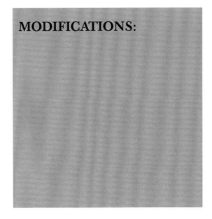

MODIFICATIONS:

Rose Lee Inn

WEST MONROE

Drench yourself with sunshine and shadows and the serenity of a midday walk along the riverbank. Let the melody of the songbirds' warble sway you like water rippling to shore. Let the fresh air remind you of crisp linen sheets and sheer drapes floating drowsily on the breath of an afternoon breeze. Bask in the afterglow of late afternoon as the stars make their nightly debut and flicker in a restless sky.

Rose Lee Inn is located on the scenic Ouachita River in West Monroe, La. It is

Everything's coming up roses at the inn.

OPPOSITE: *Check-in for Rose Lee Inn is through A&K Antiques.*

believed that the Spanish explorer Hernando De Soto, the first to be officially recognized as the discoverer of the Mississippi River in 1541, was likely the first white man to traverse the territory that became Ouachita Parish. After crossing the Mississippi River, he descended into Louisiana near the junction of the Ouachita and Tensas rivers. French colonists arrived in 1720 to settle the area. In 1769, seven years after Spain took possession of the Louisiana colony, Governor Don Alejandro O'Reilly claimed Ouachita Parish for the Spanish crown. In 1785, an outpost named Fort Miro was established, which became Ouachita Post in 1819. By the next year the city of Monroe was established and named for the first steamboat to sail the Ouachita River.

Rose Lee Inn was built in 1895 and became the Webb hotel, café and pool hall around 1905. Today, this restored hotel offers splendid bed and breakfast accommodations in antique-furnished rooms. The Honeymoon Suite, located next to the front balcony, features a wrought iron and brass queen-sized bed, marble

Eastlake dresser and a beautiful loveseat. The Mardi Gras Route room is decorated with oak furnishings, a high-back oak bed and armoire. An exposed brick wall adds New Orleans flair with Magnolia stained glass transoms. Mimi's Rose Garden is adorned with beautiful rose wallpaper. The large bath has an exposed brick wall with a window trimmed in lace above the claw-foot tub. Savana Lee's Paradise is a lovely room featuring an exposed brick wall, a large brass bed and tiger oak dresser. Sportsman's Paradise is the largest room featuring a four-poster queen-sized bed and loveseat amid hunting decor. Each room has a private bath, refrigerator, coffee maker, cable television, wireless internet service and phone.

A delicious, hearty Southern-style breakfast is served daily, at your convenience, in the quaint dining room on lovely rose-patterned china. Rose Lee's signature breakfast dish is cheesy sausage rolls served with fresh squeezed orange juice.

While visiting Ouachita Parish enjoy the Biedenharn Museum & Gardens, featuring a home, garden, conservatory, bible museum and Coca-Cola museum; Chennault Aviation and Military Museum showcasing vintage aircraft and pioneers of flight from World War I through space exploration; Masur Museum of Art displaying a permanent art collection as well as special exhibits in a Gothic home; and Poverty Point State Historic Site, a 3000-year-old prehistoric Native American earthworks in nearby Delhi. For local dining try Warehouse No. 1, Mohawk, Cormiers, The Kitchen, Waterfront Grill, Cascios, Genusas or Genos.

(Continues on page 246)

(Continued from page 244)

Rose Lee Inn is located in Antique Alley in West Monroe's Cotton Port Historic District, just one block west of the Ouachita River. This shopper's paradise has 25 antique and specialty stores with a holiday open house the first Sunday in November and a spring open house the first Sunday in May. Rose Lee Inn is located at 318 Trenton Street in West Monroe on the corner of Pine and Trenton. Check in is downstairs at A&K Antiques or by appointment. Call innkeeper Kathryn Huff at (318) 366-2412 for reservations or visit online at www.roseleebnb.com.

Return to nature at Rose Lee Inn where your room is always waiting.

A soft-shell crawfish garnishes the bisque.

CRAWFISH BISQUE

Crawfish bisque is one of those dishes in Louisiana with twin meanings. The early Cajuns created a bisque by stuffing the cleaned heads of crawfish with a spicy chopped crawfish mixture and then proceeded to simmer these in a rich roux-based stew. The Creoles with their European influence created a lighter bisque using the tail meat of the crawfish slowly simmered in a shellfish stock, finished with heavy whipping cream.

INGREDIENTS:

- 2 pounds cooked crawfish tails
- 1/2 pound melted butter
- 2 cups minced onions
- 1 cup minced celery
- 1 cup minced red bell pepper
- 2 tbsps minced garlic
- 1 cup flour
- 1/4 cup tomato sauce
- 2 quarts shellfish stock (see recipe)
- 1 tbsp fresh thyme, chopped
- 1 tbsp fresh tarragon, chopped
- 1 pint heavy whipping cream
- Salt and black pepper to taste
- Creole seasoning to taste
- 1 tbsp sherry

METHOD:

In a heavy bottom stock pot, heat butter over medium-high heat. Add onions, celery, bell pepper and garlic. Saute 3-5 minutes or until vegetables are wilted. Sprinkle in flour and, using a wire whisk, stir constantly until white roux is achieved (see roux techniques). Add tomato sauce and continue to stir blending well into the roux mixture. Add stock, one cup at a time, until soup-like consistency is achieved. Whisk constantly to smooth out the mixture. Add 1 pound of crawfish tails, bring mixture to a rolling boil, reduce heat to simmer and cook, stirring occasionally for 20 minutes. Add thyme and tarragon and season to taste using salt and pepper. Add heavy whipping cream, return mixture to a low simmer, and fold in remaining crawfish tails. Additional stock may be needed to maintain soup-like consistency. Finish the bisque with a touch of Creole seasoning. When ready to serve, ladle a generous portion of the bisque into a soup bowl and garnish with sherry (optional).

PREP TIME: 1 Hour

SERVES: 6-8

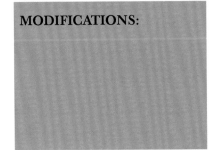

MODIFICATIONS:

PAW PAW'S SHRIMP DIP

It's amazing how many different ingredients can be folded or blended into recipes called "dips" or "spreads." In Louisiana, spinach and artichoke, smoked oysters and cream cheese, jalapeno cheese and sausage are just a few of the interesting combinations that come to mind. However, none are more famous or sought after in Bayou Country than seafood dips. When special friends are invited to the party, rest assured that Louisiana Gulf Shrimp or lump crabmeat will be the dip's main ingredient.

Collectibles abound in West Monroe's Antique Alley.

INGREDIENTS:

- 1 pound boiled shrimp, chopped
- 1/4 pound butter
- 1/2 cup minced onions
- 2 (8-ounce) packages cream cheese, softened
- 1 tsp granulated garlic
- 1 tbsp Worcestershire sauce
- 1/2 cup sliced green onions
- 1/4 cup chopped parsley
- 1 tsp hot sauce
- Salt and black pepper to taste

METHOD:

I normally boil shrimp in a prepared boil such as Zatarain's®. You may choose to chop the shrimp in a food processor then set aside. In a heavy bottom sauce pan, melt butter over medium-high heat. Add onions and saute 2-3 minutes or until wilted. Remove pan from heat and allow to cool slightly. Whisk softened cream cheese into the butter mixture using a wooden spoon. Add garlic, Worcestershire, green onions and parsley and continue stirring until well-blended. Add shrimp and fold into the cream cheese mixture. Season to taste using salt, pepper and hot sauce. NOTE: For an interesting serving tip…serve this dish with toast points made with Pepperidge Farm® thin white bread brushed with melted butter and sprinkle with garlic salt and parsley. Bake the bread in a 350°F oven on a cookie sheet.

PREP TIME: 30 Minutes

SERVES: 6-8

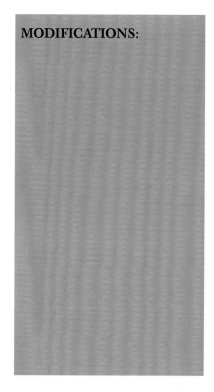

MODIFICATIONS:

$\mathcal{M}$AW MAW'S BANANA POUND CAKE

$\mathcal{P}$ound cake seems to be the greatest challenge of the bakery kitchen. It is extremely difficult to produce a pound cake that is somewhere between heavy as a brick and angel food. Relax! You have discovered the perfect formula with this recipe.

INGREDIENTS:

- 2 sticks butter
- 1/4 cup shortening
- 2 1/2 cups sugar
- 4 large eggs
- 2 1/2 cups cake flour
- 3/4 cup milk
- 1 tsp vanilla
- 2 1/2 tsps banana extract
- 4 tbsps margarine
- 1/4 cup milk
- 2 cups sifted confectioner's sugar
- 1/4 cup banana liqueur

METHOD:

Preheat oven to 350°F. Grease and flour a large tube pan and set aside. In a large mixing bowl, cream together butter, shortening and sugar. Continue to whisk until light and fluffy. Add eggs, one at a time, until all have been incorporated, beating well after each addition. Add flour alternately with 3/4 cup milk and, using a wire whisk, stir until smooth batter has developed. Add vanilla and banana extract. Pour into

the greased tube pan and bake 1 hour and 10 minutes or until cake tester comes out clean. When done remove cake from oven and allow to cool slightly. Prepare glaze by combining margarine and milk in a small sauce pot over medium heat. Bring mixture to a low boil, stirring constantly. When margarine has melted, remove from heat and add confectioner's sugar and banana liqueur, whisking constantly. Loosen the sides of the cake with a paring knife and invert onto a serving tray. Brush glaze over entire cake until completely used.

PREP TIME: 2 Hours

SERVES: 16

Cheers!

OPPOSITE: *Maw Maw had a winner!*

MODIFICATIONS:

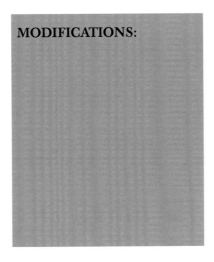

 $\mathcal{R}$ecipe for $\mathcal{R}$omance: Spiced Peaches, Poetry and a Picnic Basket

ZUCCHINI MUFFINS

The Italians brought many different vegetable breads to Louisiana that have since been transformed to muffins, cakes and bread puddings. They are not only the perfect way to get your daily vegetable requirements, but what an interesting alternative to those everyday ordinary breakfast muffins.

INGREDIENTS:

- 3 cups shredded zucchini
- 3 eggs, beaten
- 1 cup apple sauce
- 2 cups sugar
- 1 tbsp vanilla
- 3 cups flour
- 1 tsp baking soda
- 1/2 tsp baking powder
- 1 tbsp cinnamon
- 1/4 tsp salt
- 1/2 cup chopped pecans

METHOD:

Preheat oven to 325°F. Grease a compartment muffin pan or 2 square loaf pans. In a large mixing bowl, combine eggs, apple sauce, sugar and vanilla. Using a wire whisk, whip until well-blended. Sprinkle in flour and, using a cooking spoon, blend well into the egg mixture. Add baking soda and powder, cinnamon and salt. Continue to mix until all is incorporated. Add pecans and zucchini and continue blending until well-mixed.

Pour the batter equally into the muffin or loaf pans and bake 20 minutes for muffins and 40 minutes for loaves.

PREP TIME: 1 Hour

MAKES: 36 Muffins or 2 Small Loaves

MODIFICATIONS:

Exposed brick walls add to the rosy ambience.

Ahhhh…here's to the good old days.

GRILLED, SPICED DOUBLE THICK PORK CHOPS

Pork is one of the premier meats here in the South and its preparation methods are too numerous to count. Often, an interesting treatment of the meat emerges giving us yet another reason to cook pork. This is one such recipe.

INGREDIENTS:

- 12 (1 1/2-inch) thick pork chops
- 9 large garlic cloves
- 3 quarts water
- 1/2 cup Kosher salt
- 1/2 cup black peppercorns
- 1/4 cup brown sugar
- 2 tbsps dried thyme
- 1 tbsp whole allspice
- 3 bay leaves
- 1/2 cup light brown sugar
- 2 tbsps ground cumin
- 1 tbsp fresh basil, chopped
- 1 tsp fresh rosemary, chopped
- 1 tbsp Kosher salt
- 1/2 tsp cayenne pepper

METHOD:

This dish requires the pork chops being placed in a brine and marinating them for approximately 2 days. To make the brine, mash the garlic cloves and place them in large stock pot. Add water, 1/2 cup Kosher salt, black peppercorns, 1/4 cup brown sugar, thyme, allspice and bay leaves. Bring mixture to a rolling boil over medium-high heat and cook 12-15 minutes. Cool the brine completely over a bowl of ice cubes or make one day in advance and refrigerate. Divide the pork chops between 2 large containers or 3 heavy-duty sealable plastic bags. Place an equal amount of the marinade over the chops and place in the refrigerator for 2 days, turning occasionally. When ready to cook, prepare barbecue pit according to manufacturer's directions. Make a spice rub by combining 1/2 cup light brown sugar, cumin, basil, rosemary, Kosher salt and cayenne pepper. Remove the pork chops from the brine and pat dry with paper towels. Season the chops with salt and pepper then sprinkle with 1/2 tablespoon of the spice rub, patting well into the meat. Grill the chops 5-6 inches over the hot coals for 10-12 minutes on each side or until meat thermometer measures 150°F. If you wish to roast the chops rather than grill, place them on a large baking sheet in a 450°F oven for 20 minutes.

PREP TIME: 1 1/2 Hours

SERVES: 6-8

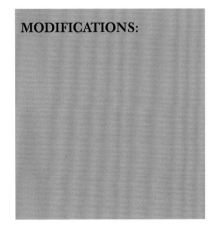

MODIFICATIONS:

Victoria Inn

LAFITTE

Just below New Orleans, where Louisiana dead ends in a watery grave, a small town rises amid the rigolettes of Bayou Barataria. A veil of salty sea air lingers over this sleepy fishing village named for the valiant and villainous pirate, Jean Lafitte, who defended New Orleans in the War of 1812. He and his scandalous band of buccaneers navigated their contraband through these murky waters like they maneuvered the concubines in their brothels. The breath of these swashbuckling rogues was stained with the dark rum that ran through their veins, and their lips, like their bodies, were bronzed by an unforgiving sun.

Local lore in Lafitte would have you believe that the treasures of these pillaging pirates are still hidden beneath the palmetto ridges and in the dark shadows of the swamp. One such treasure is the jewel of Victoria Inn.

The three-story, Caribbean-style inn is located at the end of a long, winding lane on five acres between Bayou Barataria and an expansive lake. Victoria Inn was constructed in 1985 by the owners, Roy and Dale Ross, and features dormer windows, a central staircase and a wide inviting veranda. Roy designed the home as a raised cottage, so that guests could catch the breeze from the water. There are eight spacious rooms in the inn with four additional rooms available in the Carriage House and two rooms in the innkeepers dwelling. Each room is individually and uniquely furnished and has a private bath.

The Ross' motto is to "delight and pamper" and the special treatment begins upon arrival with complimentary wine. Guests' rooms have robes, fluffy towels and linen sheets. Roy, a native of Belize, specializes in superb Southern breakfasts. His exotic menu includes such items as Mosquito Toast and scrambled eggs with fresh crabmeat, shrimp and onions.

The tropical grounds of Victoria Inn are as inviting as the heirloom-filled rooms. Delight in the tranquility of the various gardens including the Rose Garden and Shakespearean Herb Garden. Sip afternoon tea under the market umbrellas or savor lunch at one of the picnic tables. Enjoy fishing, swimming, sailing, peddle boating or water sports right from the dock.

While visiting Lafitte you will want to explore Jean Lafitte National Historical Park and Preserve where you will find an interpretive center, hiking trails, canoe trails, walking tours and boardwalks that lead right into the swamp. In the area you will find guided moonlight canoe trips and Sunday fais do-do Cajun dances. Lil Cajun Swamp Tours by Captain Cyrus travels through Bayou Barataria and includes a history of the area. Turgeon Tours offers a wonderful birding and dolphin expedition as well as a visit to the Island of Grand Terre, Jean Lafitte's barrier island headquarters arrived at only by boat. The "Jean Lafitte *(Continues on page 254)*

A pirogue in paradise.

OPPOSITE: *The gallery at Victoria Inn is cooled by a Barataria breeze.*

(Continued from page 252)

Seafood Festival" is held annually the first weekend of August. Fishing charters can be arranged as well as shrimp trawling excursions aboard a Lafitte skiff. Tours are available from the Victoria Inn dock that give you a close-up view of the islands, bays and wildlife of the area. Also available are tours of a working crawfish farm. There are four marinas for purchasing outdoor gear and two local antique and crafts shops. While in Lafitte dine on fresh seafood such as soft-shell crabs, flounder, shrimp and alligator at the local eating establishments including Restaurant des Familles, Boutte's Bayou Restaurant and Voleo's Restaurant.

Victoria Inn is located 45 minutes from downtown New Orleans, just off Highway 45 in Lafitte. For reservations contact Dale and Roy Ross at (504) 689-4757 or (800) 689-4797. You can look them up on the Internet at www. victoriainn.com.

Barataria, meaning "dishonesty at sea," was once home to Louisiana's most notorious pirate-patriot. Today, the lair of Lafitte is a natural getaway, where the traditions of South Louisiana are still an everyday part of life.

BISQUE OF THREE SHELLFISH WITH SHOEPEG CORN

There is no doubt that the abundance of shellfish on the Gulf Coast is the reason for so many fine seafood soups in Louisiana. With our semi-tropical climate, it makes perfect sense to combine these seafoods with vegetables to create an even more interesting combination.

INGREDIENTS:

- 18 (21-25 count) shrimp, peeled and deveined
- 1 pound jumbo lump crabmeat
- 18 shucked oysters, reserve liquid
- 1 (15-ounce) can shoepeg or creamed-style corn
- 1/2 cup butter
- 1 cup minced onions
- 1 cup minced celery
- 1/2 cup minced red bell pepper
- 2 tbsps minced garlic
- 1/2 cup flour
- 3 cups shellfish stock (see recipe)
- 1 pint heavy whipping cream
- 1 tbsp fresh basil, chopped
- 1 tbsp fresh thyme, chopped
- 1 tsp fresh tarragon, chopped
- Salt and black pepper to taste
- Creole seasoning to taste

METHOD:

In a heavy bottom sauce pan, melt butter over medium-high heat. Add onions, celery, bell pepper and garlic. Saute 3-5 minutes or until vegetables are wilted. Sprinkle in flour and, using a wire whisk, stir constantly until white roux is achieved (see roux techniques). Add corn and blend well into the roux mixture. Add shellfish stock, 1 cup at a time, until all is incorporated. Add whipping cream, basil, thyme, tarragon and season lightly with salt, pepper and Creole seasoning. Add 1/2 of each seafood and the oyster liquid and fold well into the soup. Bring to a rolling boil, reduce to simmer and cook 10-12 minutes. Add remaining shellfish, cook 3-5 minutes or until shrimp are pink and curled. Adjust seasonings if necessary. When ready to serve, ladle a generous portion of the soup along with an equal amount of the shellfish into 6 serving bowls.

PREP TIME: 1 Hour

SERVES: 6

MODIFICATIONS:

254

EGGS VICTORIA

There is no doubt about it, Eggs Benedict is one of the classiest breakfast entrees in America…that is until you have Eggs Victoria. Only in Louisiana would a cook consider placing jumbo lump crabmeat and crab fingers atop poached eggs at the breakfast table. Well, I guess no one ever said that we were "ordinary folks."

INGREDIENTS:

- 12 poached eggs (see recipe)
- 12 Holland rusks or English muffin halves
- 1 pound jumbo lump crabmeat
- 1/4 pound melted butter
- 1/2 cup minced onions
- 1 tbsp minced garlic
- 1/4 cup diced red bell pepper
- 1/4 cup sliced green onions
- Creole seasoning to taste
- 2 dozen peeled crab claws
- 1 cup prepared Hollandaise Sauce (see recipe)

METHOD:

In a large saute pan, melt butter over medium-high heat. Add onions, garlic, bell pepper and green onions. Saute 3-5 minutes or until vegetables are wilted. Add jumbo lump crabmeat, blending well into the vegetable mixture. Be careful not to break lumps. Heat 2-3 minutes or until

A pirate's lair.

crabmeat is heated thoroughly. Using a slotted spoon, move the crabmeat mixture over to 1/2 of the skillet and add crab fingers off to the other side to warm throughly in the juices. Set aside and keep warm. To assemble, place 2 Holland Rusks or English muffins in the center of a 10-inch plate, top each with a poached egg and an equal portion of the crabmeat mixture. Top each egg with a tablespoon of Hollandaise and 2 crab claws. Sprinkle the top of the Hollandaise with a pinch of Creole seasoning for color.

PREP TIME: 30 Minutes

SERVES: 6

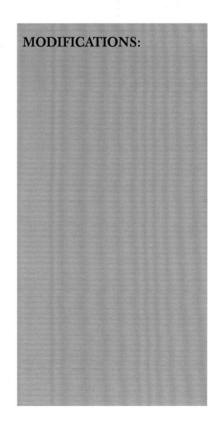

MODIFICATIONS:

BLACK-EYED PEA BATTERED SHRIMP

This is one of the most interesting treatments of shrimp I have ever run across. Dr. Bob Harrington, former dean at the Chef John Folse Culinary Institute at Nicholls State University, first introduced me to this concept of battering with beans and peas. This was one of his creations.

INGREDIENTS:

- 24 (16-count) head-on shrimp, peeled and deveined
- 3/4 cup cooked black-eyed peas
- 1/4 cup minced onions
- 1 tbsp minced garlic
- 1/8 tsp ground ginger
- 2 tsps Creole seasoning
- 2 eggs
- 2 ounces vegetable oil
- 1 cup beer
- 2 cups flour
- 1 1/2 tsps salt
- Vegetable oil for frying

METHOD:

I recommend peeling the shells from the tail of the shrimp, taking care not to separate the tails from the head. When battering the shrimp, dip only the tail portion into the batter and the shrimp will have an elegant presentation. In the bowl of a food processor, combine peas, onions, garlic, ginger

The morning sun warms the boudoir.

and Creole seasoning. Blend 2-3 minutes on high speed or until peas are coarsely chopped. Add eggs, vegetable oil and beer. Continue to blend until peas are pureed, approximately 1-2 minutes. Add flour and salt and blend once again for 1-2 additional minutes. Pour the black-eyed pea batter into a ceramic bowl. When ready to fry, heat vegetable oil in a home-style Fry Daddy according to manufacturer's directions. If a home-style fryer is not available, place 3 inches of vegetable oil in a large pot and heat to 350°F. Dip the shrimp into the batter, allowing all excess to drain off. Gently place shrimp into the deep-fryer and allow to cook until golden brown and partially floating.

PREP TIME: 30 Minutes

SERVES: 6

MODIFICATIONS:

OPPOSITE: *Bounty from the Bayou State.*

BACON-GRILLED REDFISH

Cooks along the coast, especially the German fishermen, have been wrapping striped bass or redfish in bacon and grilling them whole for generations. Although this has become an almost lost art, I think the flavor is worth resurrecting, so here it is. Give it a try!

INGREDIENTS:

- 1 (5-8 pound) whole redfish, cleaned
- 1 pound sliced bacon
- 1 small Bermuda onion, sliced
- 1 tbsp minced garlic
- 1 bunch fresh thyme
- 1 bunch fresh basil
- 1 bunch fresh tarragon
- 1 bunch fresh dill
- Salt and black pepper to taste

METHOD:

Prepare barbecue pit according to manufacturer's directions. The fish should be placed on the grill while the coals are glowing red with white ash covering them and no visible flames. Season the fish inside and out with salt and pepper. Place the seasoned fish on the backside of a large cookie sheet. Place the onion, garlic, thyme, basil and tarragon inside the belly cavity of the fish. Place the dill over the top of the fish then wrap the bacon around the center of the fish (not the head or tail) overlapping the slices. When the pit is ready, gently slide the fish onto the grill. Cover the entire fish with a sheet of aluminum foil and close the lid. The fish does not need to be turned and should be cooked when the bacon is golden brown, approximately 30 minutes. Using 2 large spatulas, remove the fish from the grill and serve.

PREP TIME: 1 Hour

SERVES: 4-6

Modern fixtures amid those of the past.

MODIFICATIONS:

FRESH BLACKBERRY PIE VICTORIA

Blackberries are one of those Bayou Country fruits that have made their way into our culinary repertoire for centuries. I cannot begin to tell you how often I went to bed at night with hot biscuits and blackberry jam with a glass of ice-cold milk. This simple recipe will be a hit for any cook regardless of expertise.

ntique English tables in the dining room.

INGREDIENTS:

- 5 1/2 cups fresh blackberries
- 1 cup sugar
- 1/4 cup all-purpose flour
- 2 tbsps fresh lemon juice
- 2 cups all-purpose flour
- 1 tsp salt
- 2/3 cup shortening
- 1/4 cup ice water

METHOD:

Preheat oven to 425°F. To make filling, combine berries, sugar, 1/4 cup flour and lemon juice. Toss ingredients gently to combine then set aside. In the bowl of a food processor, combine 2 cups flour with salt and shortening. Pulse once or twice to blend well. Add 2-3 tablespoons of water while pulsing until mixture resemble coarse corn meal. Remove the dough onto a floured surface, knead once or twice and separate in half. Flatten each half into a round disc and place in plastic wrap and refrigerate at least 1 hour. The dough may be made 1 day ahead. Remove from refrigerator and allow to soften slightly, approximately 30 minutes. Using a floured rolling pin and work surface, roll out 1 disc to approximately 12 inches in diameter. Transfer into a 9-inch pie pan, cutting the excess dough from around the pan. Roll out the remaining disc into a 10-12 inch circle and when ready, pour the berry filling into the pie tin and top with the second crust, pressing the edges together in a decorative manner to seal. Using a sharp paring knife, cut several slits in the top of the crust to allow steam to escape. Sprinkle the top crust with a teaspoon of granulated sugar. Place the pie on a shelf in the lower third of the oven and bake 15 minutes. Reduce temperature to 350°F and continue bake until crust is golden brown, approximately 45 minutes. Serve pie warm with optional whipped cream.

PREP TIME: 2 Hours

SERVES: 6-8

MODIFICATIONS:

Recipe for Romance: Café Brûlot and Sugared Bonbons

Eggs-ceptional Recipes

*E*ggs are one of nature's most perfect foods and may be served in such a variety of ways. For this reason, they are considered the premier basic kitchen ingredient. They are unsurpassed as a breakfast dish, and may be served fried, poached, scrambled or elevated to a position of royalty. An omelette can be filled with an infinite number of ingredients or, when cooked in another fashion, topped with sauces and garnishes that will entirely change their original look and character. Following are a few of the most often seen preparation methods for this unique food.

Fried Eggs

Place approximately 1/4 inch of vegetable oil in a non-stick skillet. Add 1 tablespoon of butter to the oil and heat to 325°F. Crack two eggs into a bowl, one at a time, and place in hot oil. Season to taste using salt and pepper. When white begins to solidify, using a large cooking spoon, baste yolks with hot oil to desired consistency. Using a spatula, remove the eggs and serve hot.

Scrambled Eggs

For a single order, beat 3 eggs lightly using a fork until yolks and whites are broken slightly but not over-mixed. Blend in 1/4 cup milk or heavy whipping cream then season to taste using salt and pepper. A tablespoon of fresh chopped parsley may be added for color. Place 2 tablespoons of butter in a large non-stick skillet. Heat over medium-high heat until butter is melted but not browned. Add eggs, reduce heat to medium and stir the eggs constantly with a fork until cooked to your liking. Perfect scrambled eggs should be firm but not dry. You may wish to add bits of cooked bacon or seafood such as lump crabmeat or shrimp to the butter prior to adding the eggs.

Boiled Eggs

To boil the perfect soft-boiled egg, bring 4 inches of water to a rolling boil. Place the eggs into the boiling water for 3 1/2 minutes allowing the water to boil constantly. Remove the eggs and cool slightly under cold water prior to peeling. The peeled eggs may be reheated for 1 1/2 minutes in boiling water prior to serving. An egg may be boiled to well done by following the same procedure and allowing the egg to boil a full 10 minutes. The boiled egg placed in iced-cold water for a few minutes will facilitate easy removal of the shell.

Omelette

Break 3 eggs into a bowl and season to taste using salt and pepper. Add 1/4 cup heavy whipping cream and using a fork, whip the eggs until fluffy and well mixed. If you wish to fill the omelette with meat, seafoods or vegetables, have these fully-prepared and ready for the skillet. In the case of vegetables such as broccoli or asparagus, cut into small pieces and cook fully. Into a 6-inch non-stick skillet or omelette pan, melt 2 tablespoons of butter over medium-high heat. Do not allow the butter to brown. Pour the beaten eggs into the skillet and, using a fork, break the surface of the omelette in several places to allow the uncooked egg to reach the bottom of the pan. Continue this process until the omelette starts to solidify. Place any ingredients onto the surface of the omelette and top with cheese if desired. Shake the pan vigorously to release the omelette from the bottom of the saute pan. When the omelette is loose, fold it in half onto a serving plate and allow it to rest 1-2 minutes to fully melt the cheese or heat the filler ingredients.

Poached Eggs

To obtain the best looking poached eggs, I recommend using stainless steel poaching rings which may be purchased at any gourmet store. If poaching rings are not available, simply crack the eggs directly into the water. Poaching rings allow the egg white to be contained in a perfectly round shape during the poaching process. Eggs should be poached two at a time, though, a larger pan will allow for multiple poaching. Place a shallow pan such as a skillet or baking pan onto the burner. Distribute the poaching rings evenly around the pan. Cover the rings with water and bring to a rolling boil. Season the water to taste using salt and pepper. Add 1 tablespoon of vinegar and when water has returned to a boil, turn off heat and crack 1 egg into each ring or directly into the water. Let the egg stand 12-15 minutes in the water or longer if well-done is desired. The eggs may be poached well in advance and cooled for later use. To reheat, simply place the poached egg into 200°F water for 1 to 1 1/2 minutes.

Baked Eggs

Preheat oven to 350°F. Place 1 teaspoon of melted butter into a custard cup, one cup per serving. Break 2 eggs into each cup and season with salt, pepper and a touch of paprika. Top with 1/8 teaspoon of butter and bake the eggs for 12-15 minutes for medium or 20 minutes for well done.

of butter in a frying pan and when it begins to bubble pour in the eggs. Stir them constantly over a slow fire until they are of the right consistency. They should be firm, not hard, when done, and like omelets may be varied in many ways, the extra material being added just as the eggs begin to set. A little finely chopped parsley, or ham, or a tablespoonful of tomato will give a good flavor and afford a simple change to the ordinary dish of scrambled eggs.

SHIRRED EGGS

Shirred eggs are baked eggs and may be cooked in individual dishes or in a large baking dish. Butter the dishes first, break in the eggs, put a little butter and pepper and salt on top, and cook in a hot oven until the white is cooked, but not hard, and the butter forms a glaze on top.

OMELET

Take six eggs, break them into a bowl with one teaspoonful of salt, a dash of pepper, two tablespoonfuls of milk and a teaspoonful of butter, broken into small bits. Have a frying pan evenly heated, but not too hot, put in a good teaspoonful of butter and let it run evenly over the pan, then pour in the egg mixture, slightly beaten—about twelve beats. With a fork break the surface of the omelet in several places quickly to insure more even cooking, and when cooked, but still soft on top, slip a knife under the omelet and carefully roll it to the center. Let it cook for a moment longer to set any of the egg that may have run out, then serve on a hot platter.

BEATEN OMELET

For this omelet beat the yolks and whites of the eggs separately. Season the yolks, then fold in the beaten whites and turn it into a hot frying pan in which has been melted a little butter. Let it cook until it forms a crust on the bottom, then either finish on top of the stove, folding it over, or put in the oven to set for three minutes before folding. Serve at once.

If variety is wanted in this omelet, it must be added as in the plain omelet, just before turning. Chopped peas, tomatoes, parsley, mushrooms, gra

Roux

*I*n classical cuisine the roux is the primary thickening agent. Equal parts of fat and flour are blended and cooked to create a roux. This process may produce roux of different colors and thickening capabilities depending on the cook's need. In Cajun and Creole cuisine the roux has been raised to a new dimension never before experienced in other forms of cooking.

Brown Butter Roux

INGREDIENTS:

- 1/2 cup butter
- 1/2 cup flour

METHOD:

In a heavy bottom saute pan, melt butter over medium-high heat. Using a wire whisk, add flour, stirring constantly until flour becomes light brown. You must continue whisking during the cooking process as flour will tend to scorch as browning process proceeds. Should black specks appear in the roux, discard and begin again. This volume of roux will thicken 3 cups of stock to sauce consistency.

Blond Butter Roux

INGREDIENTS:

- 1/2 cup butter
- 1/2 cup flour

METHOD:

In a heavy bottom saute pan, melt butter over medium-high heat. Proceed exactly as in the brown roux recipe, however, only cook to the pale gold state. This roux is popular in Creole cooking and will thicken 3 cups of stock to a sauce consistency.

White Butter Roux

INGREDIENTS:

- 1/2 cup butter
- 1/2 cup flour

METHOD:

In a heavy bottom saute pan, melt butter over medium-high heat. Proceed exactly as in the blond roux recipe, however, only cook until the flour and butter are well-blended and bubbly. Do not brown. This classical style roux is popular in Creole cooking and will thicken 3 cups of stock to a sauce consistency.

Creole and Cajun Roux

Creole Roux

The Creole Roux can be made with lightly salted butter, bacon drippings or lard. As with everything regarding food in Louisiana, whenever someone attempts to reduce the wealth of food lore to written material, an argument breaks out. Let's just say that Creole Roux varies in color just like classical and Cajun Roux. The Creoles, however, did use butter for the roux, whereas any butter a Cajun may have had would have been saved for a biscuit or corn bread and never put in the black iron pot for roux.

If a comparison statement can be made, it would be that generally speaking, Creole Roux is darker in color than the Blond Butter Roux it descended from but not as dark as the Light Brown Cajun Roux.

Light-Brown Cajun Roux

INGREDIENTS:

- 1 cup oil
- 1 cup flour

METHOD:

In a black iron pot or skillet, heat the oil over medium-high heat to approximately 350°F. Slowly add the flour and, using a wire whisk, stir constantly until the roux is peanut butter in color, approximately 2 minutes. This roux is normally used to thicken vegetable dishes such as corn maque choux (shrimp, corn and tomato stew) or butter beans with ham. If using this roux to thicken an etouffee, it will thicken approximately 2 quarts of liquid. If used to thicken seafood gumbo, it will thicken approximately 2 1/2 quarts of stock.

Dark-Brown Cajun Roux

INGREDIENTS:

- 1 cup oil
- 1 cup flour

METHOD:

Proceed as you would in the light-brown Cajun roux recipe but continue cooking until the roux is the color of a light caramel. This roux should almost be twice as dark as the light-brown but not as dark as chocolate. You should remember that the darker the roux gets, the less thickening power it holds and the roux tends to become bitter. This roux is used more often in sauce piquantes, crawfish bisques and game gumbos. However, it is perfectly normal to use the dark-brown roux in any dish in Cajun cooking.

Stocks

Beef, Veal or Game

INGREDIENTS:

- 3 pounds marrow bones
- 3 pounds shinbone
- 3 large onions, unpeeled and quartered
- 3 carrots, peeled and sliced
- 3 celery stalks, peeled and sliced
- 3 heads garlic, sliced in half to expose pods
- 2 bay leaves
- 4 sprigs parsley
- 15 whole black peppercorns
- 1 tsp whole thyme
- 1 1/2 gallons water
- 3 cups dry red wine

METHOD:

Preheat oven to 400ºF. Have butcher select and save 3 pounds of beef, veal or game marrow bones and 3 pounds of shin or stew meat of beef, veal or game. Place bones and meat in roasting pan and cook in oven until golden brown, approximately 30 minutes. Place browned bones, meat and all remaining ingredients in a 3-gallon stock pot. Bring to a rolling boil, reduce to simmer and cook for 6 hours, adding water if necessary to retain volume. During cooking process, skim off impurities that rise to the surface. Remove from heat and strain stock through a fine cheesecloth or strainer. Allow stock to rest for 15 minutes and skim off all oil that rises to the top. Return stock to a low boil and reduce to 2 quarts.

PREP TIME: 6 Hours

MAKES: 2 Quarts

Chicken Stock

INGREDIENTS:

- 2 pounds chicken bones
- 2 pounds chicken necks, wings and gizzards
- 2 onions, finely chopped
- 2 carrots, peeled and thinly sliced
- 6 cloves diced garlic
- 2 celery stalks, finely chopped
- 2 bay leaves
- 2 sprigs parsley
- 1 tsp dried thyme
- 12 whole black peppercorns
- 1 gallon cold water
- 2 cups dry white wine

METHOD:

Have butcher select 2 pounds of chicken bones and 2 pounds of chicken necks, wings and gizzards for this stock. Place all ingredients in a 2-gallon stock pot. Bring to a rolling boil, reduce to simmer and cook for 1 hour. During the cooking process, skim off all impurities that rise to the surface. Strain through a fine cheesecloth or strainer and allow stock to rest for 30 minutes. Skim off all oil that rises to the surface of the stock. Return stock to a low boil and reduce to 2 quarts.

PREP TIME: 1 Hour

MAKES: 2 Quarts

Fish or Shellfish Stock

INGREDIENTS:

- 2 pounds fish bones or 1 pound each crab, shrimp or crawfish shells
- 2 diced onions
- 2 diced carrots
- 2 diced celery stalks
- 6 cloves diced garlic
- 4 sprigs parsley
- 2 bay leaves
- 1 tsp dry thyme
- 6 whole black peppercorns
- 1 lemon, sliced
- 1 gallon cold water
- 3 cups dry white wine

METHOD:

Ask seafood supplier to reserve 2 pounds of white fish bones for fish stock or 3 pounds of shellfish as indicated if this stock is preferred. Combine all ingredients in a 2-gallon stock pot. Bring to a rolling boil, reduce to simmer and cook for 45 minutes. During the cooking process, skim off all impurities that rise to the surface. Add water if necessary to retain volume. Strain through a fine cheesecloth or strainer. Return stock to simmer and reduce to 2 quarts.

PREP TIME: 1 Hour

MAKES: 2 Quarts

Sauces

Guy DiSalvo's Marinara Sauce

Guy DiSalvo, from Latrobe, Pennsylvania, is the best of the best! I can't think of any Italian chef who can create a tastier pasta sauce with so little effort.

INGREDIENTS:

- 24 Roma tomatoes, peeled and seeded
- 1/4 cup extra virgin olive oil
- 1/4 cup vegetable oil
- 10 cloves garlic, sliced
- 1 cup chicken stock (see recipe)
- 12 lg. basil leaves, chopped
- 1/2 tsp cayenne pepper

METHOD:

In a stainless steel sauce pot, heat oils over medium-high heat. Saute garlic slices until very lightly browned around the edges. Add the tomatoes and blend well. Bring to a low simmer, adding chicken stock to retain moisture as needed. Cook 5-7 minutes and add basil and cayenne pepper. Continue to cook, adding stock as needed, 5-10 additional minutes. The sauce is now ready to serve as a pasta topping or a base for fish and veal. Shrimp, crab or crawfish may be folded into the finished sauce to create a seafood Creole.

PREP TIME: 30 Minutes

MAKES: 1 Quart

Blender Hollandaise Sauce

INGREDIENTS:

- 3 egg yolks
- 1/2 pound unsalted butter
- 2 tbsps red wine vinegar
- 1 tbsp dry white wine
- 1 tsp lemon juice
- Dash of hot sauce
- Salt and pepper to taste

METHOD:

Fill a blender with hot tap water and set aside for 5 minutes. Pour out water. Into the blender place 3 egg yolks then add red wine vinegar, white wine, lemon juice, hot sauce, salt and pepper. Melt the butter in a small sauce pot, swirling constantly, until the butter reaches 150°F. Blend the egg yolk mixture on high speed for 2 minutes. When well-blended, pour the butter into the egg mixture in a slow, steady stream until all is incorporated and hollandaise sauce has formed. Serve immediately. If the sauce cools, the butter will solidify. If the sauce is reheated, the butter will break.

PREP TIME: 15 Minutes

MAKES: 1 1/2 Cups

Béchamel Sauce

INGREDIENTS:

- 3 tbsps butter
- 2 tbsps minced onion
- 3 tbsps flour
- 1 1/2 cups hot milk
- Salt and pepper to taste
- Pinch of nutmeg to taste

METHOD:

In a small sauce pan, heat butter over medium-high heat. Add the onions and saute, 3-4 minutes. Sprinkle in the flour and using a wire whisk, stir until roux has formed but not browned, about 3 minutes. Whisk in milk and season to taste using salt, pepper and nutmeg. Reduce heat to low and simmer, stirring constantly until thick, white sauce is achieved, approximately 10 minutes. You may wish to strain the onions or leave them in the sauce.

PREP TIME: 30 Minutes

MAKES: 1 1/2 Cups

Louisiana Bed & Breakfasts

ALEXANDRIA

Fairmount Plantation
318-793-8254
www.fairmount
plantation.com

ARNAUDVILLE

**Turtle Cove
Guest House & Gallery**
337-280-9355
www.turtlecove
studio.com

BATON ROUGE

Great Oaks Plantation
225-927-8414
www.greatoaks
plantation.com

**The Stockade Bed
and Breakfast**
225-769-7358 or
888-900-5430
www.thestockade.com

BELLE RIVER

**La Belle Riviere
Bed & Breakfast**
985-252-9436
www.labelleriver
bandb.com

BREAUX BRIDGE

**Cajun Country
Cottages**
800-318-2423
www.cajuncottages.com

Country Charm B&B
337-332-3616
www.countrycharm
bandb.org

Isabelle Inn
337-412-0455
www.isabelleinn.com

Maison Des Amis
337-507-3399
www.maisondes
amis.com

Maison Madeleine
337-332-4555
www.maison
madeleine.com

On the Bayou Cottages
337-316-2527
www.onthebayou
cottages.com

BUSH

Splendor Farms
866-54-FARMS
www.splendorfarms.com

CHENEYVILLE

Loyd Hall Plantation
888-602-LOYD(5693) or
318-766-5641
www.loydhall.com

CONVENT

Felix Poche Plantation
Bed & Breakfast
225-715-9510
www.poche
plantation.com

COVINGTON & MANDEVILLE

**Annadele's Plantation
& Restaurant**
985-809-7669
www.annadeles.com

FOLSOM & COVINGTON

Maison Reve Farm
985-796-8103
www.maisonreve
farm.com

FRANKLIN

The Fairfax House
337-828-1195
www.thefairfaxhouse.net

GONZALES & SORRENTO

**The Cajun Village
Cottages**
225-715-6060
www.thecajun
villagecottages.com

HAMMOND

Hughes House
985-542-0148 or
985-507-7106
www.hughesbb.com

**Michabelle Inn and
Restaurant**
985-419-0550
www.michabelle.com

HOUMA

A La Maison Crochet
888-483-3033 or
985-879-3033
www.crochethouse.com

Grand Bayou Noir
985-873-5849
www.grandbayou
noir.com

Waterproof Plantation
985-872-0802 or
985-688-2200

JACKSON

**Milbank
Historic House**
225-634-5901
www.milbankbandb.com

LAFAYETTE

**AAAH T'Frere's House
Bed and Breakfast**
800-984-9347 or
337-984-9347
www.tfreres.com

Bois des Chênes
337-233-7816

**Country French Bed
and Breakfast**
337-234-2866
www.countryfrench
bedandbreakfast.com

OPPOSITE: *The inviting living room
at The House on Bayou Road in New
Orleans.*

Louisiana Bed & Breakfasts

LAFITTE

Victoria Inn
504-689-4757
www.victoriainn.com

LAKE CHARLES

**A River's Edge
Bed and Breakfast**
337-497-1525 or
337-540-3813
www.lakecharlesbed
andbreakfast.com

**Aunt Ruby's
Bed and Breakfast**
337-430-0603
www.auntrubys.com

C.A.'s House
866-439-6672 or
337-439-6672
www.cas-house.com

MANY

JuJu's Cabin
318-256-5952
http://www.toledo-
town.com/juju.asp

MARKSVILLE

Maisonnette Dupuy
318-729-9368

MORGAN CITY

**Cajun Houseboats
& Rentals, Inc**
888-508-5031 or
985-385-6621
www.cajunhouse
boats.com

NAPOLEONVILLE

**Madewood
Plantation House**
985-369-7151
www.madewood.com

NATCHITOCHES

**Cane River Cottage
& Guest House**
318-663-8239
www.caneriver
cottage.com

Chez des Amis
318-352-2647
www.chezdesamis.com

Fleur de Lis
800-489-6621
www.fleurdelis
bandb.com

Judge Porter House
800-441-8343
www.judgeporter
house.com

Levy-East House
800-840-0662
www.levyeast
house.com

**Log Cabin on
Cane River**
318-357-0520 or
318-352-6494
www.cabinon
caneriver.com

NEW IBERIA

Estorge-Norton House
337-365-7603
www.bedandbreakfast.
com

The Gouguenheim
337-364-3949
www.gouguenheim.com

**Rip Van Winkle
Gardens**
337-359-8525
www.ripvanwinkle
gardens.com

NEW ORLEANS

**5 Continents Bed and
Breakfast, LLC**
800-997-4652 or
504-943-3536
www.fivecontinents
bnb.com

1896 O'Malley House
504-488-5896
www.1896omalley
house.com

**Ashton's Bed &
Breakfast**
800-725-4131 or
504-942-7048
www.ashtonsbb.com

**Avenue Inn
Bed and Breakfast**
800-490-8542 or
504-269-2640
www.avenueinnbb.com

Bayou Saint John B&B
504-482-6677 or
504-451-4107 or
504-430-3948
www.bayousaintjohn
bandb.com

Block-Keller House
877-588-3033 or
504-483-3033
www.blockkeller
house.com

Bougainvillea House
504-522-5000
www.1822bougain
villea.com

**The Burgundy
Bed and Breakfast**
800-970-2153 or
504-942-1463
www.theburgundy.com

**Degas House Historic
Home, Courtyard and
Inn**
800-755-6730 or
504-821-5009
www.degashouse.com

**Gentry House
Bed & Breakfast**
504-525-4433
www.gentryhouse.com

**The House on
Bayou Road**
504-945-0992
www.houseonbayou
road.com

Louisiana Bed & Breakfasts

**Hubbard Mansion
Bed & Breakfast**
504-897-3535
www.hubbard
mansion.com

Lanaux Mansion
504-330-2826
www.lanaux
mansion.com

**McKendrick-Breaux
House**
504-522-7138 or
888-570-1700
www.mckendrick-
breaux.com

Parkview Guest House
888-533-0746 or
504-861-7564
www.parkview
guesthouse.com

Rathbone Mansions
866-724-8140 or
504-309-4479
www.rathbone
mansions.com

**Rose Manor
Bed & Breakfast**
504-282-8200
www.rosemanor.com

OPELOUSAS

**Country Ridge
Bed & Breakfast**
Opelousas
337-948-1678
www.cajunbnb.com

RAYNE

Hoffpauir House
337-788-1050
www.hoffpauir
house.com

**Maison D'Memoire
B&B Cottages**
866-580-2477 or
337-334-2477
www.maisond
memoire.com

SHREVEPORT

**2439 Fairfield
"A Bed and Breakfast"**
318-424-2424
www.shreveport
bedandbreakfast.com

Fairfield Place
866-432-2632 or
318-222-0048
www.fairfieldplace.com

ST. FRANCISVILLE

Barrow House Inn
225-635-4791
www.topteninn.com

**Butler Greenwood
Plantation**
225-635-6312
www.butler
greenwood.com

Hemingbough
225-635-6617
www.hemingbough.com

ST. MARTINVILLE

La Maison Louie
337-394-1872

**Old Castillo
Bed and Breakfast**
800-621-3017 or
337-394-4010
www.oldcastillo.com

SUNSET

**La Caboose
Bed & Breakfast**
337-662-5401

THIBODAUX

**Naquin's
Bed and Breakfast**
985-446-6977
www.naquinsbb.com

VACHERIE

Oak Alley Plantation
866-231-6662 or
225-265-2151
www.oakalley
plantation.com

WEST MONROE

**Rose Lee Inn
Bed and Breakfast**
318-366-2412
www.roseleebnb.com

WHITE CASTLE

Nottoway Plantation
866-445-2872 or
225-545-2730
www.nottoway.com

WINNSBORO

The Fowler House
318-435-6845
www.thefowler
house.com

**Jackson Street
Guest House**
318-435-4105
www.jacksonstreet
guesthouse.com

Louisiana Festival Guide

FEBRUARY

Camellias in the Country
St. Francisville
www.stfrancisville
festivals.com

FEBRUARY / MARCH

(Mardi Gras depends on
Ash Wednesday date)

Courir de Mardi Gras
Church Point
(337) 344-8786
www.churchpoint
mardigras.com

Mardi Gras New Orleans
New Orleans
(800) 748-8695
www.neworleans
info.com

MARCH

Amite Oyster Festival
Amite
www.amiteoyster
festival.org

Black Heritage Festival
Lake Charles
(337) 488-0567
www.bhflc.org

Celtic Nations Heritage Festival
Lake Charles
www.celticnations
world.org

Louisiana Crawfish Festival
Chalmette
www.louisianacrawfish
festival.com

Tennessee Williams Literary Festival
New Orleans
www.tennessee
williams.net

APRIL

Angola Prison Rodeo & Arts and Craft Festival
Angola
www.angolarodeo.com

Audubon Country Bird Fest
St. Francisville
www.audubon
birdfest.com

Festival Internationale de Louisiane
Lafayette
www.festival
international.com

French Quarter Festival
New Orleans
www.frenchquarter
festivals.org
www.fqfi.org

Italian Festival
Independence
www.theitalianfest.com

New Orleans Jazz and Heritage Festival
New Orleans
www.nojazzfest.com

Ponchatoula Strawberry Festival
Ponchatoula
www.LaStrawberry
Festival.com

APRIL / MAY

Contraband Days
Lake Charles
www.contraband
days.com

MAY

Breaux Bridge Crawfish Festival
Breaux Bridge
www.bbcrawfest.com

Cochon de Lait Festival
Mansura
www.cochondelait
festival.com

FestForAll
Baton Rouge
www.artsbr.org

Greek Festival
New Orleans
www.greekfestnola.com

Jambalaya Festival
Gonzales
www.jambalaya
festival.org

New Orleans Jazz and Heritage Festival
New Orleans
www.nojazzfest.com

New Orleans Wine & Food Experience
New Orleans
www.nowfe.com

JUNE

Bayou Lacombe Crab Festival
Lacombe
www.lacombecrabcook
offfestival.com

La Festival de la Viande Boucanee
Ville Platte
www.smokedmeat
festival.com

Louisiana Peach Festival
Ruston
www.louisianapeach
festival.org

JULY

Essence Music Festival
New Orleans
www.essencemusic
festival.com

Louisiana Catfish Festival
Des Allemands
www.laffnet.org

Satchmo SummerFest
New Orleans
www.fqfi.org/
satchmosummerfest

Louisiana Festival Guide

Tales of the Cocktail
New Orleans
www.talesofthe
cocktail.com

AUGUST

Delcambre Shrimp Festival and Fair
Delcambre
www.shrimpfestival.net

Gueydan Duck Festival
Gueydan
www.duckfestival.org

Original Southwest Louisiana Zydeco Music Festival
Plaisance
www.zydeco.org

SEPTEMBER

Alligator Festival
Luling
www.stcharlesrotary.
com/alligatorfestival.htm

Louisiana Shrimp and Petroleum Festival
Morgan City
www.shrimp-petro
fest.org

Louisiana Sugar Cane Festival
New Iberia
www.hisugar.org

OCTOBER

Festival Acadiens et Creoles
Lafayette
(800) 346-1958
www.festivalsacadiens.
com

German Fest
Robert's Cove
www.robertscove
germanfest.com

International Rice Festival
Crowley
www.ricefestival.com

Louisiana Gumbo Festival of Chackbay
Thibodaux
www.lagumbofest.com

Madisonville Wooden Boat Festival
Madisonville
www.lpbmaritime
museum.org

Natchitoches Meat Pie Festival
Natchitoches
www.explore
natchitoches.com

New Orleans Film Festival
New Orleans
www.neworleans
filmfest.com

St. Martinville Pepper Festival
St. Martinville
www.stmartinkiwanis.org

NOVEMBER

Abbeville's Giant Omelette Celebration
Abbeville
www.giantomelette.org

Bayou Bacchanal Caribbean Carnival of New Orleans
New Orleans
www.bayoubacchanal.org

Festival of Lights
Natchitoches
www.christmas
festival.com

Highland Games of Louisiana
Jackson
www.lahighlandgames.
com

International Acadian Festival
Plaquemine
www.acadianfestival.org

Louisiana Pecan Festival
Colfax
www.louisianapecan
festival.com

Natchitoches Christmas Festival
Natchitoches
www.christmas
festival.com

Rayne Frog Festival
Rayne
www.raynefrog
festival.org

DECEMBER

Festival of the Bonfires
Lutcher
www.festivalofthe
bonfires.org

Festival of Lights
Natchitoches
www.christmas
festival.com

Plaquemines Parish Fair and Orange Festival
Belle Chasse
www.orangefestival.com

Louisiana Specialty Products

When cooking the cuisine of South Louisiana, numerous specialty products such as cast iron pots (a 200-year-old tradition), crawfish tails and andouille sausage are utilized. Most of these unique items are grown or manufactured here in our state.

At Chef John Folse & Company, we are able to make these unique items available to you anywhere in the country. If you are interested in purchasing or obtaining information on any of the products featured in this cookbook or on my PBS series, "A Taste of Louisiana with Chef John Folse & Company," please write or phone me at:

Chef John Folse & Company
2517 South Philippe Avenue
Gonzales, LA 70737

225-644-6000 *phone*
225-644-1295 *fax*

Please visit us on the internet and take a walk through our Company Store:
www.jfolse.com

We look forward to assisting you with any special product needs or additional information on the cuisine and culture of the Cajuns and Creoles.

Acknowledgments

No endeavor is complete without the assistance of a cadre of dedicated individuals. The publication of *Hot Beignets & Warm Boudoirs* is no different.

First, a special thanks goes to the many B&B owners who responded when we searched for the 26 houses featured in this book. Though only 26 are presented here, Louisiana is home to hundreds of fantastic B&Bs. I am particularly grateful to those who provided overnight accommodations and food for my weary crew as we traveled the state producing this book and the PBS series.

A multitude of research was compiled for this cookbook. I would like to especially thank Jan Bradford of the Hermann-Grima/Gallier Houses in New Orleans for her expertise on Le Réveillon, Helene Crozat of Houmas House Plantation & Gardens in Burnside and Gwen Edwards of Magnolia Mound Plantation in Baton Rouge for sharing research on plantation breakfasts and Harry Roman of Café Du Monde for sharing his knowledge of the famous New Orleans coffee stand. Special thanks also to many of the students from the Chef John Folse Culinary Institute at Nicholls State University who contributed research to this project including Chris Gaudet, Charles Smith, Benjamin Shane, Rebecca Joseph and Brian Berry. I would also like to compliment the collections and thank the helpful staffs of the following research libraries: Troy H. Middleton Library at Louisiana State University, Baton Rouge; Hill Memorial Library at Louisiana State University, Baton Rouge; Howard-Tilton Memorial Library at Tulane University, New Orleans; and Newcomb College Center for Research on Women at Tulane University.

The historic photographs were obtained through the diligent efforts of many individuals. From The Historic New Orleans Collection, I would like to thank John Magill and Sally Stassi. From Louisiana State Museum, I would like to thank James Sefcik, Tim Lupin, Shannon Glasheen, Patty Eishen, Claudia Kheel-Cox and Owen Murphy. A special thanks is also extended to Robert Hennessey for use of the Morning Call photographs and to Thomas H. and Joan Gandy for the historic steamboat photographs. Thanks also to Warren Gandy for his assistance.

A special thanks goes to my wife, Laulie, who supports my every endeavor. My deepest gratitude is extended to the untiring efforts of the team who worked so diligently to create *Hot Beignets & Warm Boudoirs*: Pamela Castel, Ron

Manville, Philip Toups and Michaela York. Many thanks are also extended to editorial consultant Dr. J. Dale Thorn and Dawn Delhommer for administrative support. A special thanks goes to the culinary team for their expertise on the photo shoots and television series: David Reinhardt, Eric Johnson, Jay Kimball, Kevin Kaiser, Troy LeGros and Marilyn Crisp. A special thanks to Chef Carol Gunter and the students of the Chef John Folse Culinary Institute for their assistance including: Doug Barnes, Jason Coulter, Mike Losch, Katy McCarthy, Dessie Mitchell, Allyson Russell, Trey Shultz, Julie Steele and Erin Tuggle.

In addition, this cookbook and my national PBS television series would not be possible without our family of sponsors. Jointly, Zatarain's Corporation and the Louisiana Office of Tourism provide the sponsorship necessary to bring our *A Taste of Louisiana* to millions of viewers worldwide. My sincere thanks to the president of Zatarain's, Lawrence Kurzius, and his entire staff. Zatarain's, one of Louisiana's oldest and most prestigious food companies, provides many of the key ingredients that Louisianians and cooks worldwide consider a mainstay in their kitchens. A special thanks is extended to Lieutenant Governor Kathleen Babineaux Blanco and her staff at the Louisiana Department of Culture, Recreation and Tourism who bring millions of visitors to this great state each year to experience our *joie de vivre*.

I would also like to thank Viking Range Corporation for providing the professional cooking equipment used to create the dishes for these 26 programs and my previous eight PBS series'; Albertson's Incorporated for graciously providing the food for the television production, photographs and recipe testing; and Gregg Guidry of Percy Guidry Manufacturing for donating The Cajun Grill for use in the cookbook and television show.

Finally, my heartfelt thanks to Beth Courtney, President and CEO of Louisiana Public Broadcasting, Clay Fourrier, Executive Producer, Ed Landry, Production Manager, Bob Neese, Promotions Manager, Jennifer Howes, Programming Director and Donna Keith, Director of Marketing and Development. A special thanks to the LPB crew: Chris Miranda, Executive Director, Donna LaFleur, Mike Abel, Ken Fowler, Phil Beard, Sally Budd, Rex Fortenberry, Peggy Fields, Jodie Fontenot, Patrick Hardesty, Bryant Langlois, Mike MacNamee, Reggie Wade, Steve Roppolo, Ben Williams and Virnado Woods. Thanks to my LPB family for making *A Taste of Louisiana* possible season after season.

To these people and so many others, thanks for helping make *Hot Beignets & Warm Boudoirs* the cookbook I envisioned so many years ago.

PHOTO CREDITS

FRONT COVER: Chef John Folse in the Louisiana Suite at Tezcuco Plantation.

BACK COVER: Michaela York and John Mailander enjoy beignets near Jackson Square.

Ron Manville was the chief photographer for *Hot Beignets & Warm Boudoirs*.

The historic photographs were reproduced with permission of The Historic New Orleans Collection, Louisiana State Museum, Robert Hennessey and Thomas H. and Joan Gandy.

José L. García, II photographed the back cover.

Andy Breaux provided the photograph of the McKendrick-Breaux House.

Huey Stein of the *Lutcher News-Examiner* provided the bonfire photo.

Henry Cancienne provided photographs for Aunt Ruby's, C.A.'s House, Milbank Historic House, Rip Van Winkle Gardens, Rose Lee Inn and Tezcuco Plantation.

Phillip Colwart Photography provided the photographs of Michabelle Inn & Restaurant.

August Bradford provided photographs for Annadele's Plantation & Restaurant, Country French and Hughes House.

Bibliography

Amato, Gerard, owner of Mother's Restaurant. Interview by Michaela York, 6 February 1998, New Orleans. Personal interview.

Applegate, Kay. *The Breakfast Book*. Santa Fé, New Mexico: The Lightning Tree, 1975.

Arnaud's Mardi Gras Museum, 813 Bienville Street, New Orleans.

Arnaud's, menu, 1998.

Asbury, Herbert. *The French Quarter: An Informal History of the New Orleans Underworld*. New York: Alfred A. Knopf, 1936.

Bassich, Beau, King of Rex 1989. Interview by Michaela York, January 1998, New Orleans. Telephone interview.

Berry, Brian, "The New Orleans Brunch," 1998, photocopy. Chef John Folse Culinary Institute, Nicholls State University, Thibodaux, Louisiana.

Bienvenu, Marcelle, ed. *The Picayune's Creole Cook Book: Sesquicentennial Edition*. New Orleans: The Times-Picayune Publishing Corporation, 1987.

Boyd, George Andrew. "Cafe Du Monde: The Original French Market Coffee Stand." BA thesis, Tulane University, 1977.

Bradford, Jan C., New Orleans, to Michaela York, Gonzales, 27 January 1998. Letter regarding 19th century Reveillon suppers.

Brennan, Ella & Dick. *The Commander's Palace New Orleans Cookbook*. New York: Clarkson N. Potter, Inc., 1984.

Brennan, Pip, Jimmy, and Ted. *Breakfast at Brennan's and Dinner, Too*. New Orleans: Brennan's Inc., 1994.

Brown, Helen Evans and Philip S. *Breakfasts & Brunches for Every Occasion*. Garden City, New York: Doubleday & Company, Inc., 1961.

Butler, Louise. "The Louisiana Planter and His Home." *The Louisiana Historical Quarterly* 10 (July 1927): 355-363.

Café Du Monde, New Orleans French Quarter. Historic kiosks located behind the coffee house.

Camellia Grill, menu, 1998.

"Carnival Knowledge." *Arthur Hardy's Mardi Gras Guide*, 1998 Edition, 24.

Chase, Leah, owner of Dooky Chase Restaurant. Interview by Michaela York, 14 April 1998, New Orleans. Telephone interview.

Cole, Catherine. *The Story of the Old French Market, New Orleans*. Gretna, Louisiana: Her Publishing Co., Inc., 1916.

Collin, Rima & Richard. *The New Orleans Cookbook*. New York: Alfred A. Knopf, 1980.

Commander's Palace, menu, 1998.

Cooley, Esther. *Come Aboard the Steamer America: The last cotton packet boat on the lower Mississippi 1898-1926*. Slidell, Louisiana: 1962.

Culinary Arts Institute, Staff Home Economists. *Breakfast, Brunch & Morning Coffee*. Chicago: Culinary Arts Institute, 1955.

DeMers, John. "Midnight star in search of the original réveillon." *New Orleans*, December 1996, 23.

Dufour, Charles. "Early Comus Maskers Threw Fruit." *The Times-Picayune/The States Item*, 6 February 1985, Mardi Gras 60.

Dufour, Charles and Leonard Huber. *If Ever I Cease To Love: One Hundred Years of Rex 1872 - 1971*. New Orleans: School of Design, 1970.

Early, Eleanor. *New Orleans Holiday*. New York: Rinehart & Company, Incorporated, 1947.

Encyclopedia Americana: International Edition, 1992 ed. Vol.3. "Bed."

Eskew, Garnett Laidlaw. *The Pageant of the Packets: A Book of American Steamboating*. New York: Henry Holt and Company, 1929.

Famous Hummingbird Grill, menu, 1998.

Folse, Chef John D. *The Evolution of Cajun & Creole Cuisine*. Donaldsonville, Louisiana: Chef John Folse & Company, 1989.

Fox, Margaret S. and John Bear. *Morning Food from Cafe Beaujolais*. Berkeley, California: Ten Speed Press, 1990.

Galatoire, Leon. *Galatoire's Cookbook*. Gretna, Louisiana: Pelican Publishing Company, 1994.

Gaudet, Chris, "The King's Breakfast," 1998, photocopy. Chef John Folse Culinary Institute, Nicholls State University, Thibodaux, Louisiana.

Grace, William, Captain of Rex. Interview by Michaela York, 27 January 1998, New Orleans. Telephone interview.

Guste, Jr., Roy F. *Antoine's Restaurant Since 1840 Cookbook*. New Orleans: Carbery-Guste, 1978.

Guste, Jr., Roy F. *The Restaurants of New Orleans*. New York: W W Norton & Company, 1982.

Hardy, Arthur. "The History of Mardi Gras." *Arthur Hardy's Mardi Gras Guide*, 1998 Edition, 14.

Hennessey, Robert, owner of Morning Call. Interview with Michaela York, April 1998, New Orleans. Telephone interview.

Historical Sketch Book and Guide to New Orleans and Environs with Map. New York: Will H. Coleman, 1885.

Jackson, Alan R. *The Breakfast Cookbook*. New York: Simon and Schuster, 1959.

Joseph, Rebecca L., "New Orleans Brunch," 1998, photocopy. Chef John Folse Culinary Institute, Nicholls State University, Thibodaux, Louisiana.

Kane, Harnett. *Queen New Orleans: City by the River*. New York: William Morrow & Company, 1949.

Kane, Harnett. *The Southern Christmas Book: The Full Story from Earliest Times to Present: People, Customs, Conviviality, Carols, Cooking*. New York: Bonanza Books, 1958.

Kelleher, Claudia, "Any Event" Mardi Gras Coordinator. Interview by Michaela York, 27 January 1998, New Orleans. Telephone interview.

Land, Mary. *Louisiana Cookery*. Baton Rouge, Louisiana: Louisiana State University Press, 1954.

Land, Mary. *New Orleans Cuisine*. New York: A.S. Barnes and Company, 1969.

Leavitt, Mel. *A Short History of New Orleans*. San Francisco: Lexikos, 1982.

Lind, Angus & Michael Tisserand. *New Orleans: Rollin' on the River*. Memphis, TN: Towery Publishing, Inc., 1996.

Loomis, Frank. *A History of the Carnival*. New Orleans: 1903.

Louisiana State Museum, Old New Orleans Mint building, Mardi Gras Exhibit 1998, "The First Court of the Mistick Krewe of Comus."

Mme. Bègué's Recipes of Old New Orleans Creole Cookery. New Orleans: Harmanson, 1937.

Montgomery, Ann, Queen of Comus 1947. Interview by Michaela York, 27 January 1998, New Orleans. Telephone interview.

Mother's Restaurant, information packet, obtained 6 February 1998.

Mother's Restaurant, menu, 1998.

National Society of the Colonial Dames of America In the State of Louisiana. *To a King's Taste.* New Orleans: 1952.

New Encyclopædia Britannica, 1981 Ed. Vol. 5. "Hotel."

Old Coffee Pot, menu, 1998.

Ott, Eleanore. *Plantation Cookery of Old Louisiana.* New Orleans: Harmanson, 1938.

Perrow, Jonathan. "Round-the-Clock Chomping." *The Times-Picayune*, 28 April 1995, 43 (L).

Research files of Houmas House Plantation. Letters of Francis Bulekley. Burnside, Louisiana.

Research files of Magnolia Mound Plantation. Baton Rouge, Louisiana.

Ripley, Eliza. *Social Life in Old New Orleans: Being Recollections of my Girlhood.* New York: D. Appleton and Company, 1912.

Rodgers, Rick and the Delta Queen Steamboat Co., Inc. *Mississippi Memories: Classic American Cooking from the Heartland to the Louisiana Bayou.* New York: Hearst Books, 1994.

Roman, Harry, treasurer of Café Du Monde. Interview by Michaela York, 11 January 1998, New Orleans. Personal interview.

Rose, Christopher. "The 'Bird' is Humming Again; It Isn't on the National Register, But the Humming Bird on St. Charles is a Landmark that its Owners Are Struggling to Save." *The Times-Picayune*, 30 March 1994, 1(E).

Rose, Christopher. "With Fries & Flash." *The Times-Picayune*, 15 December 1996, 1(E).

Russell, William Howard. *My Diary North and South.* 1863.

Sakach, Deborah Edwards and Tiffany Crosswy. *Bed & Breakfast Encyclopedia.* Dana Point, California: American Historic Inns, Inc., 1997.

Schindler, Henri. "Throw Me Something, Mister!" *Arthur Hardy's Mardi Gras Guide*, 1998 Edition, 60.

Shane, Benjamin, "Le Réveillon: Cajun Creole Cuisine," 1998, photocopy. Chef John Folse Culinary Institute, Nicholls State University, Thibodaux, Louisiana.

Smith, Charles K., "Le Réveillon: A Christmas Celebration," 1998, photocopy. Chef John Folse Culinary Institute, Nicholls State University, Thibodaux, Louisiana.

Snow, Constance. "Counter-Intuitive Dining Thrives in N.O." *The Times-Picayune*, 19 July 1996, 32 (L).

Snow, Constance. "Golden Eggs Take a Crack at Breakfast, Crescent City-Style." *The Times-Picayune*, 10 October 1996, 1(F).

Snow, Constance. "House Boo-tiful." *The Times-Picayune*, 28 October 1994, 21 (L).

Snow, Constance. "Late Night After-Tax Dining." *The Times-Picayune*, 15 April 1994, 36(L).

Soule, Sandra W. *America's Favorite Inns, B&Bs and Small Hotels: New England.* New York: St. Martin's Griffin, 1996.

Stahls, Jr., Paul F. "Creoles and Carnival." *Arthur Hardy's Mardi Gras Guide*, 1998 Edition, 36.

Stahls, Jr., Paul F. "Return of the Reveillon." *Louisiana Life*, November/ December 1987, 48.

Tallant, Robert. *The Romantic New Orleanians.* New York: E.P. Dutton & Co., Inc., 1950.

Taylor, Joe Gray. *Eating, Drinking, and Visiting in the South: An Informal History.* Baton Rouge: Louisiana State University Press, 1982.

The Court of Two Sisters, menu, 1998.

Visitor's Guide to New Orleans. New Orleans: Southern Publishing & Advertising House, 1875.

Wayman, Norbury L. *Life on the River: A Pictorial History of the Mississippi, The Missouri, and the Western River System.* New York: Crown Publishers, Inc., 1971.

Webster, Jill Anding. "Dining Into The Night." *The Times-Picayune*, 19 February 1993, 29 (L).

World Book Encyclopedia, 1992 ed. Vol. 9. "Hotel."

Index

Note: A bold number indicates an illustration.